Stephen P. Greggo

TREKKING TOWARD WHOLENESS

A Resource for Care Group Leaders

IVP Academic

An imprint of InterVarsity Press
Downers Grove, Illinois

InterVarsity Press
P.O. Box 1400, Downers Grove, IL 60515-1426
World Wide Web: www.ivpress.com
E-mail: email@ivpress.com

©2008 by Stephen P. Greggo

InterVarsity Press® is the book-publishing division of InterVarsity Christian Fellowship/USA®, a student movement active on campus at hundreds of universities, colleges and schools of nursing in the United States of America, and a member movement of the International Fellowship of Evangelical Students. For information about local and regional activities, write Public Relations Dept., InterVarsity Christian Fellowship/USA, 6400 Schroeder Rd., P.O. Box 7895, Madison, WI 53707-7895, or visit the IVCF website at <www.intervarsity.org>.

All Scripture quotations, unless otherwise indicated, are taken from the Holy Bible, New International Version®. NIV®. *Copyright ©1973, 1978, 1984 by International Bible Society. Used by permission of Zondervan Publishing House. All rights reserved.*

Figure 7.1 on p. 146 is from Personal Relationships: Implications for Clinical and Community Psychology, *edited by Barbara R. Sarason and Steve Duck ©2001 by John Wiley & Sons Limited. Reproduced with permission.*

Every effort has been made to trace and contact copyright holders for additional materials quoted in this book. The author will be pleased to rectify any omissions in future editions if notified by the copyright holders.

Design: Cindy Kiple
Images: hikers: Jerry Kobalenko/Getty Images
            arrow: Robin Cracknell/Getty Images

ISBN 978-0-8308-2824-1

Printed in the United States of America ∞

Library of Congress Cataloging-in-Publication Data

Greggo, Stephen P., 1956–

   Trekking toward wholeness: a resource for care group leaders/
   Stephen P. Greggo.
      p. cm.
   Includes bibliographical references and index.
   ISBN 978-0-8308-2824-1 (pbk.: alk. paper)
1. Church group work. 2. Small groups. 3. Christian leadership.
I. Title.
BV652.2.G625   2008
253'.7—dc22

                                                              2008022653

P	21	20	19	18	17	16	15	14	13	12	11	10	9	8	7	6	5	4	3	2	1
Y	26	25	24	23	22	21	20	19	18	17	16	15	14	13	12	11	10	09	08		

Dedicated with love to my family.

The Lord has truly blessed our journey!

Gratitude beyond expression is due my wife, Susan,

and our daughters, Jennifer, Jessica and Elisha.

Thank you for taking this trek with me.

CONTENTS

ACKNOWLEDGMENTS

The content of *Trekking Toward Wholeness* explores the beauty of caring Christian communities for nurture and healing. Reflecting on the process, *Trekking* has not been a solo engagement. Therefore, it is essential and a privilege to express thanksgiving for the significant contributions of others whom the Lord has graciously provided.

Faculty members of Trinity Evangelical Divinity School have been a source of stimulation in academic undertakings within a biblical framework. In particular, the colleagues from the Deerfield Dialogue Group, under the sponsorship of The Carl F. H. Henry Center for Theological Understanding, have nurtured this project by their encouragement and direct input. A special thanks goes out to Scott Manetsch for his dedicated conversations. This undertaking has also been enhanced by a stellar crew of students who have served as my research assistants: Heather Armstrong, Stephen Becker, Sasa Mo Chen and Mary McClure.

As the reader will soon recognize, I am indebted to the many pastors, former clients, seminary students and counselor supervisees who have placed their confidence in my clinical leadership. *Trekking Toward Wholeness* demonstrates that the benefit of those experiences is, indeed, reciprocal.

In addition, numerous professional and lay practitioners have participated in seminars I have presented at conventions with the Christian Association for Psychological Studies (CAPS) and the American Association of Christian Counselors (AACC). Conversations with those who lead helping groups, hosted in those productive settings, have certainly shaped the material offered here. Peer reviewers, staff from InterVarsity Press and my editor, Joel Scandrett, wisely guided the transformation of my ideas into this finished form. Each important contribution is genuinely appreciated.

This admittedly limited list of acknowledgments stems from the support I've enjoyed in the recent past. God's faithfulness has been constantly evident. Looking ahead, it is my eager anticipation of the small group treks that the Lord has yet to raise up that ignites my excitement! Thus I am grateful, even now, to you as readers and future trekking guides. *May the Lord reveal his grace by transforming your helping efforts into soul care that is solace for sojourners.*

1

TREKKING TOGETHER

LANDMARKS AHEAD

This introduction casts key metaphors in motion and ties them together in service of Christian ministry. Wholeness, trekking, sojourning, shalom and soul care are discussed alongside various helping ventures in which groups participate, such as study, recovery, care, self-help, support and common theme. The first section lays out the landscape by presenting the central argument that Christian small groups are a vital means of stimulating spiritual growth. The bulk of the travel in this introductory trek involves navigating through a series of observations ranging from care ministry trends to contemporary counseling literature and even personal experience. This overview begins to demonstrate how "trekking about" together forms crucial "ties that bind." Welcome and thanks for joining!

TREKKING ABOUT

Strategic small group experiences can be superb spiritual formation ventures, strengthening those on a quest toward *shalom*. The world needs motivated, knowledgeable and transparent Christian guides who share this vision. "Open your eyes and look at the fields! They are ripe for harvest" (Jn 4:35).

Such group journeys defy simple turn-by-turn directions or exhaustive maps. This study does not describe uniform routes that promise progress or assure identical results. Small group methodology does not offer such guarantees. Sharing heartfelt dreams, relational disruptions, heavy burdens or persistent doubts brings up the unexpected. Anything can surface, from our personal best to the dreaded worst, the hidden or the unfamiliar. Groups can be relationally rich while uncomfortably messy. The intricate flow of redemptive intimacy that fosters spiritual growth will remain a vast, untamed wilderness. This is the profound domain of the Holy Spirit, who by grace transforms interpersonal intimacy into redemptive encounter.

Nonetheless it is entirely plausible to portray the demanding functions that effective small group facilitators fulfill. Leader roles and responsibilities *can* be described and demystified. The experience of those on a joint pilgrimage through the wilderness *can* be anticipated. Thus the following pages chart the territory that trained group leaders routinely traverse, following a rigorous method to a highly desirable destination.

Relationally oriented small groups certainly advance toward deeper communion and restored relationships, but the Hebrew word *shalom* best expresses the ultimate goal. Ordinarily *shalom* is understood to mean peace, completion and fulfillment. Beyond the wonder of general well-being, however, its rich biblical usage portrays the bounty of wholeness. A covenantal relationship with God that enables harmony and unity with others is the means to *shalom*.[1] *Christian small groups, this study asserts, are a route for trekking toward wholeness.*

"Trekking toward wholeness" has a personal and quite literal significance for me. When our youngest daughter was preparing to trade the nest for college life, our family stood on the precipice of a definitive transition. Aware of a strange inner mix of excitement and apprehension, my wife and I sensed this was an ideal juncture for an extended voyage. A final family fling could contain rare opportunities to instill lifelong memories. Taking advantage of the tail end of sabbatical leave, we left our Midwest suburban home and took up temporary residence in a compact row house in the university city of Cambridge, England. Our initial attempts to enter the wondrous maze of classic colleges, courtyards, cobblestone streets, "backs," church yards and shops along the Cam River yielded a valuable lesson: when exploring the beauty of Cambridge, leave the car behind and traverse its subtle riches with comfortable footwear. Walking, hiking and strolling became a family norm.

Thus it was in Cambridge that we adopted the term *trekking*. A curious neighbor offhandedly described our touring method as "trekking about." Our home base was this city of higher learning. Heading out in all directions, numerous day trips would find us in seaside and scenic villages near and far. Our conversational neighbor showed us wonderful books picturing reachable destinations. After thirty years of living and raising a family in one place, this native knew what was worthwhile and within striking distance. The neighbor's touching stories of similar trips once enjoyed with his wife, now deceased, seemed fresh and inviting. Apparently, coaching our trekking about rekindled within his internal

---

[1] Richard L. Harris, Gleason L. Archer and Bruce K. Waltke, *Theological Wordbook of the Old Testament,* electronic ed. (Chicago: Moody Press, 1999) c1980, S. 930.

travelogue the emotional vitality he had experienced in a lifetime of pleasant companionship.

Driving a rental car in the townships surrounding Cambridge involved a stick shift, reversed lanes, roundabouts, strange signage and narrow roadways. And my family never considered my driving skills up to snuff. Upon exiting the highway, persistent voices opted for parking the car and seeing the sights on foot. The intention of this unified chorus may have been to avoid playing chicken with oncoming traffic between rows of parked cars, but the clear advantage to meandering about as pedestrians was immediately obvious. In rural areas as in the antiquated cities, public footpaths do end up at popular destinations, but this is not their foremost appeal. Footpaths provide unique access to backyards and precious views that could not be secured while enduring the hazards and predictability of modern roadways. On foot, we followed the smell of fish and chips frying, sought close-up views of perennial gardens and stepped around the reminders that we were walking through occupied sheep pastures. Trekking yielded far more family pleasure than enduring dad's driving from the helpless position of being stuffed in a shrunken back seat.

Traveling via traditional footpath was nothing like following the sidewalks that strictly paralleled the roadways back home. The footpaths gave us a legitimate right of way through beautiful private estates, active farms and close-knit neighborhoods. Passing by a cemetery yard of an old church, having school children in uniform stroll by or waving in greeting to a woman hanging out the family laundry blurred the lines between tourist and townsperson, public and private, sightseeing and site sharing. Trails led to or through places that roads could not. Moving around by foot is not merely an alternative to auto transport; it is a distinct means of discovery as one traverses territory not open to motorized transportation. Trekking may lack in covering mileage, but it excels in generating close-ups of local life and charm. We have stories no touring guide can describe. "Trekking about" left a memorable impression as an intimate way to travel.

The most remarkable blessing our family received is not contained in the vast amount of photographs we took or the sights we saw. Nor do the humorous stories that now reside in our collective memories quite capture it. The blessing from those Cambridge treks flows from the cherished family bonds that were exposed, tested and refreshed. Conversations with locals often stimulated reflection and spontaneous enjoyment. Each family member's unique gifting, preferences and interests were expressed as each turn in the pathway presented new choices. In the end, our eventual family transition to greater physical distance between us and the strange quietness of the empty nest was transformed by an awareness of the close bonds that exist between us. Our trekking together strengthened the "tie that binds." Our inevitable parting did not bring overwhelming distress, so strong was the hope we found in the joining of our hearts. Trekking itself did not create this sense of family, remove any entrenched differences or eliminate friction. Verbatim transcriptions, fortunately unavailable this side of heaven, might support quite the opposite. To our delight, trekking travel in fact provided a fresh and vivid taste of how our distinctions meaningfully enrich one other.

Interpersonal and transpersonal growth produced by close person-to-person experience is the actual subject of the pages ahead. Small group treks offer picture-perfect moments to discover much about the stresses, strains and strengths of bonds between self and others. As the Holy Spirit moves, small group exploration may become the means not only to recognize, but to rely more fully on, the tie that binds.

THE TREKKING TREND

A *trek* by definition is a journey exacting personal challenge. Trekking through rigorous terrain exposes the limits of determination. Aversive elements uncover extremes in self-sufficiency, increase deep understanding and bring fragility and fear to the surface. Exhilaration and satisfaction flood moments of triumph. Trekking thus runs counter to customary modern expectations of comfort and control. And since undertaking such journeys is typically voluntary, the embedded risks are essentially the point. One treks not merely to get somewhere but to place oneself under calculated stress that will produce growth or purify moral fiber. Personal investment fuels the voyage from the familiar to the exceptional.

Trekking itself is nothing new. The earliest pioneers entered the rough and raw American wilderness with barely enough possessions and provisions to eke out a new life. The ox cart was a vehicle of choice. Slow and steady, the surly ox yoked to a stout cart could turn a dry river gulch into a roadway or a game trail into a through street. A sleek horse-drawn wagon was fast, yet it lacked the punch in low gear that the powerful ox provided in off-road conditions. Hard travel via ox cart was called *trekking*. The term today has dropped the ox and has come to mean to go on foot or to take a slow long journey that requires personal labor, endurance and strength. Slogging around in ox carts is certainly out. But strenuous tours or treks are definitely in.

Today, travelers wishing to avoid the superficiality of a whirlwind tour may opt to make their voyage as a trek. These adventurers abandon motorized assistance for a key portion of the journey and set a step-by-step pace on foot or by hoof. This allows the intricacies and nuances of a living region, filled with new people and places, to be savored rather than merely tasted. There are published guidebooks to remote places that specifically promote this primitive type of exploration such as *Classic Hikes of the World: 23 Breathtaking Treks; Trekking in Tibet: A Traveler's Guide* or *Trekking and Climbing in the Alps.*[2] Adventure travel companies host expeditions into wilderness areas for personal pleasure or as corporate team exercises designed to facilitate deeper camaraderie or esprit de corps. The trekking trend is not for everyone, but it does offer a distinct advantage for the discerning person. As enjoyable as it may be, say, to take a hike to see splendid Lost Lake, bike to the sights and smells of Hidden Harbor, or walk to sit on a porch rocker at Grand Mansion, these examples fail to capture the essence of a true trek. The end point to a trek does not take on the major emphasis. Trekking stirs thoughts of the exotic and offers the spontaneous pleasure of unplanned encounters as the press forward unfolds. *Trekking involves the journey itself and the personal effort exerted in making new discoveries along the way.*

In this era of no-risk virtual tours, hand-held Global Positioning Satellite (GPS) devices and instant global communication, a few hardy trailblazers are trekking for the rewards of the experience itself. The self is purposely put on the line to cultivate discipline, exhibit character or discover priorities. A mild-mannered accountant leaves his laptop behind to scuba dive in remote locations and photograph man-eating sharks. A college student rejects a Cancun beach resort during the mayhem of spring break to mix concrete by hand while building a meager home for poor Mexican villagers. Newlywed couples turn away from honeymoon suites and toward Nippa huts on out-of-the-way beaches or pup tents along a mountain trail. Interest surges in reaching beyond the mere appearance of adventure and entering into the pursuit itself.

One philosophical travel writer remarked that trekking has a deep and timeless significance. Traveling unaided by motorized technology uncovers the tension between two ancient lifestyles: the rooted settler versus the migratory nomad.[3] One may choose the security and familiarity of civilization or the unpredictability and freedom of the wild. This allusion casts a dramatic edge and

---

[2]Peter Potterfield, *Classic Hikes of the World: 23 Breathtaking Treks* (New York: W. W. Norton, 2005); Gary McCue, *Trekking in Tibet: A Traveler's Guide*, 2nd ed. (Seattle: Mountaineers Books, 1999); Hilary Sharp, *Trekking and Climbing in the Western Alps*, Trekking and Climbing Series (Mechanicsburg, Penn.: Stackpole Books, 2002).

[3]Robert Strauss, *Adventure Trekking: A Handbook for Independent Travelers* (Seattle: Mountaineers Books, 1996), p. 8.

subtle mystique to a trekking venture. It also unintentionally alludes to a very significant biblical term: *sojourning*. Trekking may not appear in the ordinary biblical concordance but Scripture gives considerable attention to related themes: residency and journey, inhabitants and aliens, homeland and exile, wandering and abiding, the now and the not yet.

Within Scripture, a sojourner is one who takes up permanent residence in a location beyond his former domicile. A foreigner, on the other hand, has intentions of only passing through.[4] Both of these trekker types are exposed and vulnerable. Embarking on a passage makes one dependent on the locals and subject to their whims. Pressured by famine and desperation, the people of Israel were forced to become sojourners in the land of Egypt (Gen 45–47). Slavery ensued. Following the Israelites' difficult exodus and delayed entry into the Promised Land, God established explicit guidelines for the treatment of sojourners in their midst. Aliens were given the privileges of gleaning portions of cultivated fields and seeking refuge within walled cities when threatened, and they were not to be oppressed into servitude (Lev 19:10; 23:22; Deut 14:21; 24:19-21; Jer 7:6; 22:3; Ezek 22:7; Zech 7:10; Mal 3:5). It was an incredible mandate. The alien was to be loved because the Israelite people were once themselves strangers in Egypt (Ex 22:21; 23:9; Lev 19:33-34; Deut 10:19). The implication is extremely vivid. The lessons from Israel's own historical experience were to lead the nation in treating sojourners ethically and respectfully.

Further, before the resurrection of Jesus Christ and the outpouring of the Holy Spirit at Pentecost, Gentiles were excluded from the covenant of God's promise (Eph 2:12, 19-20). Jesus Christ defused this divisive hostility, proclaimed peace and brought about reconciliation by his suffering unto death on the cross. He brought harmony between citizens of Israel and those formerly outside of God's household. But this transformation—and the resulting unity of God's people—did not bring an end to the experience of sojourning, though it altered assumptions about citizenship. Christians, members of God's kingdom family by faith, live as strangers and aliens in a sinful and fallen world. Like the nation of Israel, there is good reason for the children of God to recollect their alien history. Similar lessons should ensure that others are duly welcomed to join in the lifelong pilgrimage to live eternally with the King. Ministry leaders comfort those on a sojourn to heaven with the comfort they have received from the Lord (2 Cor 1:3-7).

---

[4]H. M. Carson, "Foreigner," in *New Bible Dictionary*, ed. I. Howard Marshall, A. R. Millard, J. I. Packer and D. J. Wiseman (Downers Grove, Ill.: InterVarsity Press, 1996), p. 380.

Trekking may be a popular form of inner and outer exploration, and all Christians may be sojourners of a sort, but here these metaphors serve a profoundly higher purpose: the improvement of biblical soul care. The imagery of trekking illustrates creative opportunities to extend and diversify the options for contemporary pastoral care. My objective is to stimulate interest in the leadership of focused, counseling care groups. My prayer is to inspire wanderlust for innovative, spiritually enriching group cohesiveness. Attaining this kind of community is not an end in itself. Instead it marks the beginning of intensive engagement within the church, the body of Christ. Jesus Christ by grace inhabits human relationships to transform hearts toward holiness and worship. *Soul care is solace for the sojourner.*

Profound spiritual transformation awaits groups that embark on well-led soul-care experiences. This is only possible as more and more leader-guided group treks—expeditions that address a multitude of concerns that inhibit, delay or detour our spiritual pilgrimage—become available. Ministry care at its core has the compelling duty of reaching out to weary souls with the hope of refreshment. Further, true soul care requires the training and equipping of leaders to anticipate the demands of their journey. Most important, pastoral care infused with the work of the Holy Spirit fosters profound relational reconciliation, bringing unity to the body of Christ. The call to group soul care is not about self-enhancement but about honoring God completely. Redemptive intimacy is a path toward increased relational adaptability, a gift found both in the process as well as in the outcome. If the Lord's command to love one's neighbor is the purest evidence of a heart that yearns to please God, the stakes are high indeed.

Sociologist of religion Robert Wuthnow rightly argued that any renewed religious inclinations within our culture are attracted by a spirituality of seeking as opposed to one of dwelling.[5] If this is so, conditions are uniquely ripe for group experiences with an intense relational mission to deepen the bonds of intimacy between self, other and God. The dated spirituality of *dwelling* is characterized by alignment with a distinctive religious denomination, history, tradition or identity. A firm identification with a cherished place or physical structure may best represent such a dwelling orientation. Faith commitment is demonstrated by joining: "The church where I am a member is the brick one just off Main Street in the center of town."

Conversely, a spirituality of seeking exhibits characteristics like questing,

---

[5]Robert Wuthnow, *After Heaven: Spirituality in America since the 1950s* (Berkeley: University of California Press, 1998), pp. 1-18.

questioning and experiencing. The *seeking* depiction of church is not as quaint or place-oriented: "A few of us gather weekly to explore how God has been instructing and sustaining us through his Word." This dweller-seeker portrayal echoes the ancient tension between settler and nomad that adventure trekking reenacts. Leader-directed groups are poised to fill the needs of a seeker faith. Care group leaders incorporate a genuine sense of openness and humility into the normal conversation of the group. Encouragement and permission to take unfamiliar interpersonal risks allow spiritual seekers fresh and unique occasions for transparent, authentic spiritual renewal.

Recreational trekking is voluntary. In the reality of life, however, people are thrust into lonely territory to sojourn for a host of reasons. Part of the ordeal stems from the perceived loss of control. An automobile accident leaves a traumatic memory or wound that refuses to heal; a blended family strives to establish a common identity while scars from the past are still tender; an increasingly disruptive addictive cycle destroys the sanctity of a marriage covenant. Helping groups seeking to strengthen and cure may soothe concerns such as these. An inner restlessness, reaching a developmental milestone, or a spiritual urge to partake of solid food over the milk of infants might also stir interest in a passage to facilitate growth (1 Cor 3:2). The responsive ministry agenda thus aims at both nurture and formation. While fine models for effective pastoral care certainly exist, the driving force here is to stir further reflection on areas where leader-guided group treks could make a unique contribution. The eventual result, should the Lord add his blessing, will be an increase in fine-tuned small group treks, where interpersonal resources contribute to spiritual formation and ultimately to fuller participation in the community where Jesus Christ is exalted. But what trends currently exist for small group care? The following discussion should establish a framework for expanding and optimizing group ministry options.

A TOPOGRAPHY OF GROUPS

Extraordinary numbers of people gather in small groups, seeking assistance in making meaningful changes. The best informed estimate suggested that over fifty million Americans have participated in these grassroots ventures.[6] The assumption beyond that snapshot was that self-help groups were a growing trend with no regression in sight. Further, the figures took no account of the increasing

---

[6]Irvin D. Yalom and Molyn Leszcz, *The Theory and Practice of Group Psychotherapy*, 5th ed. (New York: Basic Books, 2005), p. 518. The research supporting this credible yet conservative projection was conducted in the mid-nineties.

number of groups that hold regular or perpetual meetings in cyberspace. Group initiatives for helping and health enhancement are alive, well and proliferating.[7] The group movement can be loosely divided into meetings that are predominantly leader-directed and those that are pure self-help. It is best to think of these headings as anchors on each end of a bi-polar scale with many combinations in between. There are helping groups led by those with extensive training, professional credentials and sophisticated change strategies. Other groups convene with a plain acknowledgment that they are assemblies of ordinary strugglers gathered to give the best of their own brokenness. Any expertise in a self-help group comes from the thrill of personal victory or the painful agony of defeat.

Groups with a pastoral care emphasis have also become popular within ministry contexts.[8] Support networks with a faith-based foundation currently ease suffering and create a climate with exceptional evangelistic potential.[9] For example, the Celebrate Recovery (CR) phenomena started by Saddleback Church in Lake Forest, California, began as an alternative, Christ-centered local effort to the traditional twelve-step approach of Alcoholics Anonymous (AA). The recovery principles closely resemble those underlying AA with two obvious differences. First, there is a definite reference to the God of the Bible and not to a nondescript higher power. Second, the words of Jesus in the Beatitudes fasten the steps to core Christian teaching (see The Road to Recovery on page 22). Celebrate Recovery has become pivotal to the outreach of this respected church under the ministry of Rick Warren. According to CR, the support ministry has touched thousands within that church fellowship alone. Further, this movement has spawned hundreds of other host ministries worldwide where multiple groups undertake specific recovery expeditions using the CR format.[10] (Before this chapter concludes I'll describe my visit to one of these branch meetings.)

The seeker-sensitive Willow Creek Church near Chicago, Illinois, offers another example of creative, group-oriented pastoral care. Educational, psychosocial support groups address people at various developmental stages and particular life issues. The church makes direct person-to-person assistance available to relieve grief, preserve marriages, empower career changes, promote wise stewardship in financial decisions, and tame one's sexual impulses in a world that has

---

[7]Robert Wuthnow, ed., *"I Come Away Stronger": How Small Groups are Shaping American Religion* (Grand Rapids: Eerdmans, 1994).
[8]Larry Crabb, *Connecting: Healing for Ourselves and Our Relationships, A Radical New Vision* (Nashville: Word, 1997).
[9]See Dale S. Ryan, Christian Recovery International (2005) <http://www.christianrecovery.com>.
[10]Celebrate Recovery home page (updated March 10, 2008) <www.celebraterecovery.com/?page_id=4#eight>.

THE ROAD TO RECOVERY
Celebrate Recovery's Eight Recovery Principles
Based on the Beatitudes
By Pastor Rick Warren

R   Realize I'm not God; I admit that I am powerless to control my tendency to do the wrong thing and that my life is unmanageable. (Step 1)
"Happy are those who know that they are spiritually poor"

E   Earnestly believe that God exists, that I matter to Him, and that He has the power to help me recover. (Step 2)
"Happy are those who mourn, for they shall be comforted"

C   Consciously choose to commit all my life and will to Christ's care and control. (Step 3)
"Happy are the meek"

O   Openly examine and confess my faults to God, to myself, and to someone I trust. (Steps 4 and 5)
"Happy are the pure in heart"

V   Voluntarily submit to any and all changes God wants to make in my life and humbly ask Him to remove my character defects. (Steps 6 and 7)
"Happy are those whose greatest desire is to do what God requires"

E   Evaluate all my relationships. Offer forgiveness to those who have hurt me and make amends for harm I've done to others when possible, except when to do so would harm them or others. (Steps 8 and 9)
"Happy are the merciful!" "Happy are the peacemakers"

R   Reserve a time with God for self-examination, Bible reading, and prayer in order to know God and His will for my life and to gain the power to follow His will. (Steps 10 and 11)

Y   Yield myself to God to be used to bring this Good News to others, both by my example and by my words. (Step 12)
"Happy are those who are persecuted because they do what God requires"[a]

---

[a]Celebrate Recovery homepage (November 9, 2007) <http://www.celebraterecovery.com/?page_id=4#eight>.

removed many sexual restrictions.[11] The unique ministries of Saddleback and Willow Creek transcend their local impact; trends begin at such places but influence hundreds of ministries throughout the country.

Group-oriented pastoral care is not exclusive to large, multifaceted ventures. Consider the impact of Trinity Episcopal Church in Hoboken, New Jersey, as featured in the *New York Times*.[12] Its location near the World Trade Center site and its soothing traditional sanctuary positioned it to offer support groups for family and friends who lost loved ones on 9/11. Participants were filled with gratitude for the explorations surrounding their faith and spirituality in the midst of their great loss. So following their group experiences, the support group members raised funds for a new church bell. Now in Hoboken, the wonders of group work ring out like clockwork. *Groups can have profound effects on recovery and spiritual formation.*

Helping groups have been multiplying for decades because they are touted as economical and efficient. Managed care forces mental health professionals to do more with less in behavioral health clinics and social services systems. Likewise Christian ministries and counseling agencies are concerned with resource management. Groups are an appealing, cost-sensitive, *economic* option. When professionals are involved, the cost per unit of service is often lower for group than for individual sessions. Groups are also *efficient,* making the most of a group leader's time. These benefits continue outside the realm of mental health; networks like Alcoholics Anonymous or Celebrate Recovery are strictly self-help and accomplish much at a remarkably small cost.

More relevant and decisive for this discussion, group approaches are worthwhile because they are *effective;* they work.[13] The empirical case for the power of group work is so substantial that a classic text on group psychotherapy begins with this unambiguous declaration: "A persuasive body of outcome research has demonstrated unequivocally that group therapy is a highly effective form of psychotherapy and that it is at least equal to individual psychotherapy in its power to provide meaningful benefit."[14]

A spectrum of variables complicates research of group helping ventures. On

[11]Willow Creek Community Church <http://www.willowcreek.org/community_care/>.

[12]Peter Applebome, "Our Towns; A Lasting Gift, From a Terrific Club Nobody Wanted to Join," *New York Times on the Web,* (September 5, 2004) <http://select.nytimes.com/gst/abstract.html?res =F0071FF73A550C768CDDA00894DC404482>.

[13]Janice L. Delucia-Waack, "Current and Historical Perspectives on the Field of Group Counseling and Psychotherapy: Introduction" in *Handbook of Group Counseling and Psychotherapy,* ed. Janice L. Delucia-Waack et al. (Thousand Oaks, Calif.: Sage, 2004), pp. 1-2.

[14]Yalom and Leszcz, *Theory and Practice,* p. 1.

the surface, leaders and participants assess the group by how well they have achieved the group's stated goals and how well teaching, training or other direct interventions have contributed to such goals. Below the surface, multiple layers of assessment exist. How are members relating to other members and with leaders? How does each member understand the identity of the group? How do leaders address that identity? Beyond group dynamics, other factors make outcome assessment a formidable task, such as establishing reasonable controls or comparisons, isolating the impact of the group, and meeting ethical research guidelines in the midst of addressing an actual client predicament. Consider this example: in the real world of mental health treatment, group is rarely the sole helping modality. It is often used in conjunction with pharmacological therapy and individual treatment. Isolating or crediting the effects of group therapy alone is nearly impossible. Despite these hurdles, however, empirical work continues to improve. Research reviews by authors such as Gary Burlingame have applied a procedure called meta-analysis, a technique that provides systematic and thorough scrutiny of carefully selected and combined research published in peer-reviewed journals.[15] Consider these six important statements culled from the consolidation of documented research:

1. *Those who attend a group are better off than 72% of those who rely on time alone to address a major life concern.* Waiting for natural supports or individual resiliency to achieve restoration is not the ideal way to get one's life back to normal. The evidence suggests that to improve quality of life after a setback, it is best to get with a group.

2. *Clients with most any presenting problem or mental health diagnosis can benefit from group counseling.* This research finding undermines the pervasive myth that severe or complex matters are not suitable for group work. A particular person may not be a good fit to participate in a specific group at a given time, but the chief concern itself does not mitigate against applying a group approach. It is essential to evaluate personal readiness relative to the unique group mission and current member composition.

---

[15]Chris McRoberts, Gary M. Burlingame and Matthew J. Hoas, "Comparative Efficacy of Individual and Group Psychotherapy: A Meta-analytic Perspective," *Group Dynamics: Theory, Research, and Practice*, vol. 2 (Washington, D.C.: American Psychological Association, 1998), pp. 101-17; Gary M. Burlingame et al., "The Differential Effectiveness of Group Psychotherapy: A Meta-analytic Perspective," *Group Dynamics: Theory, Research, and Practice* (Washington, D.C.: American Psychological Association, 2003), 7:3-12.

3. *A common unifying theme addressed by members who are diverse in age, gender or other demographic characteristics seems to maximize favorable outcomes.* The title or central gathering call for a group provides common ground and inspires hope. Initial group structures can pull participants together despite varying factors such as age, gender or socioeconomic status. Homogeneity comes from the cognitive or psycho-educational core found in contemporary theme groups.

4. *Group benefits are best experienced under a skilled leader or when there has been explicit facilitator training accompanied by clear session guidelines.* This finding may rest in part on the reality that structured groups with trained leaders are more often invested in empirical research than informal or more broadly defined efforts. But even as differing groups submit to study, research maintains the value of a skilled leader.

5. *Placement of group members appropriately and strategically in groups is the single and most effective way of ensuring favorable gains.* Preplanning, preparing and screening members are critical ways to improve the value of the group experience for eventual members.

6. *The definition of explicit goals for the group intervention establishes targets for change that are then more realistically obtainable.* Prominent and clear objectives assist those involved in taking the required steps to realize change.[16]

These findings are derived from empirical clinical literature. But they can be generalized to speak to both the strengths and weaknesses found in the pastoral care and ministry options available today. For example, one specific limiting factor is exposed: heavy reliance on self-help groups for remediation of hurts may not be able to make use of the clinically tested counseling principles that contribute to successful outcomes. The use of general Bible studies or care groups for Christian nurture may not allow for sufficient focus on a concern or growth area, attention that would optimize the group itself as a resource. Supportive meetings can and do make a genuine difference in inspiring healing no matter what level of brokenness is represented or what the anticipated destination. Nonetheless research indicates that the dominance of self-help groups that do not make use of a trained leader unnecessarily limits the life-changing results that can come from

---

[16]Sally H. Barlow, Addie J. Fuhriman and Gary M. Burlingame, "The History of Group Counseling and Psychotherapy," in *Handbook of Group Counseling and Psychotherapy*, ed. Janice L. Delucia-Waack et al. (Thousand Oaks, Calif.: Sage, 2004), pp. 3-22.

group strategies. This shift is the one overarching concern motivating *Trekking Toward Wholeness*. Groups facilitated by trained leaders should have a significant place within the variety of care groups offered, according to overwhelming psychological research on groups. Since this book promotes a solution for this deficiency, this observation is obviously somewhat self-serving. But this book also gives readers the means to evaluate this matter by presenting distinctions between self-help and leader-guided groups. First, the following site visit samples a typical local ministry hosting an evening of Celebrate Recovery. Readers may wish to poke around their local region and enjoy a visit themselves—it might even become habit forming!

SITE VISIT

The chicken cutlets smelled appetizing as the gathering crowd moved easily into a polite food line. The mood was friendly and those with full plates quickly found companions around the folding tables set up in the church basement hall. One slightly odd-looking young fellow was seated solo at a long table suitable for ten. A well-dressed man with a few years of life experience sat down across from him before any forks hit a plate. The atmosphere was permeated with a hearty, home-style aura of comfort. If one was not known by name on arrival, it was apparent that several friendly faces would at least learn one's first name before departure. Perhaps I was the one feeling most out of place as I turned over my $3 meal money to the check-in/cashier monitor by the door, who was making tic marks on a sheet of paper. A Friday night of Celebrate Recovery was about to begin. Although I sensed the awkwardness of being in an unfamiliar place with virtual strangers, I knew exactly why I was here. For the next few hours, I would ponder my awareness of the macro group movement through a more personal micro experience. I would look into the eyes of real faces and hear how these small groups were making a difference in their lives.

Before I sat down the host and official greeter made certain that I had been welcomed and properly name-tagged. Once I identified myself as a visitor, I was given a summary of the group opportunities that would unfold as the evening progressed. After dinner, a combined opening session would commence, followed by a breakout into small groups. There was a group meeting to tame the turmoil of anxiety and depression, another introductory offering on how application of the steps could break addictive cycles, a forum for victims of abuse, a men's group focused on sexual purity and an entire separate set of meetings aimed at adolescents caught up in drinking and drugging. The evening would finish with informal visiting encouraged by plentiful desserts.

Having all these options seemed ambitious considering that this was no mega church, nor was any huge crowd piling on the chicken and rice. Obviously these would be cozy gatherings. What struck me was that the entire overview, with its smorgasbord of offerings, was typical of a multitude of meetings in libraries, town halls, hospitals, clinics, living rooms and conference rooms. Such groups meet anywhere and everywhere to help attendees lose weight, cease smoking, sustain strength while caring for a loved one, face cancer, revive a marriage, train for a marathon, curb destructive anger outbursts or relate more deeply to a holy God. This Celebrate Recovery evening was a representative slice of an "American pie" movement composed of self-help groups that are thriving across the vast array of settings where compassion and community is valued. During my evening visit, I could detect that a few trained leaders were scattered around the meeting rooms, but the prevailing weight was most definitely on the self-help side of the continuum. Our Lord is blessing this populist force for his kingdom purposes. In inward prayer, I contemplated if indeed the Holy Spirit might be whispering to visionary Christian leaders to extend these group offerings.

After dinner there were hugs, handshakes and hurried greetings leading into the worship session that preceded the breakout groups. A tearful woman with a sincere smile and thankful heart went through a pile of tissues while giving her heart-wrenching testimony. Her story was complete with a seared past and a slow but progressive faith walk. Following the old adage "what's said in group stays in group," I won't recount the specifics of her tale. Keeping confidentiality is of the utmost importance in such gatherings, worthy of being upheld even in writing intended to benefit group leaders. Nonetheless during this soul-searching autobiography I observed that her willingness to expose her struggle and broken heart was a stellar tribute to her dedicated companions. She credited those who worked steadily through the recovery steps each week with being her lifeline to the "heavenly realms" and "every spiritual blessing in Christ" (Eph 1:3). The ministry of Jesus Christ to those who are hurting becomes palpable in the life of such a cohesive community. A committed caring group with an underlying desire to serve the kingdom facilitates the vibrant experience of the presence of Jesus Christ.

While listening I compared this triumphant woman's experience with my recollection of the empirical trends in group work like those related in the preceding section. Studies in academic journals most often have trained or professional leaders. These differ greatly from the member-led support groups typical of ministry settings. This lack of investigative and evaluative efforts within Christian helping groups is both understandable and regrettable. The professional secular literature gives leaders much to consider in encouraging sturdier and sharper group offerings. Documentation of achieved outcomes communicates credibility. Perhaps greater exposure of this literature void will encourage Christian counseling and psychology programs to produce reputable outcome studies that fortify the good, faith-based programming already underway. Nonetheless the testimonies—not to mention the virtues permeating every event and conversation—I encountered on this site visit provided prototypical, anecdotal evidence consistent with the documented trends of professional group literature. The real faces I encountered revealed a hopeful confidence in the total experience of gathering for these precious conversations. This was an appointed place and time to trek together. Here was the interpersonal context to forge an intimate experience of the comfort available within the body of Christ (see 2 Cor 1:3-7). Though thoroughly impressed I mulled over a service gap that perhaps only I was in a position to notice: a lack of leader-directed groups that could offer mediated feedback on the dynamics of the bonds or tensions between participants.

WANTED: EXPERIENCED GUIDES

Evangelical ministries traditionally offer an assortment of discipleship-oriented, educational small groups that emphasize facilitated faith progression. These build on a combination of four core components that will be highlighted further in chapter five: nurture through the study of the Word, worship to honor God, community care via support and prayer, and mission or Christian service. Well-rounded Christian *nurture* is delivered in an intimate fellowship that resembles an extended family get-together where faith is shared, grounded in biblical truth and groomed into maturity.

Typically self-help groups engage almost exclusively in *community care* activity. By design, these groups give little attention to biblical nurture, worship and Christian service. If participants express interest in a more thorough kingdom orientation, leaders can make available a range of general discipleship options for honoring God, hearing the Word and reaching others. The offerings to attend a Bible study or care community may not be instantly sought, accessed or valued. Still, bringing these resources into the awareness of those receiving care provides ready access to the wider Christian fellowship experience. The invitation can be extended without undue pressure. The beauty of supportive care is that the point of contact with a seeker surrounds an immediate felt need. *How this reveals the real need for Jesus Christ is for the Holy Spirit to direct.* A small group trek within the Christian faith tradition will ultimately require a balance of input but give priority to feasting on the Word. An exciting and established trend on the ministry horizon is offering in one evening a wide assortment of groups and fellowship experiences. Sharing a meal, worship, hearing the journey story of another and a devotional from the Word can be included in the evening to supplement the self-help activity. This adds a soul-educating and faith-forming dimension to the small group experience.[17]

The self-help movement is now an established alternative to the dominant study-style small group, though not a replacement. Self-help groups are typically built on either a step or peer-support framework. Those of the step variety utilize principles adopted from the time-tested format of AA or use an application of those from the Christian-oriented CR. The structure for the group conversation flows from the specific step under consideration. Conversational rules are communicated via tradition to maintain a definite focus on personal efforts to live out the intention and values depicted by the step. Those sharing take turns. Cross-talk, feedback or advice is customarily prohibited or limited. On the other hand, support groups with a peer emphasis are not tied to the long-established step format. The structure arises out of an emphasis on sharing stories, struggles and accomplishments. There is ample room for helpful, empathetic feedback. These peer exchanges unify members and assist in recovery from a trauma such as a loss, act of violence, natural disaster, disability, disease or toxic relationship. This category of peer support group could also address those providing care to others, such as mothers of preschool children or caregivers for loved ones with a chronic illness. Either type of group may have an identified facilitator who assists with monitoring time, introducing steps or topics, and upholding group norms. The leader role in step or peer support groups is limited to managing the meeting flow. Educational material or members' stories fill the time as the most important content. There is limited room for commentary on how the group or its unique contributors are relating, engaging and utilizing the experience itself.

What might be gained if a different kind of small group was available? What would the impact be of leader-facilitated groups whose structure around a common theme allowed for more extensive interpersonal learning? This is the group

---

[17]While the momentum to install an evening of care groups must be described as recent, the use of fellowship meals coupled with testimonials, uplifting singing, inspirational messages and prayer for personal persistent problems is nothing novel to evangelical ministries. The packaging is fresh but its core of struggler assisting struggler to lean more on Jesus through caring community is a tried and true format.

trek level that I advocate. It places leaders in the role of seasoned trekking guide. Not only can leaders direct attention to the scenery and risks along the way, they can also assess how the travelers themselves are relating individually and corporately. This book contends that the prospects to move participants toward wholeness are increased considerably when a guide is intentionally positioned to assume this role. A fuller explanation unfolds in the following chapters.

Self-help groups have many similarities to those that are leader directed. Launched on a predetermined topic, both self-help and common-theme groups can have announced concerns that attract those with comparable struggles and interests. In this way, both formats place emphasis on homogeneity. The themes under discussion in either format make the content appear identical. Both group modes can complement individual counseling. But here the correspondence ends and distinctions begin.

Self-help groups of the step and support variety have an embedded operational philosophy.[18] This may be a defined set of recovery principles, steps or stages, a disease addiction model, or organizing language. Ideally these frameworks carry a struggling community through a recognized, universal and normalizing structure. In a leader-directed group, the framework is customized to the specific population based on empirical investigation, biblical principles or carefully combined material. Common-theme groups have trained or perhaps even professional leaders who can use that expertise to exercise executive function in design, screening, forming and initiating. Self-help groups have informal, volunteer guides where the basis for assuming the role is extensive internal expertise in the issue that unites the group, not from education or any external qualifications in group facilitation. Sponsors who come up through the self-help ranks are never far removed from the life concern and assume leadership to give back what they themselves have received. This layer of community care has a strong allegiance to the group and to helping others in the struggle.

The members attending self-help groups may fluctuate from week to week since there is generally an open-member policy. A common-theme group has stable attendance due to closed membership for the established duration of the group cycle. The predictability and regularity of membership allows for interpersonal exploration in these leader-guided experiences. There is a survival mentality prominent in many support groups that exclusively accents member strengths. Common-theme groups intend to promote personal, psychological

---

[18]Henry B. Andrews, *Group Design and Leadership: Strategies for Creating Successful Common Theme Groups* (Boston: Allyn and Bacon, 1995), pp. 1-14.

and/or spiritual growth by exploring the strengths and vulnerabilities that accompany automatic behavioral, emotional and attitudinal responses. Self-help programs are not inclined to engage in evaluation of outcomes because of the seemingly self-evident assumption that the system works if one works the system. According to this logic, step-based self-help groups cannot fail and their effectiveness is impossible to gauge. Leader guided groups investigate outcomes using surveys, observation, follow-up interviews and other forms of evaluation. Gathered data supplies the basis for increasing leader expertise and for refining intervention strategies.[19]

In promoting common-theme groups with leaders, I do not wish to downplay the important contribution of self-help experiences. Self-help groups can have pastoral or lay oversight and supply critical assistance on a consistent basis. Such cost effective services serve as an invaluable aid by offering a perpetual, supportive force. Throughout our travel together we will find that core corrective emotional relationships—healing encounters that extend redemptive intimacy—occur *both* in self-help settings and leader-directed experiences. There is sufficient anecdotal evidence to recognize that Jesus Christ does not discriminate when making his presence known between these distinct styles of groups.

The question when considering a potential gap in a ministry continuum is this: after thoughtful analysis of the population to be served, are there persons with growth needs who would best benefit from *mediated feedback,* commentary coached by an informed leader? Might the reason an individual is pondering a group signify a readiness or need to make adjustments in how one relates to others? Are there assumptions and relational patterns that would be amenable to communication aimed at interpersonal learning? A leader prepared to guide a group trek can seek to shape a group by using constructive feedback to identify tendencies to distort, distance, hide and wander. This is the single feature that makes a leader-guided experience unique and sets it apart from worthy self-help experiences. Mediated feedback can be offered and heard when there is an agreement at the outset to openly accept and disclose immediate experience. In professional language, participants give informed consent, acknowledging the benefits and risks of such interpersonal exercise. From the outset, leaders establish an expectation of interpersonal learning to achieve maturation, overcome isolation and reduce relational deadlocks, even though the detail and meaning of this element can unfold only within the group itself. The leader is necessary to (1) establish vision and purpose; (2) screen and secure

---

[19]Yalom and Leszcz, *Theory and Practice,* pp. 518-24.

membership; and (3) facilitate, capture and bring mediated feedback within reach. The risk to trust and relationally engage beyond automatic behaviors should be protected and praised. Leaders are not the sole messengers regarding interpersonal learning. Instead members begin to engage with each other as they speak openly about the relational polarities of self, other and God under the experienced supervision of a committed guide.

Opportunities abound for common-theme groups. Many parents have overwhelming relational baggage that stunts their parenting efforts, and they need a place to gain knowledge and techniques to train their children. Marital ministries—from pre-marital to marriage mentoring to divorce recovery—need ways to expose numerous relational concerns. Mediated feedback would assist college students establishing career, gender and worldview identity in the midst of making lifelong relational commitments. Those pursuing second careers or new priorities after mid-life often reevaluate the things that really matter, stimulating a rich awakening of relational pursuits. Seminarians and Christian leaders frequently discover that relational adaptability can enhance or hinder ministry vitality even more potently than technical skills or knowledge. Following a life crisis or severe adverse circumstances, many individuals enter a season that calls for the exploration of inner narratives and increased intimacy skills. These all hold potential for ministry application of common-theme, leader-guided groups.

Trekking together in kingdom-oriented groups may not merely ignite new insights into self. It may pull Christian believers into an ecclesial experience where there is greater reliance on the *ties that bind*. This phrase was mentioned early on to describe the rich benefit my own family enjoyed while exploring neighborhoods, town squares and backyards in a land previously unknown to us. The phrase itself has similar territorial roots in that it is borrowed from an old English poem and hymn. Country pastor John Fawcett (1740-1817) wrote these touching words to rehearse the beauty and potential of God-honoring fellowship within his simple flock. Once he gathered up his belongings, and he and his wife accepted a call to a larger church. Before he could move down the road, he realized that love for his little congregation was holding him fast. Having begun his pastoral duties at the age of twenty-six, he went on to shepherd the same Baptist congregation in the little village of Wainsgate, England, for a total of fifty-four years! Our family never visited that particular village while trekking about, but his words capture the essence of what trekking toward wholeness is all about.

Blest be the tie that binds our hearts in Christian love!
   The fellowship of kindred minds is like to that above.

Before our Father's throne we pour our ardent prayers;
   our fears, our hopes, our aims are one, our comforts and our cares.

We share our mutual woes, our mutual burdens bear;
   and often for each other flows the sympathizing tear.

When we asunder part it gives us inward pain;
   but we shall still be joined in heart, and hope to meet again.[20]

---

[20]Kenneth W. Osbeck, *Amazing Grace: 366 Inspiring Hymn Stories for Daily Devotions* (Grand Rapids: Kregel, 1990), S. 65.

Section One

TREK PREPARATIONS

2

TREKKING FUNDAMENTALS

LANDMARKS AHEAD

This chapter literally begins at the "beginning." God's creation of Adam and Eve, the rupture of sin that shattered shalom and the resulting relational fractures all form the basis for discussing some trekking fundamentals. Starting with Eden sets up the exploration of three overarching biblical motifs: walking, wandering and wisdom. The broader storyline of Scripture expands the vista of each motif. Every true kingdom trek considers the spiritual aspects that walking, wandering and wisdom represent. Leaders most fruitfully direct a communal journey when they are prepared to implement these fundamentals. Feedback related to each motif guides both participants and leaders to make immediate and long-term relational adjustments.

The chapter's close introduces the first of many trekking leaders whose reflections provide a glimpse of a group leader's inner life. In this chapter, Abby demonstrates that the courage to lead can prevail despite internal struggles.

A POCKET GUIDE

At this early juncture, I wish to establish select fundamentals of interpersonal trekking. These rudiments should be tucked neatly alongside maps for specific travel plans. Such concepts apply to hosting a group of spouses suffering through the loss of a life partner, mentoring mature Christ followers into servant leaders or directing a crew of adolescents marginally interested in avoiding mind-altering substances. This is a pocket guide to assist leaders and help groups maintain course by keeping essentials central. The intent is to reference key biblical material yet travel light. *Motifs,* or "recurring salient thematic elements," serve this purpose well.[1] The following three biblical themes—all with extensive Old Testament roots—can steer relationally oriented groups in a kingdom direction.[2]

---

[1]Merriam-Webster, Inc., *Merriam-Webster's Collegiate Dictionary,* 11th ed. (Springfield, Mass.: Merriam-Webster, 2003).

[2]The strategy of using biblical motifs in people-helping work was adopted following a message on

These motifs should be common trekking vocabulary.

GROUNDED IN THE GARDEN

Beginning with the creation account, the Scriptures tell the story of God's plan to create, call and cultivate a people who are eternally devoted to a relationship with him. Within this storyline, both basic human nature and the human state receive much attention (see Gen 1–3; Ps 139; Rom 1:18-32). In the initial chapter of Genesis, the man and woman together are the pinnacle of God's artistic effort (Gen 1:26-31). Formed by God from the dust of the earth and from the flesh of Adam, human beings are granted the nature, capability and elevated position required to have dominion over God's handiwork as his representatives and image bearers. Many of God's attributes are displayed in those made in the *imago Dei:* the ability to employ intellect and apply knowledge as rational beings; the discernment to recognize moral goodness and to practice love, mercy, justice and righteousness; and the capacity to exercise volition.[3] As God's uniquely appointed creatures exercise creation stewardship, they mirror God's character throughout the earth. This extends even to human relationships. The Trinity, the triune Godhead, is the centerpiece of Christian theology: one divine essence, three distinct yet interrelated persons. Serving a relational God whose image humans bear means that the individual and community are inseparable.[4] Small groups create a climate for growth in human beings designed for community.

From the outset of the biblical narrative, God gifts human beings with relational qualities. Adam was equipped to remain in close connection with the divine Gardener. Further, as the delegate of the male gender, he was designed to join with Eve, the female fashioned from his own flesh, to bring humanity to its complete expression. God as Creator knew each internal and external facet of the one he had formed from the dust of the ground. God was the source of the life force breathed into Adam, and God knew that Adam would yearn for a partner and for community. Immediately after God gave man his commission to work and care for the garden, he went on to explain, "It is not good for

---

this topic by author David Semands at the Second International Conference on Christian Counseling in Atlanta, Georgia; November, 1992.

[3]Louis Berkhof, *Systematic Theology* (Grand Rapids: Eerdmans, 1941), pp. 202-5.

[4]There has been extensive theological reflection in recent years on the implications of serving a relational God. One result of these discussions has been to ignite renewed interest in the link between individual and community. See Colin E. Gunton, *The Promise of Trinitarian Theology* (New York: T & T Clark, 1991); Stanley J. Grenz, *The Social God and the Relational Self: A Trinitarian Theology of the Imago Dei* (Louisville, Ky.: Westminster John Knox, 2001); John Zizioulas, *Being as Communion* (Crestwood, N.Y.: St. Vladimir's Seminary Press, 1985).

the man to be alone. I will make a helper suitable for him" (Gen 2:15-18). God had brought into existence a multitude of other living creatures to function in gendered pairs. In this regard human beings were no exception. The establishment of gender, coupled with the status of being in the *imago Dei*, is dramatic evidence of community's importance. Each individual is valuable to God as a distinct person, male or female, made in his image (Gen 9:6). Yet demonstration of community—the two coming together—provides the optimal picture of the *imago Dei*. God did not fashion a clone from Adam nor devise a divergent species with harmonizing characteristics. Instead "male and female he created them" means that two distinct but corresponding beings holistically reflect the nature of the Creator (Gen 1:27). The *imago Dei* is exposed as human gender characteristics draw separate beings toward one another and their relationship both fulfills the divine mandate and takes pleasure in God's blessing.[5] From the outset, God commanded this couple in communion to pioneer community by multiplication. This initial family portrays the eschatological destiny of the human race. God will dwell with human beings who exist together as a Creator-centered community (see Rev 21).

The Bible's opening story introduces both the satisfying and shadow sides of intimacy. Eden, God's delightful hand-planted garden, forms the setting. This place of pure *shalom* was crafted as a custom fit for Adam and Eve to be a source of continuous enjoyment. A garden is a dedicated area requiring routine attention, protection and care. In turn it produces provisions necessary for life and delicacies for pleasure. Adam and Eve were granted the privilege of caring for this special patch of well-nourished earth and their existence was infused with purpose as colaborers with the Creator.

Walking. The image of Adam and Eve walking with God contrasts sharply with the image portrayed by a verse couplet after they first sin. Prominently situated in the narrative, this Genesis passage reverberates throughout history and into the intimacy quests of contemporary human beings. These phrases may have the unnerving effect of simultaneously filling hearts with hope and eyes with tears. The imagery evokes an astonishing mixture of joy and sadness, exuberance and fear, security and shame. Immediately after Adam and Eve taste the fruit from one tree that God had declared to be toxic, an incident follows that encapsulates the core of the human condition: *God seeks while his beloved creatures hide.* "Then the man and his wife heard the sound of the LORD God as he was walking in the garden in the cool of the day, and they hid from the LORD God

---

[5]Grenz, *Social God*, pp. 267-303.

among the trees of the garden. But the LORD God called to the man, 'Where are you?'" (Gen 3:8-9). These verses reveal walking as the first biblical motif crucial for relational treks.

The perfect pair reigning in perpetual paradise would have been an idyllic situation had Adam and Eve not misused the freedom God had granted. Rebelling against or breaking God's rules, as Adam and Eve did, is *sin*. More formally, "sin is any failure to conform to the moral law of God in act, attitude, or nature."[6] Grasping this basic theological definition of sin allows us to explore the multitude of consequences and essential permanent change in spiritual status that resulted from Adam and Eve's original transgression. Sin brought death into the world and set in motion patterns of human behavior that deviate from the moral law (see Rom 3:1-23; 5:12-17). The truly fatal result of this initial sin was a fall away from openness with God, others and self. From contemplation to completion to consequence, the fall of man represents a relational rupture between creatures and their Creator. Those who were custom-made to walk beside and with the Creator God now maintain their distance. Communication becomes a distorted tool for preserving pride while suppressing shame, fear and guilt. From the point of Adam and Eve's sin forward, humans achieve relational wholeness only by overcoming the impulse to maintain distance, deny responsibility and distort intention. Joint trekking experiences demonstrate these relational patterns of distancing, denial and distortion. This relational rupture is the fallen state of wandering.

Wandering. In Genesis, the Garden of Eden faded in the distance while Adam and Eve were banished to a raw dwelling place. From that point onward travel contained threat, while tilling the soil required sweat and toil. Overtones of half-truth, blaming, scheming and deception shattered the *shalom* God had infused into the sanctity of that early garden environment. This could have begun an endless cycle of desperate running had it not been for a divine interjection of grace. *Shalom* could have been lost forever. The Creator's desire to walk with those made in the *imago Dei* brings about a new era. God in love seeks back his creatures that they might commit to walk with him.

How can these dramatic shifts in relationships be summarized for and applied toward conducting group work? In the created order before the entrance of sin, human beings had direct, unfiltered rapport with God, with one another and with themselves. God, man and woman could walk together. Such travel did not produce anxiety and fear, interspersed with the emotional elation that so charac-

---

[6]Wayne Grudem, *Systematic Theology* (Grand Rapids: Zondervan, 1994), p. 490.

terize human relationships. Prior to the Fall, divine and human intimacy was a normative state. Following the first sin, upheaval routinely accompanies human attempts at forming connections. Relational boundaries are routinely violated, intentions are misconstrued, communication is obscured and half-truths undermine trust. Sin left human beings relationally challenged and the potential for *shalom* severely compromised.

God by grace allows redemptive intimacy obtained either through human community or in a transcendent connection with the divine to flow into human experience. Grace is the activity of God that reveals his unfailing love, mercy and salvation. Grace is revealed as God enables human beings to experience his blessing despite human indifference and rebellion.[7] By grace, God makes it possible for human beings to construct the person-to-person bonds that shape our individual personalities and build the layers of relationships that support human existence. Group treks aim at cultivating novel occasions for this grace to break through and allow participants to walk more successfully together and with the Creator. Fundamentally, group trekking trains people to walk with self, others and God through the relational challenges left as sin's residue. Groups offer a means to notice subtle patterns of wandering or hiding that prohibit relational and spiritual intimacy. Trekking moves us toward wholeness when the heart places the Creator in his rightful place and longs to do his will. This infuses both sensibility and security to relationships with others. Discernment in this area reflects the biblical theme of the pursuit of wisdom in community.

Wisdom. In the Genesis account of human creation and fall (Gen 2–3), God directly and personally prohibited Adam from eating from the tree of the knowledge of good and evil (Gen 2:17). God explained that the well-being of humankind would be destroyed should Adam reject the command to abstain. Death would follow. Remarkably God granted vast freedom to human beings in this boundary-setting communication. Vegetation was plentiful. A variety of choice fruits would fill Adam and Eve's appetite and curiosity. God's restriction was limited to consumption of the fruit from one identified tree, permitting and even encouraging Adam to explore, partake of and enjoy all the remaining plant life. The text suggests that this communication was a personal, face-to-face declaration from the Creator to the creature. God's instruction left no question whatsoever about the content, meaning and details of God's command. Adam and Eve's sin in eating from the prohibited tree should be seen as a deliberate, law-breaking

---

[7]Walter A. Elwell and Phillip W. Comfort, *Tyndale Bible Dictionary* (Wheaton: Tyndale House, 2001), p 550.

action. But even before any action, a devastating fracture appears in the intimate connection and communication humans had with God. In order to fabricate a narrative that permitted deviant action, God's statements and intentions were twisted and turned. The deceiver mutated the health-promoting instructions of a loving benefactor into commands that were restrictive, unfair, selfish and belittling. Adam and Eve caught on and followed suit. God said nothing about not touching the tree of knowledge as Eve told the serpent (Gen 2:16-17; 3:2-3). He only barred the eating of the fruit. When the early representatives of the human race ate of the fruit, they broke the moral law of God. But just as important, they defamed the compassionate character of God by blatantly distorting his intentions and divine words.

Notice the motivation for the sinful course of action taken by Adam and Eve. This deadly experiment attempted to place creature on par with the Creator. When she contemplated her transgression, Eve was not drawn deeper into temptation purely by the taste and visual appeal of the fruit. She succumbed to the allure of the instant intelligence that would put her into a position of power equivalent with God's (Gen 3:4-7). In reaching for this fruit, Eve was not trying to fulfill a craving of hunger but to reposition and realign the relational order. The act of sin was a secretive, manipulative power play intended to reverse the hierarchy of creature and Creator. Thus a second biblical motif, wisdom, originates. The essence of wisdom is a wholesome fear or earnest respect for God's position, wishes and directions. Sin makes an alternative, foolish storyline seem plausible. Sin fosters an explanation for action that willfully places selfish desires over a humble determination to live out God's instructions.

The immediate consequence of this sin stands out. Human beings still experience the pain of isolation, emptiness and loneliness seen in sudden and striking results of the first sin. When Adam and Eve first noticed their nakedness and the gender differences between them, they suddenly and urgently needed clothes. They scurried to produce garments, not for warmth to resist the elements or for protection from the underbrush, but to repel the now distasteful gaze of a formally cherished other. Physical aspects of the human body that had once been exposed freely without shame required an opaque visual shield. The identifying marks of gender—celebrated features of the *imago Dei,* displaying unity and community—now became symbols of division, lust and power. Sewing fig leaves was an immediate crisis response, merely the first of infinite protective layers humans make for themselves. Other physical and interpersonal defenses perpetually divide people and diminish the likelihood of intimacy. Vain attempts to camouflage our presence or conceal ourselves psychologically may be ingenious while flimsy, resourceful but insufficient, deliberate yet disrespectful. Such defensive insulation seems necessary and advantageous but in reality distracts the wearer from authentic and beneficial relational encounters.

Adam and Eve experienced terror and fear as God approached, moving in his customary manner through the garden. The sound of God's advance no longer signaled a welcome invitation to join in a garden stroll. Now the nearness of the Creator aroused creaturely urges to conceal, evade and disappear. Exposure to the Gardener no longer meant sharing the beauty and bounty of the surroundings; rather, it implied condemnation for those responsible for its care. The trees placed in the garden by God for enjoyment, protection and nurture were transformed into objects providing seclusion. The resulting hide and seek is not a game but a useless pattern that spirals on. Human beings, the *imago Dei*, fashioned for fellowship with each other and to walk with God, now hide while he seeks. A refreshing walk where the Creator-creature relationship is enjoyed now requires delicate and dedicated effort.

WALKING

Scripture most commonly uses the word *walk* to express its literal meaning—going somewhere on foot—but also expresses a further, more demanding connotation with the same word.[8] The figurative use of *walk* conveys conviction in pursuing a pattern of life, an idea with profound spiritual significance. Two opposing paths are available for the journey of life: the bright way of righteousness, obedience and blameless moral conduct; or the highway shrouded in wickedness and evil deeds (see Prov 2:7, 13, 20; Jer 13:10; Rom 6:4; 8:4; Eph 4:1, 17). Moses employed the theme of walking when he compactly described obedience to God's laws and the best way to demonstrate faithfulness: "So be careful to do what the LORD your God has commanded you; do not turn aside to the right or to the left. Walk in all the way that the LORD your God has commanded you, so that you may live and prosper and prolong your days in the land that you will possess" (Deut 5:32-33).

Walking in the way of the Lord preserves vibrant life and fosters a healthy prosperity. The alternative direction is a destiny fixed in destruction. Immediately following these verses, Moses beautifully rehearses a list of the provisions

---

[8]F. S. Fitzsimmonds, "Walk," in *New Bible Dictionary*, ed. Derek R. Wood, I. Howard Marshall, A. R. Millard, J. I. Packer and D. J. Wiseman, 3rd ed. (Downers Grove, Ill.: InterVarsity Press, 1996), p. 1228.

available for those living in the Promised Land. The attention then turns to the source of these promises, God who is to be loved with the whole heart, mind and soul (Deut 6:1-9). Readers are to impress these commands on the next generation, living them out to preserve the nation's walk with the Lord.

Much later in the biblical story, the apostle John further explores the relationship between fellowship and internal renewal. Walking demonstrates John's central message of salvation in Christ. "If we claim to have fellowship with him yet walk in the darkness, we lie and do not live by the truth. But if we walk in the light, as he is in the light, we have fellowship with one another, and the blood of Jesus, his Son, purifies us from all sin" (1 Jn 1:6-8). These verses beautifully weave the concepts of proceeding God's way, traveling with others and inner cleansing. Walking with God and like-minded others has a sanctifying effect on the inner self.

Within our permissive contemporary culture, individual choice can be elevated to an extreme. Painting this central spiritual life choice in dramatic, plain black and white may appear rigid. But the Scriptures contrast the way of walking transparently in the light before the Lord with vain attempts to follow directions to nowhere under a veil of darkness. The culture may assert that most of life's choices are gray at best or that, given the right enhancement and filters, alternative choices have the most vivid color. But Scripture speaks in stark terms about choosing how to live before the Creator. Our walk is either proceeding toward or withdrawing from the Creator. Someone moving toward God takes seriously Jesus' Great Commandment: "Love the Lord your God with all your heart and with all your soul and with all your mind; . . . love your neighbor as yourself" (Mt 22:37-39; Mk 12:30; Lk 10:27). In contrast, a more recent paraphrase of these words illustrates the ideal walking path in a culture where self-determination reigns: "Love yourself with all your heart, soul, and mind, because you deserve it; Love your sex partner and children as yourself, but only after you have taken good care of yourself."[9] The way we walk either exposes a love for God and neighbor or reveals self-isolating and indulgent motives.

Therefore whenever trekking with others in order to change direction, strengthen one's stride, clear obstacles or expand endurance, an underlying spiritual dimension reveals one's ultimate pursuit. A group trek focused on a central uniting theme, such as parenting acting-out adolescents or reducing destructive anger, may not initially appear to be an explicitly faith-oriented journey. It is

---

[9]Jeffery H. Boyd, "Two Orientations of the Self," *Journal of Psychology and Theology* 26 (1998): 110-22.

certainly appropriate to target a specific relationship or skill for improvement when setting out on a group journey. Yet leaders with a grasp of trekking fundamentals realize that, while each journey has unique phases, nuances and specialty techniques, each trekker will ultimately be challenged to grapple with lifestyle priorities, character choices, selection of travel companions and desired depth of intimacy. The Scriptural theme of walking can shift the focus from a temporal goal to an eternal travel destination and back again.

WANDERING

Relocation into uncultivated wilderness and a relentless struggle for survival were sure signs that Adam and Eve were no longer dwelling in the cherished setting of God's garden. An even harsher reality soon hit close to home. Their family community was split wide open over the severest case of sibling rivalry. The loss of a child rips open a parent's heart like no other loss; Adam and Eve—parents of the human race—experienced a double dose of soul-wrenching heartache when one son actually took the life of the other. Both sons were lost. The destructive relational effect of sin embedded into human life surfaced suddenly, an irrefutable reality.

The Scriptures record that Cain burned with envy when God deemed worthy Abel's worship offering of the "fat portions from some of the firstborn from his flock" while his own presentation of fruits from the soil was rejected (Gen 4:3-5). How deeply ironic that a failure in worship, an unsuccessful attempt to enjoy God's favor, churned up the violent hatred that culminated in this earliest record of premeditated murder. Cain understood clearly that his brother Abel had done well in making an offering to the Lord and that he had made a serious mistake. Soon his sullen look and darkened heart were blatantly evident to God. The emotional upheaval pulling Cain sin-ward was so vivid that God described it as a dangerous predator poised to leap upon its kill. The Lord intervened with Cain to give both gracious encouragement and grave warning. "Then the LORD said to Cain, 'Why are you angry? Why is your face downcast? If you do what is right, will you not be accepted? But if you do not do what is right, sin is crouching at your door; it desires to have you, but you must master it'" (Gen 4:6-7).

God reached out once again to a wayward human being to prevent impending tragedy. The observation, empathy, instruction and admonition demonstrated in these words model the type of help that participants in a basic helping group can extend to one another. Exposing emotional pain revealed the potential for sinful action. Recognizing the inner emotional experience provided a window of opportunity for God to implore Cain to change the direction of his walk; thus, affect provides important cues for relational communication (see Mt 5:21-26). Tragically, Cain ignored God's encouragement to master his sin and instead took deliberate steps to seize the life of his brother. Another round ensued of sinner hiding while God seeks. Group work also addresses such a recalcitrant pattern of self-destructive isolation and wandering.

By acting out his murderous rage, Cain not only trampled on God's gracious words of caution but also brought down layer after layer of alienation. He cut himself off from his family only to be expelled into exile. His brother's innocent blood cursed the ground that Cain had once skillfully cultivated. The soil would never again produce crops under his care. The fruit left on the altar would be his final harvest and Cain's occupation as a farmer was ruined. Cain's sin resulted in alienation from God, from others and from the very activity that once defined his identity. Although lacking in great detail, Scripture records that Cain did not roam the earth endlessly. Eventually he became the architect of a city and fathered a line of descendants bent on wickedness (Gen 4:16-24). This is Cain's memorable legacy.

Cain may have settled down, but the wanderer never truly finds rest. For Cain there was no return to *shalom*. The city of Enoch may have been his attempt to reproduce God's Eden, demonstrating what Cain could do on his own. God permitted him to replace the community he left behind with others who more closely reflected Cain's sinister nature. This wanderer secured a place and people to quench his desire for purpose and partnership. Unfortunately for Cain, the text gives no appearance that he renewed his attempt to worship God. Cain never brought an appropriate offering before the Creator. When it came to a relationship with God, he remained a resistant wanderer. Cain is the archetype of those who stray away from the Creator and genuine community. His choices are consistently self-defeating and generally flow from a misguided self-reliance. When directing a trek with a mission of realizing *shalom*, observant leaders notice and bring awareness to this wandering pattern.

One additional dimension of this Old Testament wandering motif provides special insight for group leaders. The wanderers in this case are not representative individuals but the entire Israelite community. God had delivered the Israelites out of slavery in Egypt, and Moses and Aaron were leading the nation to a new home. God made his presence known daily through the provision of manna and the appearance of the cloud. This generation of former slaves knew that their journey was directed by a supernatural being. The time had come for God to walk with them into the place they had been promised, a land flowing with milk and honey.

In Numbers 13–14, Moses and Aaron followed the Lord's instruction and sent representatives to conduct a comprehensive survey of Canaan. In order to assess the productivity of the land, they instructed the spies to bring back samples of any available fruit. Initially following their investigation, the unanimous report declared that the land held wonderful delights. The text says it took two men to carry a crop of one clump of grapes! The spies found additional tangible evidence like sweet pomegranates and figs. The land was filled with bounty just as the Lord had described. No person of integrity could dispute its desirability. Upon sorting out the details, however, only two spies—Caleb and Joshua—believed that taking possession of this rich land was plausible. Such a magnificent place was already inhabited with people who called it home. The Canaanite stakeholders gave no indication that they would mercifully release their claim without a fight. The spies understood that the inhabitants would not surrender their land without exacting a substantial toll on all intruders. The frightened surveyors failed to trust God's explicit promise that the land would be God's gift to them. The dynamics surfacing between God and his people at this point in Exodus parallel those evident in the early chapters in Genesis. While the people would not completely return to Eden, they were poised to enter a special place selected by God for this nation at this time. Yet again God's people rejected his plan for their peace and prosperity! Dismal and distorted descriptions of the promised territory circulated. The leaders perverted God's instructions, and fear baffled and blinded the people.

The Israelite nation expressed their willingness to return to a place of oppression merely because it was familiar. Retreat was advisable; advancement, avoidable. The community lacked the courage and will to risk leaping into their biggest faith venture since tiptoeing along the edge of the Red Sea. This was their moment of choice: would they walk boldly forward with the God who had been their security or wander in the disappointment of the familiar? Was the wisdom of God's assurance of this gift to be trusted or would human reason alone prevail? The ensuing forty years of wilderness wandering resulted needlessly from the Israelite community's reticence to renounce the past, forfeit the recognizable present and appropriate God's promised homeland for the future. Even still, individuals and communities choose to wander aimlessly from place to place rather than to risk changing rituals and routine.

Those who investigate group dynamics routinely assume that a collective community dares to take on more dramatic risks than a single individual within the same group might consider prudent. Individuals demonstrate risk in the presence of others as a means to achieve status, recognition and approval. This results in the phenomenon called *risky shift*, or distributing responsibility from "I" to "we" and "me" to "us."[10] As more shoulders bear the weight of a decision, the collective is willing to tolerate a higher degree of risk. What went wrong with the people of Israel after traveling together out of Egypt under the watchful eye of their Deliverer?

This remarkable case study of group refusal requires the reader to understand the multidirectional nature of risk-taking behavior within groups. The perception of safety may exist in numbers. Recall that Adam and Eve ate the forbidden fruit after Eve spoke with the serpent. Eve took a risk after this conversation that she may not have taken without a joint conference over her options. The collective can ease discomfort with risk just as easily away from God's path as toward a walk with him. In Numbers, the people of Israel moved in the direction of a monumental risk when emotional panic permeated the collective. The risk was to reject the call for obedience and to discard God's gift. Consequently a generation meandered around a wilderness wasteland until the offending risk takers died.

The nation of Israel's extended period of wandering provides a fundamental lesson for everyone who attempts to lead a group. A leader may need to offer the realistic yet faith-centered challenge of a Joshua or Caleb not only to a single member but also as a counter to the mainstream perspective. Such leadership moments take resilience, lucidity and courage—at best, elements guided completely by the movement of the Holy Spirit. Groups may indeed provide the solace, security and support that enable risk-taking behavior. But risk does not always mean the most productive or God-honoring direction. Risk may fortify choices that result in needless and fruitless wandering. Consider the insight of Gareth Icenogle as he draws a parallel between these moments in Israel's history and the contrary behavior that can emerge in a small group.

> Israel wandered in the wilderness for forty years because the people refused
> to become self-aware of their dysfunctional group dynamics. They feared
> going on and venturing into new territory. This would challenge their set
> patterns of behavior and force them to exercise faith. To cross into the
> Promised Land meant risk, danger and threat to their desire for individual
> and group security. Every small group is confronted by such an "exodus"
> journey. Will the group wander in a long-term safe wilderness together,

---

[10]Neil M. Malamuth and Seymour Feshbach, "Risky Shift in a Naturalistic Setting," *Journal of Personality* 40 (1972): 38-49.

or will they move on into new territory, take the necessary risks, meet the interpersonal giants and experience the abundant life of a group that has the faith and courage to meet new challenges?[11]

This is where the Holy Spirit must chart a course into new territory. A leader must rely on her own walk with the Lord, preserve wisdom and protect a group from wandering. Often only a subset or a single member of the group needs such restoration. In the closing phrases of his book, James issues this charge to work with wanderers, "My brothers, if one of you should wander from the truth and someone should bring him back, remember this: Whoever turns a sinner from the error of his way will save him from death and cover over a multitude of sins" (Jas 5:19-20).

Participating in the course adjustment of a travel companion is a great honor, yet a close investment into another's life does not automatically result in a positive return. God himself came alongside Cain on more than one occasion to divert impending disaster without favorable results. Common theme groups may unite those with insight into a particular pattern of wandering. For example, the group may cluster together those battling self-destructive or relationally damaging behaviors. A leader-initiated group may gather those familiar with tricky patches of terrain, such as those caring for a disabled loved one or struggling through unemployment. Whatever the instance, members may have the insight to identify where they can successfully execute critical conversions. Such moments may also be influenced by the interventions of a group leader. A group demonstrates maximum operational proficiency when the honor of directing wanderers toward a destination of *shalom* is a shared experience not dependent solely on the leader.

WISDOM

The third biblical motif useful for kingdom-centered group work speaks to the heart of leadership discernment: wisdom. People often ask me, "What is the biblical basis for the helping groups you promote?" My response has grown firm: "Have you considered my servant Job?" (Job 1:8). The Lord spoke these words to Satan in the prologue of the book of Job. Drawing on them is not an intentional insult or defensive dodge. In the ancient Hebrew Scriptures, the biblical book of Job could be read as the transcript of a helping group addressing the most poign-

---

[11]Gareth Weldon Icenogle, *Biblical Foundations of Small Group Ministry: An Integrational Approach* (Downers Grove, Ill.: InterVarsity Press, 1994), p. 189.

ant themes of our day and in our lives. "When Job's three friends, Eliphaz the Temanite, Bildad the Shuhite and Zophar the Naamathite, heard about all the troubles that had come up on him, they set out from their homes and met together by agreement to go and sympathize with him and comfort him" (Job 2:11). Job's wife started the conversation with her crude advice to "Curse God and die" (Job 2:9). Job himself offered early on a most profound response: "Shall we accept good from God, and not trouble?" (Job 2:10). His friends labored long, spouting many words over powerful matters such as good and evil, suffering and sin, faith and fortune, hope and despair. In later chapters, Elihu droned on, searching to explain integrity, evil, fate and the fragility of life. Finally the Lord himself put the critical matter to rest by asserting his role as the Designer, Sustainer and Creator of the universe. The dynamic exchange reached a clear conclusion: God is wisdom. Faith is to rest in him and not on any philosophy, religious methodology or vain self-righteousness.

Folk wisdom insists, "Misery loves company." Group research attests to the healing effect of universality, the relief that comes with realizing others encounter suffering similar to our own.[12] Biblical wisdom and clinical evidence best support the following revision of folklore: good company can mitigate the miserable isolation of suffering. Those who experience and share comfort from the Source of all comfort and Father of compassion are good company (2 Cor 1:3-7). Job's friends attempt to assist from a framework of persuasion and advice-giving, not a desire to give comfort. Job deals with God through the human exchange and eventually God intervenes directly and introduces the basis for wisdom.

The dramatic dialogue of the book of Job reveals how one can relate transparently and wrestle vigorously with self, others and God. The text tells us that while he was blunt, emotional and at times explosive, "Job did not sin in what he said" (Job 2:10). God eventually forced Job's friends to repent for offering foolish counsel and issuing too many useless arguments. They were nonetheless personally present with Job throughout his suffering and God forgave them for their erroneous utterances. What poetic beauty when in the epilogue he who had suffered such horrific loss offered intercessory prayer on behalf of those who intended to be his comforters. While the wisdom of God actually set matters straight, Job offers an observation of interpersonal support, intensive give-and-take exchange, and purification of faith. Job walked closer with God after this experience. To their credit, his friends did not leave him to wander alone dur-

---

[12]Irwin D. Yalom and Molin Leszcz, *The Theory and Practice of Group Psychotherapy*, 5th ed. (New York: Basic Books, 2005), pp. 6-8.

ing the darkest days of his life. God made his presence known and his wisdom plain within this small community. The book of Job provides a biblical example of intimate group conversation that loses its grip on comfort yet with the Lord's help, embraces wisdom.

What relevance can Job's friends' failed attempts to administer God-honoring comfort have for leader-guided group treks? The friends mistakenly presumed that Job was wandering from God's intentions and challenged him for it. They should have gently encouraged Job to walk through his painful suffering in absolute trust. But it seems that their words of support were the best these friends had to offer even though they did not reflect divine wisdom. God's intervention in their group conversation provided a meaningful new perspective. Did not God offer feedback that returned the direction of the group toward a walk of faith? A leader follows this example here by citing a metaphor, posing a question or reflecting on the direction, progress or rigidity of group dynamics. Certainly trekking guides should proceed more tentatively and humbly than God did in this encounter. Still, entering into the fray of the group and calling others to reconsider the dominant relational process demonstrates the benefit of mediated feedback. Wisdom takes its place at the table.

Wisdom is "the ability to direct one's mind toward a full understanding of human life and toward its moral fulfillment."[13] Wisdom is a multidimensional concept that combines adeptness in practical life-coping skills with the pursuit of a lifestyle dedicated to ethical conduct. The current secular contamination of wisdom elevates the importance of superior intellectual resources. In contrast, biblical wisdom is never reserved for those with stellar minds but permeates only those whose hearts are passionate for God. The conclusion of the book of Job provides a firm foundation for understanding wisdom, one that Scripture echoes elsewhere: "The fear of the Lord—that is wisdom, and to shun evil is understanding" (Job 28:28; see also Prov 1:7).

Fundamentally any kingdom-centered helping group embarks on a wisdom quest. Specifically this means the fostering of a faith that values obtaining wisdom, discerning prudent action, increasing stamina in self-discipline and deepening moral fortitude. The Scriptures declare that the pursuit and application of wisdom promise a return beyond any price, the experience of life as pleasurable and a path of peace (Prov 3:15-20).

Wisdom is frequently personified in Scripture (see Job 28; Prov 1:20-33; 3:13-18; 8:1-36). The writer of Proverbs pictures wisdom as a woman crying

---

[13]Elwell and Comfort, *Tyndale Bible Dictionary*, p. 1304.

aloud in the streets (Prov 1:20-33). In the New Testament, the wisdom theme is expressed as the *word* that became flesh with the incarnation (Jn 1:1-4; see also Col 1:15-20). Jesus Christ is wisdom in actual flesh and blood. In helping groups, wisdom makes a grand entrance when the presence of Jesus Christ becomes undeniably real in interpersonal exchanges infused by the ministry of the Holy Spirit. When a group encounter turns heavenward, participants recognize wisdom as a work of grace. Loving company ministers to misery. As Jesus Christ reaches out through others to wipe tears and whisper wisdom, individuals discover spiritual benefits even in their suffering.

Pulling the three motifs together, to walk in obedience and right relationship with God is to abandon wandering according to our own wishes and to appropriate wisdom by living in dependent accountability to the Creator.

REACH AND REMEMBER

Abby gazed around the small room now that the empty stacking chairs had been moved into position.[14] The members of her new Reach and Remember group, a choice setting for grief sufferers to exchange comfort, would soon warm those seats. The sound of steam starting to sizzle in the coffee pot brought her focus closer to the current moment but she refused to come to the present just yet. Instead she allowed her emotions to return her to a distant place, back to an evening long gone. Her mind temporarily traveled to a dimly lit restaurant where the startling loss of her own husband made that anniversary meal unforgettable. His heart attack had been like a sudden and ferocious storm that was over in a flash. Her heartache began in those terror-filled seconds, only to persist with the predictability of the returning tide. The ache would rise and fall, come and go, advance and retreat. How could she presume to invite others to share their grief with the hope that the unbearable sadness in their hearts might fade when her own loss could surface again and again with such a soul-crippling effect?

There had to be a reason she had started this grief group—it was about to enter its third cycle, after all. Two previous crews had trekked through a grief recovery experience with her as their guide. Had those groups been helpful? What stories of loss would this new cycle bring? Would these tales of separa-

---

[14]Throughout this work such group examples are clinical composites woven together from a variety of personal, consulting and anecdotal experiences often relayed by supervisees. These are not real life leaders, specific groups or a retelling based on transcriptions. Actual events will be related in the first person or by acknowledgment of the specific source. Even in those instances where there is a recollection of a first person event, the names and details are changed to preserve confidentiality.

tion be too fresh to be put to rest? She needed to recall her own memories now or she was in danger of losing her own courage to lead. What had happened in the bereavement support group at her church that she had joined a few months after her loss? What choice moment had convinced her to offer to take others on a similar journey? She could sense a ball of tension start to form in the center of her chest right near the ache. She knew that tears were not far away. The memory of saying good-bye to those who had once trekked with her was returning now and their presence would soon provide her the courage to give a warm welcome to the newcomers who would arrive very soon.

The depth of Al's soft tone was the first voice she recalled. He had thanked each group member one by one for their support as he dealt with the dreaded cancer that had robbed him of his wife. There was no doubt in his mind that he would not be around had these fellow grievers not assembled each week. He relayed that the overpowering isolation of his suffering had caused him to abandon the love of life that had been his trademark. On the darkest of days, he planned to let the car run in a pitch black garage while he quietly fell asleep behind the wheel. The temptation to flee his despair and unite with his partner of nearly thirty years was so compelling that it mesmerized him. Somehow the powerful stories he had heard from others had restored enough hope in his heart that he never moved from the stuffed recliner in his living room to the leather seat in his automobile. The darkness did not take over, he mastered the sin crouching at his door and he never wandered too far from those he knew were there to sustain him. Yes, Abby could hear Al's voice and her courage began to ascend.

Her mind now raced to recall a name that refused to be retrieved. The woman had reddish brown hair and a touch of an accent in her speech. What was her nationality anyway? Her handkerchief had functioned like a security blanket. Perhaps it was because the woman had spoken up so rarely that her name was difficult to recollect. Abby could not even correctly assemble the details of the defeat she had suffered. It was associated with the sounds and smells of a hospital complete with surgery, medical wizardry at its finest and being by a bedside while her loved one exhaled his final breath. The woman had spoken about the hospital chapel being a place that God never visited. Her prayers hit the ceiling and bounced right back. When this grieving traveler said her group farewell, her muttering ceased and a statement of clarity broke through: "My prayers are reaching heaven again." Answers were not flowing down, but the messages were surely getting through. The woman with the reddish brown hair who hardly spoke up had apparently taken much in. She credited the group with helping her to pray again and to resume a walk of faith. True, she had admitted that it was feeble even on her good days, but practices had returned that had long been absent from her routine.

Now Abby's own parting phrases entered her mind. For her the injustice of a fatal heart attack interrupting an anniversary meal and abruptly ending her marriage kept forcing its way into her thoughts. The confusion, helplessness and unfairness of that restaurant experience could never be undone. It was ironic and inexcusable. The effect of this repetitive echo drowned out every word of rebuttal. The former joy of an anniversary approaching on the calendar was suddenly transformed into a remembrance of tragedy. How had that taunting message been tamed? No group member had ever addressed this internal nightmare. Her perspective on universal justice was never challenged. There were no lessons with three sure steps to curtail compulsive thoughts. Her parting words had been to simply thank everyone for sharing their separation stories. A word of wisdom had broken through as she endured the ritual of each one speaking about his or her deep personal loss until the practice turned into encouragement.

There is never a good day to lose a loved one; nor is there any justice in loss. It does not matter if the departure is anticipated or unexpected, slow or instant, before a birthday or shortly after a new birth. There is always an upcoming celebration that will not be shared or a moment of achievement that will not be savored together. Death itself is unjust. The circumstances are not the issue. Every loved one experiences separation as if evil was winning out. The affectionate faces of that group along with their irreplaceable stories sparked Abby's courage. She could smell the coffee now and someone was walking down the hall toward this room. Abby would embrace this approaching group member because wisdom might once again show up among common accounts of grief and produce an uncommon comfort. After all, the journey through grief is never welcome and the warmth of being together is a small but extremely worthwhile consolation.

Trekking toward wholeness does not return people to the Garden. *Shalom* is never fully or permanently restored. Yet in spite of that earthly limitation, miracles do happen. A group trek may be a time when God calls out to those in hiding: "Where are you? Would you like to walk together?"

3

EVERY TREKKER TELLS A STORY

LANDMARKS AHEAD

A personal story begins and ends the trekking lesson in this chapter. A silly fishing "trauma" sparked vivid memories of my early training in group work. This provides the backdrop to introduce the technical terms content *and* process, *critical concepts for discussing leader-guided groups. My early training left a memorable impression of communication just beneath the surface that inevitably displays relational assumptions, vulnerabilities and hopes. A second feature is a tour of the small group "bands" of John Wesley. This refreshing visit to one of the great care group efforts from the evangelical faith heritage introduces the four major leader functions: vision and structuring, caring, affect and attachment stimulation, and meaning attribution. Be on alert for five orientation principles, which will be summarized at the end of the chapter. These establish the unique formation value of groups where mediated feedback is encouraged. Trekkers are enabled to observe and then transform their own relational stories.*

HOOKED

It was a sunny, breezy, lazy August afternoon and I was fishing on a glorious body of water nestled between beautiful hills. I routinely enjoy spending as many of my summer leisure hours as possible on this deep glacial lake. The wave from a passing Ski Nautique hit at the precise moment I was snapping a brand new rebel lure onto my leader. Instantly my hands were intricately joined. One of the sharp treble hooks found its way into the thumb on my left hand and barbed harpoons lodged themselves into several of the fingers on my right. I looked down at the situation with stunned admiration. The hooks had inserted themselves with surgical precision. I squirmed and wiggled my fingers in a variety of positions in vain attempts to free myself from the fishing lure that now bound my hands as if handcuffing me for some crime. New empathy welled up in me for lake trout, who cannot break free when in a parallel predicament.

Two hours later a non-squeamish family member and I had exhausted our first aid skills and I agreed to go to the local ER. It was the first time I had been back to the hospital where I had begun my professional journey well over two decades previously. In this same teaching hospital the potency of people helping within group counseling burned itself into my memory. The place did not look the same, but distinctive features jogged my memories of the experience. The facility was much larger and quite contemporary given its rural country setting. But the folks and surroundings still conveyed a friendly, warm, hopeful and professional atmosphere. I had not returned after my earliest training experience on the inpatient psychiatric unit. It had been here, way back then, that I was introduced to therapeutic group work. As I sat with legs dangling off the side of a hospital bed and a fake minnow holding my hand, my mind wandered. I traveled back to those nervous moments when I had greeted patients sitting in a similar position—that is, minus the menacing minnow. My task as an intern, presumably, had been to collect background information for the ER physician and psychiatric team. In hindsight, perhaps my role was actually to keep agitated patients distracted until real help arrived.

Fortunately in my current predicament, the good-natured medical staff kindly welcomed this hook-tied patient. They avoided the quips dancing around in my own imagination that would be fitting to use on the worst excuse for an amateur fisherman ever to wet a line in their state. Before tackling my mini-medical crisis, the nurse dealt with my most serious injury, a bruised ego. With apparent enjoyment, she told me in great detail about a comparable predicament she had witnessed a few weeks earlier. Her story was indeed humorous, yet it sent a compassionate message. Another klutzy sportsman had hooked not only both his hands but another portion of his lower anatomy at the same time. He was obviously in extensive pain with his body locked—hook, line and sinker—into a considerably more embarrassing pose. Hearing that sordid fishhook story did much to soothe my wounded pride, which was in need of more immediate attention than my impaled fingers. Next that smiling nurse offered an interesting tidbit of information: "We just so happen to have an attending physician on duty today whose specialty is removing fishhooks." This hospital had a reputation for its fine roster of specialists but I never expected to hear that fishhook removal was on that list. Is there really board certification for treating angler-related injuries?

The nurse had not exaggerated regarding the proficiency of this particular Doc. An advanced intervention system belied his strong theoretical background. His well-honed technique involved reversing the snagged entry using fishing line and a flick of the wrist that mimicked the art of fly-casting. The only painful aspect of the procedure was that several medical interns were on hand to observe my predicament or, more accurately, the advanced remedy. My misfortune provided the occasion for them to learn the fine art of barbed hook removal to assist future self-destructive fishermen. Memories of being the center of such attention as a result of a careless moment don't exactly warm my insides. The humbling experience brought back the lessons of an earlier teachable moment. I mentally traveled back twenty-five years when I had been the eager intern and like these open-mouthed students had watched a master craftsman at work. My recollection landed on days when a therapeutic milieu and a mentor who enjoyed being transparent about his craft shaped my sputtering attempts to be helpful.

Way back when, Dave was the veteran psychiatric social worker who directed the treatment groups on the inpatient unit. His expertise extended from conducting family therapy sessions to gleaning insights from patient group encounters. Dave could sense, name and utilize the invisible cords that connected the conversations of seemingly isolated and disinterested participants. Like the fishhook removal specialist, this master could see entry and exit paths invisible to the naked eye. With what seemed to be magical ease, Dave choreographed an intimate dance where the casual observer might notice nothing more than confused persons wringing their hands and colliding in hopeless, random repetition.

This seasoned social worker placed his neophyte psychiatric interns as facilitators of an adjunct therapy group that utilized poetry as its focal point. It wasn't hard to figure out that my poetry therapy-group assignment was an ingenious way to keep a fairly useless undergraduate psychology student occupied while not seriously endangering any struggling patients. Or was there genuine therapeutic value in this trendy approach? Patients were encouraged to share their favorite verse selections, echoes from intriguing folk songs or even their own poetic material. We student intern leaders carried sample pieces around in our pockets so like faithful scouts we were always prepared to prime the pump. One of those sessions centered on the famous Robert Frost poem "The Road Not Taken." Picture six psychiatric inpatients ranging in ages from twenty-two to seventy-two and struggling with deep discouragement, a loose grasp of reality or moods that changed without warning. This was not your typical literary book club. Odd as it sounds, these group members reflected on the phrases of that traditional poem in a way that prompted lively self-disclosure and intimate emotional exchange. The sturdy metaphor of paths intersecting and winding onward evoked emotions on a spectrum from peaceful resolve to frightening panic, from crippling uncertainty to brash impulsivity. The poet depicts a solo hiker soulfully contemplating a country crossroads. A decision is made as roads diverge. Could destiny be designed by small, insignificant choices?

About one month later, the therapeutic team watched the videotape of this session. As a novice, I was sorely embarrassed by my own blundering attempts to imitate the sophisticated skills of my supervisor, a person who was so subtle and sharp in stimulating exchanges, highlighting critical insights and prompting deeper disclosure. I forgot these insecurities, however, when the camera caught a dark-haired, unshaven, forty-two-year-old single man named Jim, who was suffering from major depression. He pondered over treasured phrases like: "sorry I could not travel both," "I took the road less traveled" and "that has made all the difference."[1] Every traveler makes choices. Regrets are all too real.

How thin and sad he was as he spoke of the recent loss of his mother. His hand touched the colostomy bag hanging at his side, reminding observers of his medical crisis at that time. A growing sense of determination arose in his voice as he spoke. An elderly and frail female patient in the hospital for a series of Electric Convulsive Therapy (ECT) treatments replied with comforting words of hope and challenge. Her counsel seemed to fit so perfectly with the courage that was stirring within him. No one would deny that there was life in that therapeutic exchange between those deeply hurting patients. The video left with me a lasting impression. *The member-to-member component of group counseling is a powerful tool for observing and activating relational intimacy* (Orientation Principle 1).

Sadly, several weeks after the session was recorded, Jim successfully took his own life. As a result of that bleak reality, the otherwise bland educational review of students doing poetry therapy gained an emotional intensity. The entire exchange was now deciphered with new insight, and Dave provided the indispensable commentary. Was that patient explaining a line from a poem to a fellow struggler or was he internally making a life and death decision? Was he hearing the kind voice of a gray-haired widow speaking encouragement out of her own hurting heart? Or did the voice of his controlling mother fill his ears during that moment of relational connection? Thus a second lesson was locked into my therapeutic repertoire. *There is much more to group interpersonal process than meets the untrained eye. Skilled leaders view, access and utilize relational communication* (Orientation Principle 2). In order to make sense of the layer beneath, a group leader needs to see like Dave. He could discern messages about emotions and

---

[1]Robert Frost, "The Road Not Taken," in *Robert Frost: Collected Poems, Prose, & Plays* (New York: Literary Classics, 1995), p. 103.

relationships revealed via hopes and fears. On the surface, six psychiatric patients had spent a relatively benign but entertaining ninety minutes with three young helpers discussing a dated and well-worn piece of verse. After considering Dave's insights and my own deeper review, I could now see the road less traveled. In my therapeutic work, seeing pathways of interpersonal connection, as well as relational misses and rejection, has made all the difference.

The pages ahead explore lessons on how person-to-person interactions in structured group experiences can be effective for personal, relational and spiritual growth. I admit to still being "hooked" on a few basics: (1) our most troubling or embarrassing predicaments may not be as isolating or unique as the scream down deep in our soul declares, (2) a wise leader may offer freedom from situations that seem impossible to untangle and (3) fellow travelers on the journey of life can be an invaluable resource for the trek. These points were novel and inspirational to me once, but I have come to recognize that the Holy Spirit gave parallel insights to evangelicals in the past who had a deep passion for comprehensive pastoral care. My unintentional trip to the hospital where I was first introduced to group work can provide other insights as well. At the end of the chapter I will give some transparent attention to those beneath-the-surface elements. But first, let us roll the clock back much farther and turn our attention to four central functions of a leader.

WESLEY'S GIFT FROM A CHRISTMAS PAST

In the pursuit to understand human motivation, the phrase "there is nothing new under the sun" takes on deeper meaning (Eccles 1:9). There is indeed nothing new in recognizing the potential of social groups to become living organisms that foster life. Jesus' followers have harnessed this supportive force for kingdom purposes since the advent of the best news the world has ever heard. Consider this poignant example.

Three centuries ago, John Wesley (1703-1791), passionate preacher and master of pastoral care, articulated a purpose, plan and procedure for group discipleship. His methods reveal an uncanny resemblance to the intimate gatherings advocated here, as do his critical assumptions. Pilgrims on a spiritual journey toward holiness travel best when closely united, or in Wesley's words, *banded*. A living faith requires more than momentary personal expression. Believers must encourage each other toward excellence and zealous devotion as followers of Christ. Ongoing sanctification—progress in becoming holy—requires mutual support. John Wesley was convinced that Christians were able, in cooperation with the

Holy Spirit, to live out high and holy standards. Consider the hefty charge in the inspirational statement known as Wesley's *Rule*.

> Do all the good you can,
> By all the means you can,
> In all the ways you can,
> In all the places you can,
> At all the times you can,
> To all the people you can,
> As long as ever you can.[2]

These stirring sentiments echo key teachings of Jesus Christ, goals particularly relevant for those committed to being his representatives in this world: "Love your neighbor as yourself" (Mt 22:39); "love your enemies" (Mt 5:44); "I tell you the truth, whatever you did for one of the least of these brothers of mine, you did for me" (Mt 25:40). As followers of Christ, our souls testify that this calling is extreme; we are too weak. The unlikelihood of serious sustained effort to reach such a lofty selfless standard sends shivers down our spines. Such a rule would make a splendid plaque for the office wall or a stimulating sermon quotation. A humble follower of Christ might stutter when offering this prayer in solitude, but the corporate practice provides additional challenges. Seeking to do good while living authentically in relationship is an awkward journey not intended for the weak. Committed movement in this direction as a community requires great grace, considerable courage and a cherished bond with fellow travelers. But the heartfelt support of likeminded souls actually sustains such a worthy advancement. Living out Jesus' teachings with the help of others undeniably qualifies as trekking toward wholeness.

John Wesley is best known as an evangelist and circuit preacher associated with remarkable revivals in England and America. He deserves the reputation; he preached more than forty-four thousand times over a span of fifty-four years. The prolific author and teacher became the reluctant founder of the Methodist denomination because he sought to preach the Word and breathe new sacred vitality into the Church of England. Wesley was profoundly concerned with the pastoral care of those who professed a new faith in Jesus Christ. His widespread flock included many who were illiterate, socially outcast or otherwise unsophisticated in relating according to accepted social norms. Thus he developed elaborate

---

[2]John Wesley, *Rule*, in *Bartlett's Familiar Quotations*, ed. John Bartlett (Boston: Little, Brown, 1980), p. 346.

systems of organizing converts into *societies* and *classes* where worship, spiritual instruction, encouragement and admonition would preserve the fruit of conversion. When these large to mid-sized gatherings did not fully influence the actual behavior of these fledging Christ followers, Wesley advocated even smaller, single-gender groups of five or six members called *bands*. Further, within these units were pairs of spiritual friends or *twin souls*.[3]

"Wesley, it must be acknowledged, had a tendency toward the proliferation of small groups."[4] Societies consisted of twenty-five to two thousand persons who met Sunday afternoons and Wednesday mornings to hear the Word, pray together, sing hymns and press on in the challenging task of living wholly consistent Christian lives. Those who wished to remain in good standing within their society were expected to routinely attend a weekly class with twelve other members. There the preaching from the recent society meeting was carefully reinforced. Central to this session were *examinations*, candid conversations that scrutinized each member's application of this teaching in everyday actions and relations.[5] Some disciples resisted the intensity of these examinations, saying they were too threatening among so many. Also, the time allotted was not sufficient to establish the depth of fellowship necessary to facilitate the espoused degree of holy living. The plan for the more intimate band was introduced in response to these problems.

The model for these small spiritual accountability groups was probably influenced by Wesley's various past experiences. For instance, much earlier John's brother Charles established a fellowship for intensive discipleship among university friends at Oxford. John later directed that group. The meetings consisted of communion, prayer and investigation of the Scriptures. Members invested determined effort in making faith the backbone of all their university learning. Their driving purpose was to pursue personal devotion, holiness and an uncompromising commitment to honor God; their method, to adhere unashamedly to Christian theological tradition. This fellowship mockingly became known as the "Holy Club." Other derogatory terms were tossed about such as the *Bible moths* (because these men fed on the Bible as moths on cloth), *Bible bigots, Sacramentarians*, and perhaps prophetically, *Methodists*.[6] Strategically meeting together to

---

[3]Rupert E. Davies, ed., *The Works of John Wesley: The Methodist Societies: History, Nature, and Design* (Nashville: Abingdon Press, 1989), p. 77.
[4]Ibid, p. 13.
[5]Gary Cockerill, Donald Demaray and Steve Harper, *Reflecting God* (Kansas City: Beacon Hill, 2000), p. 132.
[6]J. D. Douglas and Philip W. Comfort, eds., *Who's Who in Christian History* (Wheaton, Ill.: Tyndale House, 1992).

bring about spiritual formation was not popular in Wesley's wider social context; such zealousness exposed the shallowness and hypocrisy of those who held to an imputed spirituality via church affiliation, participation in religious rituals and other meager traditions. Given the revolutionary ministry that members of this Holy Club—such as the Wesley brothers and George Whitefield—eventually undertook, it would appear that God blessed their effort even though their peers did not embrace it.

John Wesley's second impression of group potency came several years later when his own compelling renewal occurred within another cluster of believers, the society on Aldersgate Street. He vividly remembered the Holy Spirit's work within that fellowship group on one particular evening. Finally, during his voyages to America and travels to Germany, Wesley encountered Moravian believers who incorporated a durable peer network to further develop the faith of converts. Their influence probably convinced him that rigorous spiritual fellowship provided an enormous benefit to persons wishing to be sanctified and edified.

During the same historical period, visionary leaders had formed many small, voluntary groups to achieve a lifestyle change or to pursue a mission impossible as a solitary undertaking. Wesley had sufficient prototypes available to shape his bands of believers. What matters most for our purposes is the remarkably solid structure for formation groups that Wesley put into place on a Christmas day in 1738. These groups were designed to foster the utmost transparency and ultimate spiritual support.[7] This Christmas gift of a formation group format may be an antique, but it nicely illustrates basic principles from the four essential leader functions of contemporary helping groups: (1) vision and structuring, (2) caring, (3) affect and attachment stimulation and (4) meaning attribution. These global leader functions were derived from careful analysis of data involving leader behavior and member experience in various therapeutic encounter groups.[8] Now they serve as categorical starting points for exploring leader characteristics and practical implications. These functions also serve as the overarching themes for the remaining chapters.

Wesley's inspiration for group work came from the epistle of James, known for its practical wisdom in the pursuit of a real-world faith: "Therefore confess your sins to each other and pray for each other so that you may be healed" (Jas 5:16). The ingredients of mutual confession, individually targeted prayer and realized

---

[7]John Wesley, *The Works of John Wesley*, 3rd ed. (Grand Rapids: Baker Books, 1992).
[8]Morton Lieberman, Irvin D. Yalom and Matthew B. Miles, *Encounter Groups: First Facts* (New York: Basic Books, 1973); Virginia Brabender, *Introduction to Group Therapy* (Hoboken, N.J.: Wiley, 2002).

healing from the effects of sin were carved into the procedures Wesley authored and circulated to guide the advancement of bands. Vision and structuring are quite evident in the biblically anchored, compelling mission statement. The verse plainly articulates the intended group destination, or *vision:* that you may be healed. Likewise it acknowledges a member's responsibilities: gather together to openly confess and to pray. The message behind the biblical term for *confession* implies revealing of a secret or making an admission. This solid New Testament practice—open communication to God regarding hidden faults, prideful rebellion, and sins of omission and commission—is modeled plainly within the Lord's prayer (see Mt 6:9-13; Lk 11:2-4). This passage from James, however, does not emphasize confession as voicing agreement with God about an internal state of sin or speaking privately to a spiritual or therapeutic authority. Rather, it calls for the persistent, ongoing practice of person-to-person, mutual exchange filled with frank, honest, solemn statements of commitment and pledges of faith. The healing promised in James accompanies transparency and intercession within an intense interpersonal context. Wesley's application of this verse to his bands supplies a biblical foundation for his prescribed praxis. The leader function of *structuring,* or setting up a group with maximum potential for success, goes further in Wesley's version. Formal questions were put in place to determine entrance eligibility, highlight the group's purpose and discern a proper match with the perspective member's spiritual goals. In contemporary group work, this prescription would be described as steps for screening, selection and member preparation. Wesley's specific meeting plan for bands detailed six procedures: (1) meet weekly, (2) begin on time, (3) start with prayer or singing, (4) take turns honestly speaking about one's own spiritual condition, (5) end with prayer that benefits each participant and (6) examine one another regularly using a routine set of probing questions.[9]

In our day, these rules or external conditions may appear too rigid—a restrictive death trap for true fellowship or a formula for psychological intimidation. This applies in particular to the notion of examining one another regularly. Granted, implementing these guidelines places much at stake, but each point served an intended purpose, and needed to be skillfully enforced under the care of a leader engaged with a unique combination of participants. The deep concern of a pastor's heart comes through fervently in Wesley's presentations, which illustrates the second leader function: *caring.* These guidelines could indeed help

---

[9]John Wesley, "Rules of the Band Societies," in *The Works of John Wesley,* vol. 9, ed. Rupert E. Davies (Nashville: Abingdon Press, 1989), p. 77.

create safe conditions for soul-to-soul sharing. In order for members to trust and thrive, each had to recognize that the intended exchange, namely, committing to make visible one's inner world, meant receiving effective and nurturing care in return.

A third group leader function involves providing *affect and attachment stimulation* to further the growth of group members; that is, encouraging the appropriate expression of emotion and fostering healing relations among group members. Wesley offered a prescribed pattern for members to examine one another that demonstrates this particular task. Imagine what it would be like to give weekly account of one's spiritual status guided by this updated version of Wesley's detailed questions:

1. What spiritual failures have you experienced since our last meeting? What known sins, if any, have you committed?

2. What temptations have you battled this week? Where do you feel the most vulnerable right now?

3. What temptations have you been delivered from this week? Please share with us how you won the victory.

4. Has the Lord revealed anything to you about your heart and life that makes you want us to join you in taking a second look at what might be sinful attitudes, lifestyle and motivations?

5. Is there any spiritual problem that you have never been able to talk about to us or even to God?[10]

Could it be that such anticipated conversation with others every week would deter or influence moment-by-moment thoughts, feelings and actions? Not only would this expose vulnerabilities in terms of heart and behavior, but also, done well, it would encourage an intense connection to the companions of one's journey. This type of confessional practice—the sharing of intimate struggles between old and new self and the open expression of blessings, hopes and dreams—creates a rich reserve of social support. This exhibits the last group leader function: *meaning attribution*. The band was one layer of a comprehensive spiritual care system. There, personal spiritual priorities and sinful pressure points could be woven together into the lifelong story of a pilgrim's progress. The pains and joys of everyday life, many related to the inward and outward effects of sin and vic-

---

[10]Cockerill, Demaray and Harper, *Reflecting*, p. 133.

tory, reveal their place in a unique narrative centered on a heavenward walk of faith. The close bonds of affection found within the band would influence and invigorate the faith story of each sojourner.

This historical example of group work requires three important qualifications. First, the band was a link in a sturdy pastoral care chain. Exposure to an in-depth proclamation of the Word of God supported the interpersonal exchanges of confession, prayer and spiritual life review. *Transparent interpersonal exchange, the means for redemptive intimacy, is a necessary but not sufficient condition for spiritual maturation* (Orientation Principle 3). Submission to the ministry of the Word is imperative. Second, the plan for the band meeting may not be as transferable as it first appears. The use of penetrating queries to provoke holy living, like any set of helpful techniques, must be applied with wisdom and the prompting of the Holy Spirit. *Group experiences are redemptive and refreshing when leaders and members practice sensitivity to the proceeding of the Holy Spirit for the sake of the gathered souls* (Orientation Principle 4). A group leader must assist members to manage the delicate balance between pursuit of the group program and individual preparedness. Third, even with this elaborate discipleship plan, some converts were like the seeds that fell on the rocky soil or amid the thorns; the sprouts withered for lack of nurture or were choked by aggressive competition (Mt 13:1-23). Christians who struggled to remain true to their vow to live for the Lord, called *penitents*, were gathered into special bands to overcome troublesome behaviors or episodes of inconsistent growth. This creation of bands targeted toward unique spiritual needs will be of particular interest in the current work. *Mutual edification can occur even between struggling souls and the benefits may be increased by guidance from understanding pastoral leaders who are familiar with particular pitfalls, predators and persistent urges to sin* (Orientation Principle 5). Both guides and fellow trekkers are useful when traversing rough terrain.

Long before contemporary researchers studied human relationships within small helping groups and identified the four leader functions, labeling and refining the terms, John Wesley incorporated the essence of each into a fine helping group model. Wesley's groups had a firm kingdom purpose. A leader with spiritual maturity pastorally guided the band toward wholeness and holy living.

RELATIONAL COMMUNICATION WITHIN STORIES

Before this orientation concludes, two essential terms from the group literature need to be identified and afforded a kingdom perspective: content and process. *Content* straightforwardly represents information offered, stories told and themes brought to the surface. In the world of groups, content refers to the topic or subject matter under consideration. The term *process* refers to relational communication beneath the surface content. Process is not concerned about what is said but who says it, how and to whom. What effect does the communication reveal about relational patterns? How does that communication shape relational bonds?

As author and reader, we are engaged in an ordinary manner of communication via the printed page. To illustrate a central premise regarding the promise of group methods for stimulating Christian growth, it may be useful to reflect on the two levels of contact operating here in this chapter. The primary intention has been to introduce, with a hint of passion, key organizational assumptions regarding group work. By now readers are aware of my underlying conviction that our heavenly Creator designed human beings to experience relational intimacy—to know and to be known. Sin isolates and distorts our attempt at interpersonal connection. *Shalom* is disrupted when sin ruptures our relationships with God, self and others. We approach wholeness when by grace we attain relational harmony. Groups offer a forum that reveals the hits and misses in personal efforts to connect. Small group interaction represents a powerful reservoir that can be the source of hope or harm, health or hurt, sanctification or self-centered sin. The wisdom and skill to tap into the dynamics of a helping group may be sought and applied in service to our relational, holy and triune God.

I interjected five Christian group-trekking orientation principles throughout the narratives and historical investigation of this chapter:

1. The member-to-member component of group counseling is a powerful tool for observing and activating relational intimacy.

2. There is much more to group interpersonal process than meets the untrained eye. Skilled leaders view, access and utilize relational communication.

3. Transparent interpersonal exchange, the means for redemptive intimacy, is a necessary but not sufficient condition for spiritual maturation.

4. Group experiences are redemptive and refreshing when leaders and members practice sensitivity to the proceeding of the Holy Spirit for the sake of the gathered souls.

5. Mutual edification can occur even between struggling souls and the benefits may be increased by guidance from understanding pastoral

leaders who are familiar with particular pitfalls, predators and persistent urges to sin.

This summary captures the *content* of our trek thus far. If all this seems familiar, content-level communication has occurred between writer and reader. Next, let's reflect on imbedded examples where personal attitudes and ideals aided or hindered our relational connection. Considering this level of exchange is known as *process.*

At this point of acquaintance between author and reader, indirect statements within this narrative exposed substantive material. Take my fishing-trip-turned-ER-excursion as an example. Was that story merely a way to set the stage for the recall of an early group training experience or did it provide insight into me as person, helper, child of God and soul in need of restoration? Did the style and tone of my story facilitate a connection or drive a wedge between us? I am consciously aware that my helplessness in hook removal symbolizes an entrenched personal tendency to avoid turning to others for assistance unless absolutely no other option appears evident. Is this trait indicative of a healthy self-reliance or might it represent a private pride that the Holy Spirit desires to refine? In the interest of the type of confession described earlier, the answer does indeed go both ways. There are numerous implications for the underlying self-disclosure and this material contributes a critical layer in the communication now underway.

I selected the hook experience for inclusion because it bears a message about the value of expertise, experience and quality care. Although I may initially recoil from revealing vulnerabilities and seeking aid, my own resistance softens in the presence of gifted, seasoned or genuine support. When a fellow traveler with a pressing need finally seeks guidance, our Lord is honored when the seeker is given the best assistance that wisdom has to offer. Take for example the initial miracle of the Lord Jesus during the wedding feast at Cana, where at the request of his mother, Jesus transformed water into a most excellent wine (Jn 2:1-11). Drawing a common table variety from those stone water jugs would not have diminished Jesus' creative action. Nonetheless, his gift was scrutinized in a blind taste test and designated to be among the finest. A similar message embedded in my selected story mirrors my prayer for myself and for readers: "Lord, may the cup of cool water provided from our supplies to thirsty sojourners represent the best that we have available to offer. Increase our appreciation for the potency of redemptive intimacy for doing good and add to our proficiency in guiding relational treks as you accomplish your purposes." Notice that this prayer reflects the messages that I included either with deliberate intention or at least self-awareness. It also exposes other aspects of my inner self and relational patterns that were not premeditated or brought to the surface by mindful choice. My filters are not fine-tuned enough to catch, or even to sense, all that I expressed as this narrative unfolded.

What if this communication was being conducted within a live group setting and not as a book to a reader? What if others had the opportunity to speak openly about what they gleaned about my perceptions, personality and purpose? Rich insights would move from below the typical threshold of communication and become the subject of direct conversation. Further, this would open to investigation my facility in enhancing or detracting from the variety of relationships being forged within the group. Did the effect of my communication match my intentions? Were my attitudes and the resulting behaviors consistent with the fruit of the Spirit (Gal 5:22-23)? What is the relational impact of my disclosure? The ebb and flow of relational shaping below the content or surface is *process;* reflection and discussion regarding this level of communication in group work is *processing.* Consistent with the vast professional group work tradition, *content* will reference topical communication and *process* will indicate relational communication.[11]

A small group offers an ideal forum for content delivery. Members exchange information, insight and good teaching. Ministry settings have long recognized this potential in selective group gatherings. But what about the confessional experience that Wesley envisioned for those struggling to live authentically as followers of Christ? Are the hooks holding penitents back from relating intimately with Jesus Christ and others best removed via topical or relational-level communication? Are evangelical ministry leaders available who can sensitively, safely and wisely tap the potential of the relational communication known as process? Even in groups where trust is carefully cultivated, the potential to gain access to the underlying transmissions between souls is frequently left outside of the cordial and casual conversation. Since authentic spirituality involves relating ever more deeply to the Lord through his Son and then in turn increasing one's depth of love for others, access to a force for shaping relational schemas can have tremendous value for soul care. More leaders need to be empowered to love sojourners with compassionate, multifaceted and relevant care.

---

[11]Irvin D. Yalom and Molyn Leszcz, *The Theory and Practice of Group Psychotherapy,* 5th ed. (New York: Basic Books, 2005), pp. 143-50; Donald E. Ward and Michele Litchy, "The Effective Use of Processing in Groups," in *Handbook of Group Counseling and Psychotherapy,* ed. Janice L. Delucia-Waack et al. (Thousand Oaks, Calif.: Sage, 2004), pp. 104-19.

Remember my hook-tied hands and the nurse who informed me of the hook removal expert? Imagine the heartfelt comfort and hope that would burst into life when a wounded soul hears, "It just so happens that this ministry has a focused group with an experienced leader that specializes in assisting seekers with needs and goals just like yours. Please know that you are welcome to trek with us."

4

PRIORITIES WITH A PIOUS HERITAGE

LANDMARKS AHEAD

The trail ahead affords readers the opportunity to look back at a pivotal point in the history of group therapy. Two questions give the desired coordinates: (1) How do seasoned guides actually enable interpersonal connections to flourish and redemptive intimacy to thrive? (2) How do we know that increasing group opportunities in ministry settings does not require the ill-fated import of secular therapeutic techniques into a domain where the Holy Spirit should freely reign? The itinerary initially explores the history behind the identification of the four leader functions, which emerged from the Encounter group rage of the not-so-distant past. The next stop exposes the religious heritage of interpersonal groups in which transparency was emphasized. These groups had a spiritual formation core. The heritage influences evangelicalism still today. At the close of this tour, the Christian helper will be able to link intimate group encounters of tomorrow with a past, yet hearty, Christian tradition.

A CUSTOMIZED PURPOSE

Before Abby invited a single participant to Reach and Remember, a grief support group, someone recognized and nurtured her emerging passion to minister to fellow sufferers. A superb caregiver exhibiting a gentle spirit, an empathic heart and a conspicuous inner map had directed the community Abby traveled with when her heartache was acute. He was no novice to trekking through the dark territory of suffering. His interior plan was informed by extensive hospice training in bereavement groups. The particular excursion he steered when Abby was a participant had been a mere eight weeks. Each session appeared to flow naturally from the previous one. The smooth gatherings gave the impression that a mutual unity guided the discussion. Throughout her journey, Abby was alert to the underlying direction offered by their seasoned guide. Usually, it seemed as if he was barely in the room. Still Abby was cognizant that this leader was at ease

introducing themes, balancing contributions and respectfully presenting hard
matters for personal reflection. As soon as she shared with her pastor a sense
of the Lord's leading toward grief ministry, she contacted the person who had
been her inspiration. This former leader graciously presented three gifts: recommendations on select reading materials, tips on how to prepare herself to guide
and profound encouragement regarding her capacity to care for those lost in the
aloneness of grief. Borrowing from the pattern that had been helpful in guiding
her, she applied a soft structure to Reach and Remember. As needs arose among
hurting sojourners under her watchful care, she had access to two consultation
partners: a prayerful pastor and a seasoned guide. These resources formed a constructive match of spiritual nurture and technical expertise. One other advantage
empowered Abby, one that lay subtly beneath her conscious awareness: her previous positive group encounter with others. She entered their company empty after
hope had departed her life. Not long after, hope slowly appeared on her horizon.
Her vivid memories of being in a healing community supplied a durable internal
motivation for leadership. Voices that once comforted pain continued to soothe
angst and sustain momentum.

Even without Abby's favorable support, numerous tried-and-true formats
for similar treks would have been readily available. Medical and mental health
clinics as well as many churches widely promote grief recovery groups, giving leaders and potential members a general sense of what to anticipate. In
the bereavement area, there are published group manuals,[1] national networks,
training seminars,[2] and even Christian-based videos complete with discussion
guides.[3] Given a reasonable research effort, leaders will locate well-articulated
and compassionate strategies. The rich information available for leaders like
Abby would discuss issues of guilt, regret, loneliness, adaptation, moving on
without the one who was the reason to move on, letting go and relating anew.[4]
In addition, a major loss inevitably places core religious convictions under intense review, an aspect that also receives attention in secular and faith-based
grief resources. Death provokes turbulence in one's perception of the transcendent. For Abby and many like her, this openness to considering matters of faith

---

[1]See <www.goodgriefgroups.com> or <www.americanhospice.org>.

[2]In the past the Mayo Clinic website <www.mayoclinic.org/support-groups> listed three resources
for information on bereavement groups: Grief Watch <www.griefwatch.com>, Grief
Share <www.griefshare.org> and Compassionate Friends <www.compassionatefriends.org>.

[3]See Grief Share <www.griefshare.org>; Ann Dickerson, "Survivors Helped to Deal with Their
Grief," Atlanta Journal-Constitution, January 4, 2007.

[4]Irvin D. Yalom and Molyn Leszcz, The Theory and Practice of Group Psychotherapy, 5th ed. (New
York: Basic Books, 2005), p. 479.

and spirituality during such a crisis period is the most intriguing aspect of all.

Careful preparation communicates compassion. Abby began Reach and Remember with a good idea of who the group would attract, what they would do, and how she would help. A more technical way to describe her expectations would be that she had a comprehensible purpose, target membership, topic cycle, meeting format and facilitator model. This foundation provides a tremendous benefit when negotiating the responsibilities of group leadership. In fact, the major challenges facing those who desire to invite others on a group trek often stem from failing to define the expectations closely enough. For example, they are faced with a daunting series of inquires: (1) Who would benefit most from this service? (2) What are the specific needs and resources? (3) When will members know they have actually grown? (4) How can diverse individual concerns be unified and addressed via key themes? (5) What are the best options for meeting format and flow? And most important, (6) how might the leader contribute significantly to the group trek without becoming either the center of attention or a needless distraction? A genuine small group experience, particularly a leader-directed one, does not revolve around the person who brought it to life—that is, not if the guide effectively activates the potential of the group to care exceptionally for one another. The ultimate expression of group leadership is to guide in a manner that makes a guide appear unnecessary.[5] Attaining this level of proficiency requires experience acquired with a few bumps and bruises along the trail. Nonetheless, undertaking the trek becomes easier with a touch of the following "book learning."

A LEGACY OF ENCOUNTER

When a leader has the inner enthusiasm to launch a cooperative helping venture with a kingdom purpose, the intricate maze of leadership may appear more obscure than obvious. Those aspiring to invest in the group helping ministry proposed here will benefit from a comprehensive picture of the behaviors, attitudes and tasks that seasoned guides demonstrate. Veterans with field experience can use this portrait of successful leadership to compare notes, conduct self-assessment and explore new areas. The four leader functions, introduced in

---

[5]The verse that I frequently share with Christian group leaders on this point is pulled from Paul's words to Timothy (1 Tim 1:5). Consider how Eugene Peterson paraphrased these lines in *The Message:* "The whole point of what we're urging is simply *love*—love uncontaminated by self-interest and counterfeit faith, a life open to God." Guiding a group is motivated out of a love for others, since the credit for any healing or growth is not likely to be tagged to your account or reputation. If one prefers the return of accolades, stay with one-to-one counseling.

relation to Wesley's bands in the previous chapter, here again provide the structure. This chapter continues to tease out the meaning for small group leaders of vision and structuring, caring, affect and attachment stimulation, and meaning attribution.[6] Leaders have a lot to juggle. Forming a group means inviting folks, already under strain or pressure, to accept the additional dimension of a journey with others. It entails encouraging them to expose stories, shame, strategies and successes. The entire endeavor requires conviction regarding duty, purpose and mission. This proposal contends that therapeutic literature provides valuable insight for Christian ministries that wish to offer leader-guided group experiences. These groups access the relational communication or process layer and also introduce appropriate content. Since both the leader functions and the method of using groups themselves as strengthening resources share a common lineage, this chapter will explore the background of these premises. While the empirical investigation of these notions is distinctly modern, the roots of the group movement have a heritage useful for those in ministry to ponder.

The leader functions describe what seasoned guides of productive groups actually do. These four main groupings collect diverse skills and functions that were initially detailed in a research study conducted during the early 1970s.[7] The seventies period is commonly associated with *The Brady Bunch*, "The Hustle," *Apollo* moon landings and *Roe v. Wade*. But it was also an era when the "encounter group" phenomena reached the peak of its previously prolonged popularity. These small assemblies purported to unmask self and deliver the ultimate community high. Primarily they served as unstructured alternatives to psychotherapy and attracted those without serious mental illness searching to become more sensitive to others while exploring their own emotional crevices. Such efforts to "get real" proliferated in colleges, secondary schools, business settings, retreat centers, living rooms, churches and synagogues. Strangers transformed into an intimate company became the means to promote personal growth through self-awareness and intense interpersonal awakening. This fashionable rush into the depths of naked interpersonal experience was as controversial as the applications were popular. Researchers dramatically described the encounter movement as an enigma, the "interpersonal equivalent of skydiving."[8] Here is what one group of researchers had to say about these provocative gatherings:

---

[6]Virginia Brabender, *Introduction to Group Therapy* (Hoboken, N.J.: Wiley, 2002), pp. 119-58.

[7]Morton Lieberman, Irvin D. Yalom and Matthew B. Miles, *Encounter Groups: First Facts* (New York: Basic Books, 1973).

[8]Lieberman, Yalom and Miles, *Encounter Groups*, p. 3.

Encounter groups have varyingly been looked at as an antidote to alienation, a modern-day revival without the deity, fun and games for adults who cannot play without a token offering to the Protestant ethic, an inexpensive form of psychotherapy for the masses, a Communist plot to undermine American morals, a way out of the havoc of the industrial revolution. Those who have made themselves available to lead encounter groups may have been prepared by long years of training in a prestigious professional institution, by participation in a two-week institute, or purely by personal commitment.[9]

Notice at least four features of encounter sessions revealed in this description. First, there was an intentional dual agenda: assist participants to get in touch with a personal inner reality and reach out with relational authenticity. Second, for the most part, this was a secular happening where the proponents were zealously sacrilegious and against formal religion. Third, this fad was closely tied to the revolution of social trends and conventions. Fourth, while encounter groups were hosted and loosely planned, leadership was charismatic with no uniformity in approach, conviction or procedure. While these distinctive qualities might appear to place the encounter movement well outside of the modern therapeutic movement, there were definite events in the history of therapeutic groups that supplied the necessary fuel for this craze to catch fire.[10] Therefore let us take a side trip to review some notable tales from earlier in the twentieth century. For the sake of brevity, I have included in this capsule history only select and distinct contributions leading up to the encounter movement.[11]

The modern storyline of psychologically oriented group work is typically tied to the work of Joseph Hershey Pratt. In 1905, this physician incorporated social interaction into the treatment plan of patients with tuberculosis.[12] Massachusetts General Hospital held a weekly program, The Emmanuel Church Tuberculo-

---

[9]Ibid.

[10]A comprehensive analysis and discussion of these encounter groups was included in the now outdated fourth edition of Irvin D. Yalom's 1995 classic *The Theory and Practice of Group Psychotherapy*, 4th ed. (New York: Basic Books, 1996). Chapter 16, "Group Therapy and the Encounter Group," was reprinted and is available on Dr. Yalom's webpage, <www.yalom.com/books/> (click on the book, then click on "Encounter Groups" on the left side; last updated May 28, 2008). Most interestingly, Yalom raises a significant question regarding the possibility that remnants of the encounter movement are now evident in the church-related self-help groups. His hunch, independently conceived, corresponds well with the proposal offered here.

[11]A succinct, readable and informative history of the modern group counseling moment is available in Virginia A. Brabender, April E. Fallon and Andrew I. Smolar, *Essentials of Group Therapy* (Hoboken, N.J.: John Wiley & Sons, 2004).

[12]William B. Kline, *Interactive Group Counseling and Therapy* (Saddle River, N.J.: Merrill Prentice Hall, 2003), p. 8.

sis Class, with twenty-five members. The intervention aimed to offer education regarding this deadly illness and advance conversations between patients. The prognosis for those in the late stage of the disease at that time was predictably poor. Remarkably, Pratt reported the survival rate of those in the group treatment to be 75 percent. Pratt was the first to document focused use of the following approaches: (1) the pronounced application of a psycho-educational experience; (2) emphasis on treatment of the patient, not the disease;[13] and (3) strategic increase of social support to manage a serious medical condition.

In the 1920s and 1930s, group approaches were extended to psychiatric patients and prisoners experiencing crippling isolation within the large institutions that arose during that period. Jacob Levy Moreno offered groups in prisons and psychiatric institutions where inmates and patients played out stories that facilitated the promotion of new perspectives. His approach differed markedly from the psychoanalytic model dominant not only during that period but also in his own training background. He preferred to describe his method of activating the spontaneous reactions of participants to each other as "working out" issues as opposed to the passive analytic technique of "working through."[14] His book, *The First Book of Group Psychotherapy*, came out in 1932. It claimed Moreno invented this method of psychological assistance and provided a basic empirical footing by describing interactions in detail. Moreno was firm on two points that carry through to the present. First, he noted that individual work between patient and physician, with defined superior and inferior participants, is asymmetric. This posture presents a definite predicament when attempting to connect with those who reject authority, are inherently suspicious and distrust the motives of others. This situation was and is common with inmates and psychiatric patients. In a group situation, Moreno said, "the therapeutic process streams through their mutual inter-relationships. Every man has an equal rank. The roles are plastic and the situation is symmetric."[15] Second, Moreno believed that issues of scale prevented one-to-one rehabilitation methods from succeeding; the need for treatment that operated on the internal domain of the patient exceeded the resources available for working with patients individually. Moreover, he asserted that the popular and entrenched dyadic method was inferior because it did not take advantage of the here and now. Spontaneous behavior between persons, he noted, is vibrant and directly accessible.

---

[13]Yalom, *Theory and Practice*, chap. 16.
[14]Jacob L. Moreno, *The First Book of Group Psychotherapy*, 3rd ed. (New York: Beacon House, 1957).
[15]Ibid., p. 61.

At an impressive gathering of prominent medical, psychiatric and penal authorities attending the 1932 American Psychiatric Association meeting at the Bellevue-Stratford hotel in New York City, Moreno was asked to defend his novel, somewhat grandiose claims. His recollection of that meeting is included in the third edition of his group therapy text. The unfolding exchange is as fascinating as it is powerful. Instead of rehearsing data and diagrams freshly available in his monograph, Moreno proceeded to make observations on the current relational dynamics in his immediate surroundings. What followed was commentary on the social activity his peers had just enacted. He turned the conversation from content toward process. He demonstrated primarily that spontaneous behavior in instantaneous situations revealed extensive information regarding deeply ingrained personality patterns. Why engage in extensive analytic excavation to unearth psychological material buried in the unconscious when the interactions of the moment were readily available? Thus Moreno transformed (at least by his account) a proper and technical professional meeting into an impromptu therapeutic demonstration of his convictions. Could a more dramatic attempt to validate the construct related to the importance of the "here and now" be offered today?

Next, this historical overview of group movements must mention a serious research group effort in 1946. Social psychologists and educators under the leadership of Kurt Lewin had a mission that encompassed a daunting task: devise a method to equip leaders to reduce interracial tension in communities. On the tail end of the battles of World War II, a profound racial war in America was commencing. Could deeply ingrained racial bigotry and destructive racial prejudices be addressed using the tools of social science? The State of Connecticut enacted legislation on fair employment practices, but no law of the land could change prevailing attitudes. Some Connecticut communities attempted to solve racial problems by organizing interactive small group experiences. The work of Lewin to develop basic skill training groups coalesced into the National Training Laboratory (NTL) research program and moved to Bethel, Maine.[16] The groups became known as *intensive talk sessions*. Researchers observed meetings detail-by-detail and relationship-by-relationship. Their focused observations were then carefully scrutinized to ascertain which dynamics produced attitudinal and affective modifications. During the course of this study, an event oc-

---

[16]Sally H. Barlow, Addie J. Fuhriman and Gary M. Burlingame, "The History of Group Counseling and Psychotherapy," in *Handbook of Group Counseling and Psychotherapy*, ed. Janice L. Delucia-Waack et. al (Thousand Oaks, Calif.: Sage, 2004), pp. 3-22.

curred that is occasionally referenced as *the great mistake*. Apparently participants in the research groups expressed an interest in hearing the discussion taking place between the researchers. When participants were allowed to eavesdrop on what was shared, the insights altered their interactions in subsequent groups. This set the mechanism in motion for "feedback" to become the prime feature of this style of intervention.[17] Training or "T" groups caught on as a means to orchestrate social change because individuals were given directive feedback on how their communication affected others. Such feedback was as candid as it was intoxicating. The commentary topics could range from the intentional messages to the inadvertent, from conflicting and statements to the unambiguous. Researchers identified consistency and inconsistency between the verbal and nonverbal. Participants became immediately aware of their negative vibes or covert communication. In particular, members heard clearly about the harmful and adverse impact their communication had on others. Following this blunt enlightenment, members were expected to take steps to successfully harmonize with their fellow participants through transparent, direct expression. Within the safety of these groups, participants learned to question long-cherished stereotypical beliefs triggered by external characteristics. Freed from these hang-ups, group members could invest their effort in seeking honest familiarity with the people beneath the skin.

As the national mood tuned in and accepted the notion that it was preferable to "let it all hang out," Carl Rogers, the founder of the person-centered counseling approach, endorsed the experiential group methodology. He is said to have coined the term *encounter* and characterized these planned, intensive experiences as a means of self-realization via affirmation. In 1970, this humanistic psychologist claimed that the basic encounter group was the "most rapidly spreading social invention of the century and probably the most potent."[18] Other psychological theorists joined the bandwagon and popularized parallel versions of a close-knit collective experience.[19] The starting gun had fired and the race was on to legitimize each distinct helping approach.

Partisan proponents of each particular group model thrust their competing claims of effectiveness on the general public. Professional and scientific circles needed someone to scrutinize the testimonial endorsements of a particular theo-

---

[17]Yalom, *Theory and Practice*, chap. 16.

[18]Carl Rogers, *Encounter Groups* (New York: Harper & Row, 1970), p. 1. See also Thomas C. Oden, *The Intensive Group Experience: The New Pietism* (Philadelphia: Westminster Press, 1972), p. 56.

[19]Marianne Corey and Gerald Corey, *Groups: Process & Practice*, 7th ed. (Belmont, Calif.: Brooks/ Cole, 2006).

retical approach or therapeutic style. To establish a convincing empirical base for credible group work, Stanford researchers Lieberman, Yalom and Miles undertook a large scale study, publishing their first results in 1973.[20] The project involved two hundred and ten college students; eighteen groups including two controls; sixteen experienced professionals with diverse theoretical views; and roughly five hundred hours of encounter! Twenty-seven discrete leader behaviors (such as intrusive modeling, limit-setting, release of emotion by demonstration, charisma, etc.) were catalogued under the following five areas: evocative behavior, coherence-making, support, management and use of self. Members rated their leader's behavior by quantifying perceptions, experience and impact. The resulting data was crunched using the statistical procedure known as factor analysis, effectively a mathematical search for relationships between variables. This effort established behavioral clusters describing leader style, action and emphasis.[21] The Stanford project generated the four leader function categories that have since been refined, accepted and transferred to other psychological studies. As the knowledge base regarding group efficacy has vastly increased over the ensuing decades, these functional roles continue to be proven useful.[22]

Leader behaviors that allowed or pressed members to take emotional or interpersonal risks were placed under the broad label of *emotional stimulation*. A leader might take center stage to model an approach well outside the ordinary repertoire of one or more members. Perhaps a leader would taunt or dare a member into expressive activity. The net effect was direct and forceful confrontation to engage in self-disclosure or make advances toward the expression of empathy to others. In order to capture the emotional or affective activity and the relational enhancement aspect of these leader behaviors, the heading *affect and attachment stimulation* will be applied here.

Numerous reports of gestures by leaders that demonstrated or induced shared moments of compassion were recorded. Researchers recalled instances of warmth, comfort, affirmation, praise, compliments or recognition. These behaviors were collapsed under the general heading *caring*. When leaders aided the group as a whole or particular members, helping them find words to capture experiences, recognize self-defeating patterns or communicate heartfelt desires in more effective ways, participants discovered meaning embedded in methods of relating. Using themes, metaphors or ideas to clarify, interpret or convey previously un-

---

[20]Lieberman, Yalom and Miles, *Encounter Groups*.
[21]Yalom, *Theory and Practice*.
[22]Brabender, *Introduction to Group Therapy*, pp. 121-40.

recognized or unexpressed dimensions of self in relation to others became known as *meaning attribution*. Participants achieved clarity on how to transport a lesson lived out within the miniature social group to their actual life in community.

Last, wide arrays of organizational, time management, boundary shifting or protecting, and norm-setting behaviors exemplified the *executive* aspect of leadership. Leaders appeared to have a sense of what the group could be and how the connections in between could be enriched. Leader activities within this category are extensive. In order to bring out how these behaviors could infuse vitality and safety to group experiences, these executive style behaviors will here be referred to as leading with *vision and structure*.

The study of Lieberman, Yalom and Miles did not end debates over the advantages of distinct theories of human functioning and empowerment applied to group approaches. Rather, it shifted attention from how various psychological theories utilized group methodology to how intrapsychic or interior psychological growth was produced within the group phenomena itself, insofar as the research addressed interpersonal skills and relationship enhancement. Interest increased in a broader enterprise, namely, investigating the complexity of individual-community-leader variables. *Small groups are dynamic human systems where member–group–leader interactions are associated with eventual outcomes in relational adaptability.*

A LESSON FROM RELIGIOUS HISTORY

As social science researchers were analyzing the encounter group movement empirically, noted theological and long-time Drew University professor Thomas C. Oden offered an important thesis concerning the group therapy movement.[23] His insightful little book, titled *The Intensive Group Experience: The New Pietism*, gave a theological, pastoral and historical critique to the growing trend. In church history, Pietism refers to the revitalization movement that attempted to reignite the spiritual zeal of German Lutheranism. Pietism arose during a period when the dominant orthodoxy was dead and distant from the lives of ordinary citizens. Preaching in the pulpit was doctrinally and philosophically sophisticated, but average folks were left unaware of the need or insufficiently motivated to live lives that honored God. One deliberate and effective response was the organization of informal devotional meetings outside of routine worship and instructional preaching. Small groups sprung up under the pastoral urging of Philip Jacob Spener in 1675. His pastoral heart was determined to shepherd his

---

[23]Oden, *Intensive Group Experience.*

sheep toward *pia desideria* or "pious desires."[24] Over time, Pietist ideals migrated to other Christian traditions and revival campaigns.

What possible connection could there be between this historic discipleship revival and modern group approaches? In short, Oden equates the encounter movement of the late twentieth century with an enlightened and psychologically retooled pietism. The book's preface makes it evident that his research methods included extensive direct participation in encounter groups at distinguished training centers.[25] Thus the observations Oden offers are not the limited abstract ideas of an outsider looking in. Contemporary evangelicals may be surprised that he does not offer a rampant theological deconstruction of this grassroots movement. Instead, he writes with the authority of practical experience and with appreciation for the constructive feedback one can attain via well-orchestrated group work. Oden mines several veins that need to be brought to the surface.

Relationally demanding groups of the twentieth century conspicuously appealed to people because of their fresh, novel and progressive quality. Encounter groups were modern; they were "hip." In fact, this very quality may be what raises evangelical skepticism about encounter groups. After all, Carl Rogers, a premier representative of humanistic philosophy, endorsed them. Even the four leader functions, gleaned from investigating the benefits of those groups, share a non-religious history. But Oden asserts that the group movement's claim of novelty is essentially like the emperor who had no clothes. Such a statement may come across as rude, but it is certainly not naive. According to Oden, the acclaimed radical turn to transparency in small community was no avant-garde invention. Rogers wrongly attributed these groups a recent derivation. Encounter groups were more accurately characterized as a homecoming to a recurring historical pattern within religious communities. In particular, this so-called advanced social science movement had significant correspondence with traditional religious Protestant and Jewish pietism of the seventeenth and eighteenth centuries.

> The encounter group is a demythologized and secularized form of interpersonal encounter and community that is familiar to the history of religious communities in the West. The basic prototype of the encounter pattern is found in Protestant and Jewish pietism, which emphasized here-and-now experiencing, intensive small group encounter, high trust levels in group interaction, honest confession amid a caring community, experimental mysticism, mutual pastoral care, extended conversion marathons,

---

[24]Philip Jacob Spener, *Pia Desideria*, ed. Theodore G. Tappert (Philadelphia: Fortress, 1964).
[25]Oden, *Intensive Group Experience*, pp. 14-15.

radical accountability to the group, an eclectic amalgam of resources for spiritual formation, intimate personal testimony, gut-level self-disclosure, brutally candid feedback procedures, antiestablishment social attitudes and the laicization of leadership.[26]

Oden builds this main thrust of his argument piece by piece. He carefully aligns the values, expectations, norms and methodology contained in encounter groups with priorities articulated by religious leaders influenced by pietism.[27]

Spener determined that personal religious growth would be optimally developed within dedicated small groups committed to intensive dialogue and reciprocal care. These small groups fostered a deep sense of human duty to the Creator God. The assemblies became known as the *collegia pietatis*. Similar to the origin of the term *Methodist*, the label *Pietist* was no compliment. This life-penetrating form of piety was associated with cultish, reactionary and non-intellectual activity. The emphasis centered on a group experience where extensive accountability cultivated a heartfelt faith that colored every activity and perspective.

Consider these peculiar ideological parallels between traditional Pietism and the later encounter movement. First, the moral decline in his parish agitated Spener, who saw no potential within the political or ecclesial elite to influence common peasants and laborers.[28] Spener sought major social reform through the individual practice of a vital faith that included good works and lived righteousness. The forerunners of the encounter movement were ambitious enough to tackle an audacious challenge involving one of the most venomous moral issues of their time: pervasive racial prejudice. Neither movement designed any comprehensive social program to initiate top-down change. The old and new pietists

---

[26]Oden, *Intensive Group Experience*, p. 56.

[27]Oden brings out a fascinating secondary linkage that stirs the imagination. Several of the foremost names associated with the encounter movement had direct ties through therapy, training or teaching appointments to Frankfurt, Germany. The following leaders each had close associations with Frankfurt: Frederick Perls, promoter of Gestalt therapy and group techniques; Martin Buber, the Jewish philosopher who deeply impressed many psychological theorists including Carl Rogers and Jacob Moreno, who launched group psychodrama as well as coined terms such as "group therapy" and "here and now"; Kurt Lewin, known as the father of social psychology and the originator of T groups; Paul Tillich, a theologian who made substantial contributions to the encounter movement; Kurt Goldstein, a psychiatrist and Gestalt therapist; and Erich Fromm, social psychologist and philosopher. It is not simply the geographical connection during the 1920s and 1930s of these key figures that is so striking. Rather, three hundred years earlier in the same city of Frankfurt, Spener spurred on spiritually focused groups with many similar features. Oden points out this piece of group history trivia as he makes the following claim: while Vienna may be known as the heartland for psychoanalysis, Frankfurt is the "seminal heartland" of both pietism and the encounter culture. Oden, *Intensive Group Experience*, p. 79.

[28]Peter C. Erb, ed., *Pietists: Selected Writings* (New York: Paulist Press, 1983), p. 5.

quietly began a countercultural faction whose impact multiplied through created intimacy in small groups.

Second, intellectual persuasion was not the tool of choice for changing behavior. Spener was wholeheartedly committed to the Reformation principle that all those who knew the Lord through conversion and were indwelt by the Holy Spirit could comprehend the Scriptures and make immediate life applications. The informal faith discussions of the *collegia pietatis* were all about letting the Word of God govern everyday choices and lifestyle as common believers shared biblical insights with other devoted Christ followers. Encounter groups were likewise a means to empower commoners to make meaningful adjustments through ordinary but intensified interactions. The relational or revolutionary role changes uncovered in gritty face-to-face revelation did not need legitimization from extraordinary theory-based insights. Third, both movements tended to bypass professional authorities in favor of informal leaders who earned status by action and not memorized verbiage. Fourth, Pietism and encounter groups granted inner personal experience and emotional sensations a position of influence that could conceivably trump tenets of doctrine, logic or scientific psychological theory. Both encouraged the pragmatic discovery of one's robust internal guidance system. Last, both religious Pietists and modernist secular group proponents trusted in the potential of any small cluster of human beings to exercise sound judgment and propose reasonable direction to participating members. Presenting these similarities does not endorse the effectiveness or evaluate the difficulties that may accompany implementing these assumptions, but it does unmask the ideological credit that secular encounter groups owed their historic religious predecessors.

Oden illustrated the practical resemblance between the encounter groups of the sixties/seventies and the traditions of Pietism by comparing leader quotations between the centuries. In terms of the pragmatics, ponder these overlapping areas: (1) the small group format and method; (2) the zealous pursuit of honesty; (3) the elevation of immediate here-and-now experiences; (4) the nurture of intimacy; and (5) the concentration on marathon revival sessions. Oden never accused the leaders of the encounter movement of deceptiveness. Nonetheless, he suggested they had ignored the religious tradition that formed the expectations and served as the essential archetype for the modern secular experience. Those devoted to Jesus Christ and to the advancement of a Christian worldview find a useful connection here. The religious connotations associated with this now extinct group movement are often thought to be predominantly Eastern.[29] In fact, the assumption of an Eastern foundation may have magnified the popularity of encounter groups among those undermining the Western religious establishment. This association has carried forward to the present day.[30] Oden makes a convincing case that modern small group initiatives have deep roots in Western religious traditions that strongly influenced Christian evangelicalism.

Oden offers another remarkable comparison in his book. He compares an entry in an encounter participant's journal quoted by Rogers with the conversion account of John Wesley, known as his "Aldersgate experience." Wesley's words depicting his deep inner sense of acceptance and grace as his heart was "strangely warmed" parallel the participant's "turning point" when he felt touched, accepted, affirmed and loved by the group.[31] Even secular researchers have noted such similarities, labeling the encounter movement a "modern-day revival without the deity."[32] An immediate experience of being vitally and intensely joined in togetherness creates an amazing sense of being grounded in and merged with a communal reality. This memorable decisive moment is often equated with a religious experience or sensation of the transcendent. If viewed only from a psychological perspective, this encounter might mistakenly be attributed to humanistic efforts and forces. On this point Oden's review provides depth and theological insight not bound by the trends of an era.

According to basic Christian tenets, sin and an intrinsic sinful nature separate humans—corporately and individually—from the Creator. The impact of the core relational rupture between God and man was summarized earlier in the themes of walking, wandering and wisdom. Oden contends that the encounter movement mistakenly restricted the internal experience of estrangement to disconnection from self and others, thus removing any supernatural or spiritual implications. In its radical humanistic form, such alienation from others results from a chasm deep within. Something severs the experience of one's innermost feelings. One way to remediate this universal phenomenon is through a supervised encounter with others where feelings of guilt are identified, expressed and appeased. The group experience invites acknowledging one's profound sense of wandering alone (confession), which is followed by a purging of deep emotions

---

[29]Oden, *Intensive Group Experience*, p. 87.
[30]The characters in Yalom's recent group therapy novel draw their ideas from existential philosophy and Eastern mysticism. See Irvin D. Yalom, *The Schopenhauer Cure* (New York: HarperCollins, 2005).
[31]Oden, *Intensive Group Experience*, p. 63.
[32]Lieberman, Yalom and Miles, *Encounter Groups*, p. 3.

that brings an overwhelming experience of acceptance within the familiarity of the small group (thanksgiving), and ultimately results in hope-based behavioral change (commitment). This accounts for the group member's affective experience with religious overtones. The group offers an opportunity for redemption on a human level through genuine and immediate contact with others.

Salvation in this sense, from the Latin *salvis* (meaning health), is mediated not through ideas but through relationships that enable persons to overcome the demonic power of anxiety and guilt. What changes people is not mere cognitive knowledge of their predicament, but entering into a new relationship in which they know themselves to be positively valued by others and accepted without conditions of worth.[33] The group, in effect, takes the hand of the person and descends with him into his hell of fear, despair, hatred or helplessness. Yet the group is not like a professional therapist who is paid to do diagnostic work. The group's service is a gift, which may be part of the reason why groups can be more effective.[34]

Within the secular group movement, religious terms and experiences are reduced exclusively to a human plane. One response to this secularization of fundamentally spiritual concepts might be to discourage participation in any such group ventures. Doing so would avoid the spiritually destructive error of flattening rich theological concepts into mere psychological jargon. Salvation in Scripture is never portrayed as a gift of social affirmation. It is the remedy for sin, receiving the divine grace that flows through the sacrifice of Jesus Christ on the cross. Christians who hold the gospel message dear place tremendous value on sacred terms with crucial theological meanings such as *conversion*, the Lord's turning our hearts to honor him; *redemption*, the payment for the penalty of human sin by means of the cross; *justification*, altering our legal standing under divine standards of holiness; and *regeneration*, the imparting of a new birth experience. These reflect a supernatural reality revealed faithfully by the Holy Spirit through the authentic Word of God. Without rejecting the importance of such theological concepts, Oden urges his readers to see the value even in secular group approaches. Rather than shunning or dismissing powerful small group experiences, he takes a different tack. He maintains that intimacy and community may marvelously occur even in secular small groups. When this happens,

---

[33]Oden, *Intensive Group Experience*, p. 108.
[34]Ibid., p. 109.

"God's love is present incognito, received indirectly but not confessed."[35] Even in a community where a Christian worldview is never openly endorsed, God is still God. He is never limited and may freely make himself known within human experience.[36] This sense of earnest community is a foretaste of Christian fellowship or *koinonia*, where the implicit grace of God becomes an explicit matter of praise and worship. Just as "the heavens declare the glory of God" and "the skies proclaim the work of his hands," creatures made in the *imago Dei* may in honest unity reflect God's goodness, nature and love (Ps 19:1). To paraphrase the words of our Lord himself, God in his grace sends the refreshing rain of positive human emotions that occur within community to fall on the righteous and the unrighteous (Mt 5:45).

A CHARGE TO SEASONED GUIDES

This concludes our retrospective look at a group movement that faded with the fads of a bygone decade. I have no intention of appealing to renew that outbreak of instant encounter camaraderie any more than I crave the fashionable return of flared polyester pants and satin shirts. Instead I contend that current ministry challenges require contemporary solutions with a distinct kingdom orientation. Nonetheless, this nostalgic voyage has a valuable purpose.

Committed Christian leaders need not be apprehensive about helping groups that make extensive use of transparency to cultivate mutual trust, explore the here-and-now experience and nurture intimacy. Such ventures have been the source of spiritual formation in believers for centuries, are solidly within our Christian tradition and are consistent with the evangelical faith legacy. Therefore ministry through small groups with an emphasis on accountability and redemptive intimacy represents the recovery of practices that enhance the application of faith, not the appropriation of secular humanistic technology or accommodation to Eastern religious influences.

Modern therapeutic groups placed under empirical scrutiny have validated the effectiveness of small groups that use education to expand psychological awareness, build networks of social support and care for the whole person beyond a

---

[35]Ibid., p. 93.
[36]The theological basis for this argument is referred to as *common grace* or the unmerited favor of God bestowed on all human beings. This is the blessing of God on the just and the unjust. The benefits of social groups to members were first framed into human nature made *imago Dei* and remain evident in ongoing human experience through God's sustaining hand. No statement is being made regarding any salvific or eternal consequences. The transcendent quality of human encounter is merely being credited as a gift of God (see Jas 1:17).

single perplexing issue. On the contemporary scene, ministry-oriented helping groups apply similar approaches in self-help and step-style supportive endeavors, among others. Therapeutic counseling researchers have extensively investigated the use of the group as a self-contained social system that can serve as a resource for developing vigorous social ties and increased relational adaptability. Such research has identified and described the techniques that leaders have at their disposal. These involve assisting members within groups to offer constructive feedback to one another on patterns of communication and interaction. In addition, relational risks taken with the group can produce greater human connection beyond the group. The wealth of insight regarding this type of leader-guided small group technology may be appropriated into useful ministry application. Instead of rejecting these notions because of a presumed secular source, let us investigate their potential in light of their deeper religious roots.

The leader functions refined in the psychotherapeutic literature provide valid assistance in guiding present-day groups with wisdom. Gleaning material from the existing helping group literature, which is informed by empirically derived principles, can increase the precision of our support efforts and character crafting strategies. Here, such applications accord with our broader kingdom mission (Mt 28:16-20).

The popular encounter movement was associated with a tide of social change that had low regard for traditional Christian spirituality. When interpersonal intimacy was intensely present, a transcendent experience appeared to be at hand. Because of the humanistic climate at that time, groups inevitably attributed something to the divine that was inconsistent with a biblically informed worldview. However, when leaders are committed to honoring the triune God of the Scriptures, a breakthrough in people relating with depth and intensity might correctly be viewed as a "God thing." More attention will be given to this dimension in chapter nine, "Entertaining Trekkers Unaware." For the moment, simply recall the fundamentals. When a group enables its members to cease wandering and turn toward an intimate walk with one another, there may be a fresh awareness of the Lord's voice inviting each to embrace wisdom and walk with him.

Group leaders seeking to assist others in service that honors Christ might repeatedly return to this heart-gripping prayer for small group ministers, lifted from Spener's *Pia Desideria:*

> Let us, all of us together, now do diligently what we have been appointed to do, namely, to feed the flock which God has bought with his own blood and therefore at a very great price. . . .

Let us remember the rigorous reckoning which faces us at the hands of him who will call us to account for the souls which have in any way been neglected.

Let us remember that in the last judgment we shall not be asked how learned we were and whether we displayed our learning before the world; to what extent we enjoyed the favor of men and knew how to keep it; with what honors we were exalted and how great a reputation in the world we left behind us; or how many treasures of earthly goods we amassed for our children and thereby drew a curse upon ourselves. Instead, we shall be asked how faithfully and with how childlike a heart we sought to further the kingdom of God; with how pure and godly a teaching and how worthy an example we tried to edify our hearers amid the scorn of the world, denial of self, taking up of the cross, and imitation of our Savior; with what zeal we opposed not only error but also wickedness of life; or with what constancy and cheerfulness we endured the persecution or adversity thrust upon us by the manifestly godless world or by false brethren, and amid such suffering praised our God.

Let us therefore be diligent in investigating ever more deeply our own shortcomings and those of the rest of the church in order that we may learn to know our sicknesses, and then with a fervent invocation of God for the light of his Spirit let us also search for and ponder over the remedies. . . .

Let us not abandon all hope before we have set our hands to the task. Let us not lay down our rod and staff if we do not have the desired success at once. What is impossible for men remains possible for God. Eventually God's hour must come, if only we wait for it. Our fruit, like other fruit, must be borne in patience, and the fruit in others must be cultivated by us with perseverance. The work of the Lord is accomplished in wondrous ways, even as he is himself wonderful.

Philip Jacob Spener; September 8, 1675[37]

This is a beautiful prayer and a high calling to serve the Most High God. No focused, short-term, common-theme group could undertake such a vast mission. Rather, this is the vision for the body of Christ living in worshiping community. A seasoned trekking guide will recognize that there is a grander mission to which our abbreviated ventures only contribute. We look to make the immediate journey continuous with the whole. Short-term small groups with an emphasis

---

[37]Spener, *Pia Desideria*, pp. 36-38.

on community are not an end but a means; ministry leaders must understand and accept this. Sojourners in need of support or refreshment experience the benefits of redeemed community through the resource of leader-guided trekking. Along the way, trekking together affords an extraordinary opportunity for the Holy Spirit to instill and increase the pious desires Spener names.

With this heavenly and holy destination in view, we now turn to consider the many ways modest small group treks can explore territory much closer to home.

Section Two

LEADING TOWARD VISION
AND STRUCTURE

5

DETERMINING DESTINATION

LANDMARKS AHEAD

Ministry care leaders are barraged with care needs that range from alleviating a stunning crisis to seizing a choice season for spiritual growth. But a unifying purpose for helping groups rarely arises simply from a leader's awareness of genuine concerns. This chapter retells a sturdy parable about helping that demonstrates how to discover a clear vision for reachable destinations. Trekking guides can follow a basic approach for assessing whether group needs center on redemptive, adjustment or advancement purposes. From this point, leaders can communicate reliable directions and optimal procedures to support the expedition. Such empowered leadership vision contributes to creative and successful groups. Participants and leaders alike find far more help and fulfillment trekking toward attainable destinations than bushwhacking aimlessly in uncharted terrain. Leaders with foresight can develop a strong sense of necessary "days on trek" and prepare site visits meant for assembly, rest or departure.

RENDEZVOUS AT POINTS OF NEED

Randy and Erin are ministry leaders. The Holy Spirit appears to be prompting each to convene a caravan. Sojourning alone is getting treacherous for those to whom they offer care. The idea of a group experience takes hold in their mind and releases a surge of adrenaline. The urge to unify hurting folks with similar concerns stimulates their imaginations. Surprisingly, opposing sensations cool this initial enthusiasm all too soon. Their focus clouds as the mixture of participant expectations, preferences and excuses make a collective undertaking daunting. The following scenarios illustrate how leaders must tackle the critical decision of destination early in their planning and before any group members are recruited. The stories of Randy and Erin demonstrate how leaders can plan for a collection of strangers to journey together, receiving personal benefit while increasing their devotion to the Lord.

Randy copastors a steadily growing congregation commissioned as a church plant. He sees a need to cultivate stable volunteer leadership out of the largely erratic pattern this vibrant worshiping fellowship has seen. A cluster of men expresses a desire to quench a growing thirst for the sacred. Though the buzzwords are distinct, each indicates a readiness to kick their spiritual lives up a notch. They are receptive to mentoring, ready to dig into a discipleship plan and excited about the possibility of pursuing intensive scriptural investigation. Randy has been earnestly praying with his associate that the Lord would anoint elders from this pool of dedicated seekers. Yet for reasons he does not fully understand, he hesitates to initiate a full-blown recruitment effort for leadership training at this juncture. Neither Randy nor his colleague has had substantial contact with any of these men. They lack a firm assessment of each man's moral fiber, theological conviction or Christ-honoring maturity. Several men freely admit to persistent marital tension and hint that their distress may be reaching an explosive stage. Another man candidly questions if his numerous work-related commitments clash with family loyalties. His wife has complained that his priorities blow about like "lost leaves in a winter wind." These men primarily request guidance on how to achieve a healthy dose of relational and motivational transformation. Several others request nothing short of becoming spiritually centered. Perhaps this theme would draw these scattered faithful into sustained conversation on soul sculpting. Not only would this be thrilling pastorally, but it could also provide the very leadership core the fledgling fellowship desperately requires. How might Randy commence a joint trek? What is the ideal route to get there from here?

The natural next step for Randy is to identify "here" and "there" more precisely based on the actual needs of the men. First, Randy uses response cards from the conclusion of a potent worship series to identify seventeen men with leadership interest and spiritual cravings. He makes it a priority to sit with each and every one at a nearby coffee shop. His sleep is affected by two weeks of candid conversations and too much French Roast. For these men, brutally intense competition abounds for the precious commodity of time. It becomes swiftly evident that only eight, maybe nine, men would rank convening with others high enough to make consistent contact viable. While this is a jolt, it is not the foremost surprise. When pressed for an honest statement about their impetus for worship and pursuit of a "God thing," six of the potential candidates state that a serious disruption or persistent dissatisfaction with work or within family life drives much of their spiritual searching. The frankness of these admissions is both a compliment and unnerving concern. These men want God as a fix for the predicaments in their lives. Their press for weekly, personal, pastoral presence weighs heavy. The unstated plea for Pastor Randy to summon the Almighty to miraculously intervene is a powerful stimulant. Or is that just the caffeine?

Erin has thrived in her position as a counselor on a Christian college campus. Working routinely with bright, talented and energetic students is a rare privilege for which she routinely thanks the Lord. Her crammed appointment calendar is a daily reminder of a crucial reality: the terrific students attracted to this educational institution are loaded down with more than hefty backpacks. This compassionate counselor simply cannot ignore their burdens of extensive personal pain. Well-wishing parents drop off their adolescents as students at college with new bedding, stacks of snack food and turbo-charged computers. Surprisingly, they also carry a hefty supply of emotional baggage into those dorm rooms.

Consistent with national reports across college campuses, Erin's caseload has a substantial percentage of women who appear to be facing either an immediate crisis or a chronic struggle related to the simple, everyday function of eating. The phrase *food network* could take on a whole new meaning if a collective group of these clients could share face-to-face. Perhaps the beauty of soothing Christian community could quell their shame and inspire strength to conquer old patterns. Unfortunately, the opportunity to form a united front in this intensive food fight has remained elusive. Erin's mind races with perplexing questions: Should the common denominator for a group be those who binge, purge, or starve? Are those who occasionally succumb to one of these behaviors in the same cohort as those who bear daily battle scars? Would not a serious, clinically oriented therapeutic group be the ideal fit? What nutritional, medical and mental health resources would be necessary? Erin learned in graduate school that groups are an effective approach for those plagued by eating disorders. But should she ignore, acknowledge or refer elsewhere more isolated but disturbing reports of cutting or self-mutilation? Perhaps a wiser path would be to address a core spiritual issue that hits gross distortions in self-esteem. A biblical inquiry into God's deep, gracious love for his children could surely address the cavernous distortions in self-perception and acceptance. A retrospective search that considers earlier broken and distorted family relationships is yet another potential solution. Might this remedy enable these young women to land firmly on their adult feet and thereby feed themselves during their college years? Neither of the available prototypes for group therapy targeting eating disorders or women's Bible studies on appropriating grace fit the clients with whom Erin is meeting weekly. As her caseload grows, she wonders if the counseling care she distributes is truly what these clients need, desire and deserve.

Erin has enough savvy to commence her own detective-style investigation. In conjunction with a colleague, she conducts an assessment of the needs throughout the center's caseload. They piece together a basic grid noting the main initial request, the top three items on the symptom profile and the agreed-upon goals for the treatment direction. They then assemble a careful count of recent clients who exhibited some variation of a food-related struggle. Not surprisingly this list easily tops ten. The confounding datum that surfaces is that not one of these students came to the center to fix a food-related issue. Their typical concerns were relational frustrations, bouts of anger or anxiety, floundering self-confidence, spiritual discouragement and dealing with dark dispositions. These issues, not food, dominated the distress of her clients. They sought help to overcome recurring dismal moods, mild depression and intensely annoying inner anxiety. Erin does the simple math. She is doing steady work sifting through and diminishing disparaging inner conversations with nearly 70 percent of these clients. Eating issues were a striking and, in select cases, alarming symptom. Strangely, they were not the major voiced concern. What could Erin do with her new insight regarding the concerns of her clients? Erin's grasp of the variety of her clients' struggles brings one immediate benefit; this knowledge equips her to discern principles and programs from professional literature that speak to her setting. She can now shift her research toward discovering how other groups with college students make progress in distilling useful material, themes and methods. Erin continues to listen to her clients as she prays. She reads to sharpen her perspective.

The dilemmas that Randy and Erin face are not unique. Care leaders and counselors confront numerous barriers to the formation of cooperative treks. The first and foremost is: what type of group can address divergent needs? What will fit and what won't? Further, as the pragmatics of availability and time constraints are evaluated, the notion of a common venture becomes increasingly tenuous. Having sat with many helpers such as Randy and Erin to sort out serial questions, establish realistic priorities and to determine an intended outcome, I have found that an old anecdote known as the "prevention parable" comes in handy. I was introduced to this well-traveled tale during my psychological training. As a Christian, I had learned that parables in the Bible are to be treated as earthly stories with a heavenly meaning. The source of this yarn was not Scripture, of course; it was relayed to me as a psychologically oriented allegory. The oral tradition was passed down without any spiritual insight, so I take full responsibility for the faith perspective I've imposed on it. This contemporary Good Samaritan tale can assist future group leaders like Randy and Erin to select a tactical destination.

THE RELUCTANT RESCUER: A HELPING PARABLE

One day, a man was driving over a bridge that crossed a great river. To his astonishment, as he reached the center he caught a glimpse of a person struggling in the current below. When the man was over the bridge, he rapidly pulled his vehicle to a place where he could attempt a rescue. He waded into the water far enough to grab the drowning person and drag him to shore. By this time, several others had noticed this rescue attempt. They also turned aside and came to offer assistance. The instant that the unfortunate victim was on dry land, a bystander screamed that now a woman was floating down the river and would soon reach the extraction point. The man went back into the river. This time a bystander handed him a set of jumper cables, for he had to go further into the current to reach out to the struggling woman. This required linking several sets of helping hands and the use of the trusty cables to get far enough out into the water to execute the saving maneuver. Once the second victim was on the shore, more cries rose up indicating that additional sufferers were being carried by the current and in need of rescue. A team began to form. An ad hoc method took shape for bringing those who were drowning to safety. Soon exhausted, the rescuers motioned for more help from the drivers passing over the bridge. As fresh volunteers joined the effort, it was agreed that this place in the river was too treacherous for so many rescuers. Therefore, under the direction of the original hero, a second team moved to a peninsula where the river was narrower and the liberation of victims was less dangerous. After numerous successful rescues, the hero suddenly ceased his efforts and climbed out of the water. He began to walk away. When the others asked him where he was going, he replied, "I'm heading upstream till I find the son-of-a-gun who is throwing all these people in."[1]

The details of this story are subject to the whims of the storyteller. Those drowning in the river represent any person with a medical, mental health, rela-

---

[1]The source of this story has not been successfully traced. My initial exposure to the story was in 1987 through my professor, academic advisor and expert in school-based consultation, Joel Meyers. The story is associated with key names in prevention such as George Albee, Emory Cowen and The National Institute of Mental Health (NIMH).

tional or developmental concern. The inner struggle provoked by these needs can also rouse spiritual restlessness. The preliminary rescue site, where victims were yanked from the river moments before impending death, signifies corrective efforts targeted to relieve a fully developed disorder or actual crisis. The psychological and epidemiological term associated with intervention at this late phase is *tertiary prevention*. Helping interventions attempt to reverse the course of the disease or crisis and prevent the existing condition from worsening, spreading, harming others or further disabling the individual. Only a portion of the assistance seeks a cure. When the suffering and related conditions are not likely to change, helpers do best simply to manage or contain the disruption. The intervention earns the term *preventative*, indicating the aim to minimize the adverse impact of the affliction wherever and however possible. In the case of Erin, one or more of her clients may have a clinically diagnosable eating disorder. Tertiary prevention strategies would seek to curtail its severity and avoid long-term health consequences for the individual. Such a problem would indicate treatment to directly reduce or eliminate the risk behaviors. From the prevention angle, remediation could reduce any behaviors that might compromise educational endeavors, disrupt relationships, or most importantly, create a risk of immediate physical harm.

Common-theme ministry groups that reach out to those in this category suggest the label *redemptive*. Abby's Reach and Remember group introduced earlier ideally operates at this prevention level. That group came alongside those who had already suffered a severe loss. Their distress produced the meeting point. Abby embraces a destination strategy of walking with the group through shock and dismay until members begin to regain their bearings. This style of grief group may only run for eight or ten weeks. The leader understands that a redemptive journey requires a certain number of sessions, which are hereafter called *days on trek*. The length represents a bare minimum of meetings for such a major crisis. Then after a pause or break, another cycle typically begins. Participants may return for a second round or even begin to assist others through the turmoil of early grief experiences. The introductory, leader-guided, themed group may be followed by a less formal support group where participants drop in weekly as necessary. This term *redemptive* indicates the intention to honor God in the restoration of capabilities and resources. The victim experiences a loss due to the death, separation and the effects of sin. In a ministry context, redemptive assistance aims to expand coping and self-management skills during a period of significant emotional, relational and spiritual upheaval. Further, redemptive groups facilitate the reestablishment of fulfilling bonds with others and ultimately strengthen confidence in one's walk with the Lord.

Referring back to the parable, the more suitable rescue site in the narrower section of the river represents the intervention level termed *secondary prevention*. Here, a helper tries to catch people who are at risk, early on the course of a progressive dilemma. Reaching out as early as possible aims to slow or deter potential progression toward a crisis, thereby avoiding increasingly serious concerns. This prevention level offers action before the difficulty reaches a detrimental phase. An immense potential exists for developing common-theme groups in this category, here termed *adjustment*. Across the human lifespan, relationships and responsibilities vary, accumulate or stagnate over time. Individuals are confronted with the constant press to accommodate. Children grow, parents age, employment demands increase or shift, health conditions deteriorate or fluctuate. If an internal or external force inhibits a person from making the required responses or modifications, increased stress, relational strain or even separation from seemingly permanent resources bring increased risk. Life transition periods thus increase vulnerability to destructive currents.[2] Groups aimed at facilitating adjustment provide valued benefits like sharing information and resources, sharpening skills, and expanding one's social network.

For example, Randy is alert to the messages that he has heard in his personal pastoral dialogues. He recognizes that the hints at marital tension, if left unattended, could progress and ultimately threaten the vitality and survival of the marriage. Randy heard another hazard in these conversations. One or more of these men is vulnerable to an involuntary employment change, which could result in financial ruin, esteem destruction and family fragmentation. Fortunately the inner restlessness of these fellows sent them looking in the best possible direction. They admit their real needs, and the Holy Spirit is moving in their circumstances. They are actively looking beyond themselves and their situation. toward a spiritual remedy. No pastoral care provider should miss such signs of potentially deeper issues on the horizon. When facing transitions, faith seekers benefit from the wise counsel of others who have walked circumspectly with the Lord through similar challenges.

Finally, the spontaneous hero's attempt to venture upstream to identify, apprehend and suppress the culprit tossing people into the river represents *primary prevention*. Such tactical intercession involves inhibiting the development

---

[2]Jane Goodman, Nancy K. Schlossberg and Mary L. Anderson, *Counseling Adults in Transition*, 3rd ed. (New York: Springer, 2006), pp. 22-82.

of conditions or vulnerabilities that may give rise to a later malady. Public service announcements touting healthy lifestyle choices, parenting classes, retirement seminars, substance abuse warnings and information circulated from positive psychology are everyday examples of intervention at this prevention level. The worship and preaching series at Randy's church resulting in those survey responses could be considered a form of primary prevention. It inspired constructive action where no critical concern rose up demanding help. Group destinations that enhance skills, increase resiliency, deepen relational ties and strengthen spiritual resources have virtually no limit. Common-theme groups that fit this category will be tagged *advancement*, as these efforts build hope toward a brighter future. A Christian perspective recognizes that even troubling circumstances and suffering may produce future spiritual benefits (Jas 1:2-7). Groups at this level seek to maximize personal strengths, improve self-awareness, hone interpersonal competence and establish discipline that molds character. In a Christian setting, these groups encourage ordinary faith practices such as prayer, worship, Scripture

Table 5.1. Three Group Types

Group Category	Prevention Level	Common-Theme Group Examples
Redemptive	Tertiary	Bereavement Divorce Recovery Addiction Management Celebrate Recovery Weight Reduction
Adjustment	Secondary	Parenting Children and Adolescents Caregiver Support Premarital and Marital Communication Relational Coaching Financial Stewardship
Advancement	Primary	Bible Studies Men's & Women's Discipleship Groups Mother of Preschoolers (MOPS) Spiritual Formation/Covenant Groups Leadership Skill Development

study and fellowship. Thus formation activities are placed under this advancement category even though any level group has intentions of moving members toward a more intimate walk with the Lord. See the chart Three Group Types for a summary of these ideas.

SPIRITUAL DISCERNMENT OF DESTINATION

This secular parable illustrates three points of intervention for public health and medical and mental health initiatives. Evangelical ministries will not run identical or substitute services for those that specialists make available in hospitals, clinics and community outreach programs. But the needs of many people remain unaddressed; some still float down the river with no rescuers in sight. Ministry applications flow from this parable too. The allegory identifies how to create helping ventures that make use of the strategic places where rescue stations can at least get folks to shore. The destination is not at the mouth of the river or in a remote location miles away; it is the network of rescuers operating near the most suitable location on the shoreline. When people experience critical needs, helpers consider the risk level and design the simplest route to safety. Even better, could they look for ways to keep people out of the river or equip them with the skills or devices necessary to keep them afloat? Use these images as the inspiration to envision the type of group and its mission, as well as the common elements uniting them, at one particular point of need.

My original orientation to this well-worn tale was a solemn educational moment. I clearly saw that new categories of thinking about groups could revolutionize Christian ministry. I glimpsed a vision of secular and sacred helping models converging to offer God's very best to hurting people. Ministry assistance would never be identical to medically oriented offerings and outreach. Nonetheless, service layers that aim to protect folks from severe crisis or to ensure safer passage most certainly apply to both contexts. If suffering must be faced, Christian ministry assists by offering reachable lifelines to community. Comprehensive care strategies must not wait for a crisis to set in. The plan: identify key opportunities to extend a helping hand when the benefits can have the greatest impact. In ministry endeavors, anticipated group outcomes do appeal to immediate individual needs as well as yearnings for self-improvement. Ministries are distinct in that they are nested within the broader agenda for Christian formation and sanctification. The following implication, drawn from the biblical narrative, provides a needed consideration for ministry leaders like Erin and Randy.

As many times as I have retold or thought through the story of this reluctant rescuer, my theological convictions have never been able to rest peacefully on the shoreline while the hero heads off into the horizon. The culprit is the river. Picture that deadly river with its demanding current. Does it have a name? What is its source? Might it be the Pishon that winds through the entire land of Havilah? Was it the Gihon that flows through the entire land of Cush? Could it be the Tigris that runs along the east side of Asshur or perhaps the Euphrates? Any one of those branches might eventually lead the trustworthy rescuer back to the river that watered the Garden of Eden. What would happen when the hero reaches the cherubim and the flaming sword that the Lord placed there to prevent a return to Paradise and the Tree of Life? He would not be able to enter; human beings are no longer permitted to travel into that pristine garden. Only in that God-tended garden would no one fall or be thrown into the water. Stated without references to Eden, humans cannot return to the days before their fall from God's holy presence. Only in the direct presence of the Creator could the rescuer reach a place where no victims are floating down the river's current. Those who hold Scripture dear set their vision on "Jesus, the author and perfecter of our faith" (Heb 12:2). Our gaze is not restricted upstream to follow a deterministic line of cause and effect. We look forward to the day when Jesus Christ will wipe away each and every tear. He will quench parched tongues and desperate thirst through the spring of life (Rev 21:1-8).

Sin is the source of the river flowing with pain, toil, sweat, thorns and thistles, family strife, conflicting desires, relational paradoxes, decline and death. No discovery or disentanglement of conditions will reveal the ultimate origin of suffering. The source of suffering is this: created beings no longer walk within the garden or with the Creator. The separation due to sin is now woven into the fabric of creation itself (Rom 8:22-23). Human beings rebel and reject the Creator, who is the only security for life, well-being and safe passage.

As beings made in the *imago Dei*, humans were qualified by God to exercise stewardship over creation and charged them with developing productive civilizations to fill the earth. Wanderers are able to turn a place of wilderness into a neighborhood oasis. Scripture's wisdom can serve as a protective fence around lethal sections of the river. Jesus himself pulled victims from devastating currents when he supernaturally healed the sick, fed the multitude, empowered sinners and embraced outcasts. His disciples were given a similar ministry. Our parable's hero may honor the Creator through acts of compassion and redemption by successfully eliminating nasty villains and natural threats along the riverbank. He could post danger signs at treacherous bends. Bridge construction might provide

effortless crossing. Even so, the river itself will continue to flow and human beings will be pushed or pulled, fall or jump in. My obsession with the metaphor of
the river as a symbol of sin within this parable does not negate its hopeful lesson
nor feed a fatalistic view of helping others. It is quite the opposite. Helpers can
establish stations of grace, or rest stops. This is stewardship of soul care, solace
for sojourners.

The parable provides useful insight about helping group destinations. Leaders
may direct rescue teams to pursue redemptive, adjustment or advancement purposes. Thus the river's edge gives us a picture of numerous small group ministries
with outstanding kingdom potential. Recall the lesson previously explored from
either the traditional Pietists or the encounter group proponents. Targeted groups
steadily and substantially contribute to a much larger spiritual and social change.
Informal and humble group gatherings may appear to be incidental or limited.
After all, the number of people influenced initially is so pitifully low. But those
who benefit tend to remain involved by bringing others to the same types of caring networks that were instrumental in getting their feet firmly on shore. Further, those touched at critical moments in their lives may by grace merge deeply
into the community of the body of believers for a lifetime. This holds promise
for personal renewal, gospel realization and kingdom impact. Such groups have
far-reaching implications. In this pluralistic, secular and self-focused age, small
group helping ventures with embedded spiritual perspectives may function as
mustard seeds and yeast when offered in honor to the Lord (see Mt 13:31-35).
Consider these four applications drawn from the prevention parable.

First, folks fighting to barely tread water may be most willing to grab the
hand of the one who has risked entering the river to assist them. Christians who
offer authentic assistance using a method within reach of those with an earnest
need will find that empty seats gradually fill, even if the setting is not flashy
or the participants are not eloquent. Such offerings need not be structured as
overtly evangelistic enterprises. Those on the receiving end naturally become
curious about the lives, values and source of renewable strength for those serving
as rescuers. The Holy Spirit may use this openness to allow the heart to inform
the mind that Jesus Christ is indeed the Way, the Truth and the Life. The old
adage proves itself again and again: news travels fast when it involves one beggar
telling another beggar where to find bread.

Second, teams offering group support ideally exhibit the love that Scripture
commands us to share (see Mt 22:39; Mk 12:33; Lk 10:27; Jn 15:12; 1 Jn 3:11).
This is a way to be obedient (see Mt 25:37-40). Note that the word *love* may never

be referenced when rescuers care in a small-group helping ministry. They just "do unto others," demonstrate compassion, and help because it is the right thing or it returns a favor. This is love in action just the same.[3]

Third, the experience of community within a group connects with a universal and acute human need for connection. In fact, people frequently wander into the river of sin in a misguided attempt to drown out an inner ache spiraling out of a core void of vital relatedness. Thus a group may provide intimacy, connection and relational relief that individuals long for. The sense of being touched by a caring group may pave the way for eventual Christ-centered fellowship. In a Christian context, leaders never intend the common-theme group as an end in itself. It offers an exercise in communion that invites the participant to join the church, the bride, as she awaits return of the bridegroom, Jesus Christ. His free gift is the water of life (Rev 22:17).

Fourth, there will never be a shortage of victims in the river. The journey of life inevitably brings every human being into contact with the river's currents. This seems to be how the Lord consistently reminds his creatures that he desires to travel with us. When we find ourselves overwhelmed by the currents of life, we listen intently and we may recognize his voice calling, "Where are you?" Helplessness in the river motivates us to answer.

CHARACTER MATTERS AND RESHAPING THE IMAGE

Randy's dreams have focused. He first worked through the vision and structure function of group leadership so that he could design a trip toward a worthy destination. The Holy Spirit empowered him to sort through what he heard in his investigative conversations. With great clarity, he is now able to separate his own wishes for a quickly anointed leadership core from the needs of those he desires to shepherd. He knows now that he cannot allow the urgency for stable church leadership to override the heart cries the Spirit has given him ears to hear. He recognizes that pastoral care should be multifaceted and long-term. A leadership development retreat for building elders and igniting enthusiasm for this church will come. But this is not the immediate destination toward which Randy is

---

[3]The biblical term *love* is applied in this section. The insights of Robert Wuthnow obtained through extensive survey research are important here. He asserts that those who help others through religious organizations prefer in the current day to describe their work as "caring, caregiving, helping, assisting, serving, and in some cases showing compassion." Love is viewed as too intense, intrusive or as violating a boundary. While alternate terms may be the socially permissible ones currently, they reflect the biblical concept of love. See Robert Wuthnow, *Saving America: Faith-Based Services and the Future of Civil Society* (Princeton, N.J.: Princeton University Press, 2004), p. 262.

to direct these men. For a season, that advancement effort must be separated from the adjustment effort necessary now. A less glorious and more modest trek appears on the horizon. In fact, Randy sees that it is ideally suited as an inaugural expedition. He will make a personal appeal to interested men, asking for a two-month commitment of weekly contact in a group entitled Character Matters. Traits from Colossians 3:12-14 (compassion, kindness, humility, gentleness, patience, bearing with one another, forgiveness and love) will serve as themes. The group's main press will be to make everyday applications in key relationships. Those who commit should be willing to strip down to transparent talk, risk honesty and listen for the Holy Spirit. This group exemplifies the *adjustment* level of intervention because it is for those dealing with an inner restlessness to move toward an authentic Christian experience. Brokenness exposed will not be a surprise; frankly, it is expected. Randy may not have the details ironed out, but this iron-sharpening-iron trek is nearly ready to roll. Once he establishes Character Matters through a couple of cycles, a new leader for subsequent treks may become apparent.

The behavioral symptoms of her most challenging clients no longer mesmerize Erin. She carefully collected and screened referrals and resources for those who need intensive care. Specifically, those few women who need more extensive mental health services than the college can supply will receive guidance from professionals in agencies equipped to offer the required comprehensive care. In addition, Erin communicated with other student life support entities on campus to raise awareness of her concerns, and they know about her strategy to provide assistance. For the time being, this networked approach for providing reasonable care in severe cases is the best she can offer. Her own efforts on the local campus simply cannot assist all possible clients, but Erin is convinced that she can help many of them. By educating the other invested stakeholders about her concern and sketching a strategic system for assistance, Erin can also forge a groundswell of enthusiasm for the mission of a group approach within the wider social and organizational context.[4] Erin has explored the literature enough now to realize that broader organizational cooperation facilitates both the recruitment of members and their eventual level of engagement. Each group member must eventually take risks with others to reach personal goals. Thus the endorsement and encouragement of the trek purpose by on-campus peers and mentors bolsters the entire undertaking.

Like Randy, Erin has tightened her purpose to address one meager but ob-

---

[4]Virginia Brabender, *Introduction to Group Therapy* (Hoboken, N.J.: Wiley, 2002), pp. 121-40.

tainable redemptive area. Instead of seeking to reverse the scourge of an eating disorder that has captured a victim on her campus, Erin will lend a helping hand toward curtailing the plague from gaining a foothold. Those with pressing needs will find aid via networking with other providers while Erin will assist those with milder symptom expression, a category that includes many on campus. Further, radically reforming the self-concept of these young women is a project that the Lord will have to address in his own time through comprehensive maturation experiences. Perhaps the broader Christian college community with its host of spiritual growth activities can contribute in this regard. Erin's invitation will go out to those who desire to reduce pain stemming from body image concerns. Her Reshaping the Image group will be an exercise in tuning in to myths, ideals, lies and outrageous thoughts that stir negative emotions into a frenzy. These can be tamed, and Erin knows how to do so using a variety of techniques to catch cognitive distortions and emotional deadly traps. She has already started working through similar techniques in individual sessions. The group will not automatically replace existing appointments, and the blend with her ongoing counseling work is still brewing. Erin prays God's thoughts will enter into the crevices as minds are jointly renewed through reciprocal encouragement.

While these treks may not be grand, each is doable. Once leaders select a destination, the directions are not hard to establish. Contemporary common-theme groups often have a limited focus and fixed time frames, and they target specific member profiles. With such attempts, a leader brings compassion and knowledge together so that the Lord may transform lives through wisdom. No one claims that such small group adventures will revolutionize anyone's entire life. But recall the effectiveness of the group movements of the seventeenth century and the seventies. Who knows what might happen if trust transforms individuals into a community where mutual care and honest confession become the norm? These small gatherings might be the catalyst for God to do a great work. He has and he can!

6

PACKING ESSENTIALS

LANDMARKS AHEAD

The challenge of guiding relational treks can stir apprehension. Leaders, particularly novices, may tend to react to the intensity of their inner battles by packing sessions with fascinating exercises or materials that distract from the central vision. A personal account of a leadership experience that placed my conviction on the line supplies this chapter's prologue and epilogue. This chapter answers the question: how can leaders produce the optimal structure for igniting the interpersonal dimension within a group? Here are the essentials necessary for judicious and prudent packing, or structuring. This chapter accentuates two priorities: balancing educational and member interaction, and instilling holistic relational expectations. Take a tip from guides who know; pack wise and well, then trek by faith in the potential of what members can achieve. The Word may enter those encounters!

A TREKKING PARADOX

Lugging an awkward brown shopping bag instead of a black professional briefcase down the school hallway felt peculiar. I approached the meeting room for my new group and froze in the doorway. I knew for certain only that my insides were stirring with uneasy sensations, my heart was pumping hard with anticipation and my head was spinning with doubt. There was irony in this inner ambivalence. What was about to commence was the result of my own convictions, ideals and design. Not only had I volunteered for this assignment, I was its advocate and engineer. A familiar voice had persuasively asserted, "Counselors should occasionally leave the familiar comfort of the one-on-one office session to explore the possibilities of focused group work." Wasn't this supposed to be natural for me?

This extraordinary opportunity would merge extensive youth ministry acumen and advanced psychological training. I had the chance to assist a handful of needy young adolescents. Further, I was pioneering this effort within a long-

established social service agency already doing fine work with this taxing population. The group approaches we had instituted with these rebellious boys had,
bluntly, gone bust in recent years. I blamed my uncomfortable hesitation on how
silly I must look holding the wrinkled bag with the jute string handle ripping off
and its bulges revealing irregularly shaped contents.

Once safely in the room, I placed the bag plainly in view and well within my
grasp. There was to be no question about its ownership or control. After arranging the cushioned chairs, I attempted to greet the boys as each one charged, slid
or strolled into the room. I facilitated the introductions, dispensed instructions,
and hurriedly issued the ground rules with firm intensity. The minimal regulations boiled down to basic respect and would be revisited at regular intervals or
as crises dictated. The group was ready to embark. The mysterious sack made
its way to the center. Out of the paper bag I pulled a sturdy claw hammer, a few
ten-penny nails, and a wide, fat board. The wooden-handled tool handed down
to me by my father had served well on less ambitious projects. The objects were
placed on the floor in the midst of our small circle. I could sense a dozen eyes
intently checking me out. Allowing for a poignant pause, I stared back at the assembly of squirming, male adolescents surrounding me and closing in fast.

The stocky one with curly black hair had an earned reputation for being impulsive and aggressive, and for having a roaring foul mouth. Wonderful! The
blond-haired youth with the squint in his eye would not face anyone. His chair
was pulled away from the others even though I was reasonably sure that this
was not its original placement. His face revealed a distant glare that gave the
impression he was not entirely in the room. The rigidity of his body screamed
tension. A spontaneous word never left his lips. Phrases from his psychological
paperwork flashed across my mind: poor reality testing; possible latent schizo-
phrenia; depression; and questions regarding "psychotic features." Beneath the
jargon, I could plainly ascertain this was a perplexing kid whose odd ways would
make him a target of ridicule here as he customarily was everywhere else. Two
of the boys were not all that distinctive. This might be explained by their obvious distractibility. Conversations with them were choppy and peppered with
phrases such as "uh, yes," "uh, no," and the ever popular "uh, don't know." Their
unrelenting inner activity and outward perpetual motion made a physical description hard to establish. Then there was the articulate, charming youth with a
nymph-like quality. His main reason for being in this residential school for boys
who find and stir trouble could bring the most hardened grown man to shed a
tear. His wandering parents were reportedly drugged-out in places unknown.

Then his devoted caregiver grandmother had a severe stroke leaving her feeble and bedridden. Such a young boy could not be left to wander the streets without restrictions; that is, no longer than the six months that he had already spent doing so while remaining truant from school. Welcome to my new counseling group, designed to increase emotional self-regulation, curb behavioral impulsivity and cultivate stronger decision-making skills.[1] The last set of eyes portrayed a stunned look and belonged to the young social worker who was there to co-facilitate. I knew that he had been drafted to learn from me how to run such an outrageous yet presumably therapeutic venture. Out of the corner of my eye, I noticed the hammer and nonchalantly moved it nearer to my own feet.

Each one of these boys had been to my office for an official pre-group screening and orientation. They felt different now as a collected mass. While in my stark, coffin-style office, tucked away in the quiet corner of the professional clinic, each had seemed quiet, timid, suspicious, curious and most important, manageable. In that setting, one on one, I saw behavior representative of those who were out of place, caught off guard and momentarily outwitted. I held no delusions that these fourteen-year-olds had in any way volunteered to join this venture, though the idea of missing an academic class twice a week had been appealing. I was under no illusion that I had won anyone over with the warmth of my invitation to develop effective tactics to deal with the dilemmas and people surrounding them. The tightening now in my throat added *hopeless* to the sensations identified earlier. I was no longer in the safety of my assigned space. We were in school—their school. I was in the midst of the social world that these boys faced each day. Numbers were no longer in my favor. My leadership instincts indicated that the most pressing matter was to display a comforting sense of confidence. Where might that come from?

I pointed out with careful explanation the objects now before them on the floor. The hammer triggered a brief warm memory of father-son carpentry projects in days gone by. But as the child of a high school industrial arts teacher, I was about to risk my reputation and leadership role in this assembly. The moment had arrived to lay down the challenge. I picked up the hammer and explained that

---

[1]The group design and approach was customized specifically for this alternative school setting. It was based on a standardized treatment manual available at that time. See David Wexler, *The Adolescent Self: Strategies for Self-Management, Self-Soothing, and Self-Esteem in Adolescents* (New York: W. W. Norton, 1991). My including this reference should not be viewed as an endorsement of this material for other settings. Such a decision is made carefully after a comprehensive assessment of the population to be serviced. Note that the wise use of treatment manuals in the hands of trained leaders is encouraged and can have positive results.

each of them would be given a nail, three chances to swing the hammer, and an opportunity to send their nail deeply into the board. The winner would get one of the prizes that remained stashed away in the brown bag. The contest was on and there was life in the room. After each near miss or wild swing, there was the sound of swearing, moaning, whining, challenges to the contest rules, unabashed begging for more turns and explanations for why "that one didn't count."

The stunt was not entirely without redemptive results. Not one of these youth did much of anything to put a nail into the fat board. While my own three hits were nothing remarkable, relatively my efforts were quite impressive. At least when I swung the hammer it made direct contact with the head of the nail. My mind did not wonder for too long about the possible presence of angels. My success with the hammer allowed me to proceed as planned with an explanation to this frustrated and baffled crew. Our meetings together over the next quarter were designed to equip them with more personal power. My promise was to increase their unique influence to get things done by "hitting the nail on the head." My pitch ran along these lines: Everyone in the room already had enough physical strength to send any nail deeply into the board. Each lacked a well-honed strategy to point energy in the optimal direction. If they would be willing to work with me and with each other, I would virtually guarantee that every single group member would gain more personal power to earn privileges and influence teachers, parents, authority figures and perhaps more importantly, their peers. I would be available as their coach or "shrink" to enable them to take more control over their own future, that is, if they had the guts to invest in this trip. The clock struck the magic minute, the alarm sounded, and our minutes together were gone. One session was done; only fifteen more to follow.

What kinds of relationships might form among this unlikely cast of misfits? Who would most modify his behavior through this tricky and tumultuous trek? Which member might carry off lasting impressions of lessons learned? Truth be told, I may be the one who experienced the most productive reshaping. My leadership tactics, style and strategies were hammered out through those fragile bonds and sputtering conversations. My growth spurt within that unique assembly of individuals went beyond the reinforcement of principles. The dynamics were not all that unusual given the poor baseline skills and lack of participant readiness. This trek was not about what I could hand off to each member during the combined helping time but what the group itself could be. Here is a basic trekking premise and a leader paradox. *As a helping group comes to life, the identified change agent may no longer be the most influential agent of change.* The group takes on a life of its own. Any and all of those who are invested may be influenced, including the leader. This particular journey exposed my own assumptions and weathered my confidence. It became evident that the increase in personal power I advertised would be grounded less on changes made within these boys and more on how they related with one another. The subtle interplay between intrapersonal and interpersonal, growth within and growth between, was portrayed in vivid color.

There are three common misconceptions regarding what makes a group a potent force for healing and growth. A popular myth is that the motivation level of the members themselves produces a promising trek toward wholeness. A second assumption is that success depends on the characteristics or quality of members. The third error attributes the eventual outcome to the material and themes the group explored. All three of these factors do indeed influence how pleasant the gatherings will be, but none of them ensures the realization of the group's potential. I contend that neither motivation, nor member skill nor the significance of the topics sets great groups apart from mediocre ones. *Superior groups build on and derive meaning from the interactions between members.* There are at least a dozen packing essentials that influence the interactive force a group experiences (see Twelve Trekking Packing E-ssentials). Ministry settings routinely promote a number of these essentials. Two in particular, however, distinguish the style of group leadership promoted here. They will be addressed for their value in assisting leaders to undertake the necessary vision and structure their groups require.

Twelve Trekking Packing E-ssentials

1. Plan the anticipated balance between the **educational** and interpersonal components of the meeting sessions.

2. Shape member **expectations** prior to the start, reinforce these as the trek gets underway, and then refine these as members discover the value of being together.

3. Highlight how watching the progress of others **enriches** all participants.

4. Encourage members to reflect on the immediate **experience** of relational support and challenge.

5. Help participants to find ways to express gratefulness when risk taking and genuine communication result in a meaningful **encounter** between members.

6. Use the remarkable benefits of group cohesion as a resource to **empower** members to make and maintain change.

7. Take care to invite, receive and appreciate productive **emotional release** that results in closer ties between members.

8. Build on the sense of trust in the group by coaching the **exercise** of effective social skills in member interactions.

9. Seek to take maximum advantage of those rich occasions when personality patterns—consistent ways of thinking, feeling, and behaving—are **exposed** in group interactions.

10. Allow time and opportunity for members to **explore** how they are relating to and affecting others.

11. Match expressions of self-**evaluation** with immediate group feedback to facilitate the development of new perspectives.

12. When a participant risks to implement change, notice and **embrace** this victory by offering group members an invitation to compliment the accomplishment.

Christian groups frequently struggle to anticipate the balance between the educational and interpersonal components of a group. Further, leaders enhance a group experience when they shape member expectations prior to the start of the group and then refine them as the group develops a sense of unity, togetherness and commitment. At this later stage, members can work toward, recognize and reap the benefits of shared community. This is training to enjoy the blessing of Christian fellowship.

EXPECT THE UNEXPECTED

In my opening recollection, the ugly brown bag bore the blame for my heightened sense of self-consciousness. The source of anxiety was surely within. It is obvious that this brash helper had deep concerns about launching that group and stepping into this leadership role. After ample opportunities to train numerous novice leaders and review the broader literature, I know that my early subjective experience was not unique.[2] In fact, intense leader anxiety is such a universal and conceivably destructive weight that professionals strongly urge or mandate group leaders to be under supervision. The counseling community views guidance in managing inner turmoil and uncomfortable feelings as a leader's ethical responsibility.[3] Unfocused and unfiltered helper concerns within can inadvertently inflict harm. Or in less austere terms, incapacitating leader tension can inhibit member investment and eventual gain. Leaders obviously benefit from training and comprehensive supervision. More critically, leaders serve the best interest of those under their care when they comprehend and receive direction regarding methods to harness their own inner state. Picture this angst as a fire that produces warmth and ambiance if contained in a stunning fireplace complete with hearth. If sparks start to fly out of control, the damage could be costly.

Leaders legitimately worry that member personality clashes, a participant crisis, or a thousand other uncontrollable variables could turn a cohesive team into a chaotic mob. Generally, however, apprehensions of group leaders flow from five distinct, equally valid sources. First, leaders often fear that they will lose control of either a single session or the group progression as a whole. Group *dynamics* is the appropriate label to depict the intensity of the relational forces. Dynamic relationships stoke the heat to forge change. With too much heat, these may explode like dynamite, which is exactly what the term implies. Leaders must not view their fear within as the signal of an ignited dynamite fuse; it is instead a memento of group potential. It serves to remind a leader to respect the power within the interacting members. Second, a related worry stems from a threat to self-image. Leaders acknowledge nagging intrusive thoughts that their incompetence may be displayed before the group they are charged to guide.

The matters revealed within a group form a third avenue of leader anxiety. People bring forward a wide range of complex and perplexing concerns. The talk can turn on a major crisis or a lifelong struggle; a recent spat with an angry stranger or a split with a marriage partner; a minor medical incident or impending death. As concern after concern enters the conversation, they eventually expose the idiosyncrasies of personality. At this point leaders may become over-

---

[2]Janice L. Delucia-Waack and James Fauth, "Effective Supervision of Group Leaders: Current Theory, Research, and Implications for Practice," in *Handbook of Group Counseling and Psychotherapy*, ed. Janice L. Delucia-Waack et al. (Thousand Oaks, Calif.: Sage, 2004), pp. 136-50.
[3]See "Section C: Professional Responsibility," American Counseling Association Code of Ethics (2005), <http://www.counseling.org/Resources/CodeOfEthics/TP/Home/CT2.aspx>.

whelmed. An alert and conscientious trekking guide visualizes the sheer magnitude of the material that could be addressed and starts to calculate the nearly
infinite options. Questions start to fly concerning who, what, where, when and
how. Admittedly, one's mind can become muddled. It should help to consider
that this occasion has the inherent makings of becoming intimate. The hope
of connection stimulates story sharing and behavioral self-disclosure. Members
confess their struggles and this becomes the content for discussion. Simultaneously each member demonstrates interpersonal trademarks or typical ways of
walking with others. Group work may be messy in this respect, but this mix also
sets up the conditions for members to develop connecting skills. Nonetheless,
when awareness of the heightened relational dynamics mimics the experience
of looking out over a vast precipice, a trekking guide can get dizzy and begin to
wobble.

A leader can make a directional turn with a group that suddenly runs into a
roadblock, dead end or rough conditions. These images represent a fourth familiar fear. Leaders wonder if they will make a mistake that prompts a premature
member exit. What if the group veers off course? Could a participant refuse to
return due to disappointment with the experience? Such departures are dreaded
because infectious doubts over the viability of the entire venture spread rapidly.
A leader trapped by trepidation over offending one or several members may be
ineffective in bringing important observations to the surface.

Last, a group guide realizes that entering this helping zone means that both
personal and professional weaknesses are not likely to remain hidden. A slip of
the tongue may insult and reveal a bias or flaw; a display of emotion may say
more about a personal vulnerability than about what actually occurred; and a
missed opportunity or a misreading of intentionality may point toward a glar-
ing hole in the leader's experience. Denying the risks cannot dispel these fears.
Rather, the leader comes to realize that the people sitting around the circle have
corresponding thoughts and feelings. Thus leaders can use this sense of disequi-
librium to create commonality rather than distance. This source of leader inner
turmoil may be worth an entire chapter. Yet for our purposes here, let us turn our
attention toward ways leaders can keep this trepidation in check.

Christian helpers seem particularly prone to a reflexive response to inner discomfort aggravated by the presence of relational risks. Frequently, they increase
the volume of educational material to secure relief from such anxiety. Teaching
demonstrates expertise. Unfortunately ideas, concepts, and models can take the
attention off persons and place it on principles. Leaders may bolster content and

discussion while inadvertently fortifying boundaries prohibiting interpersonal exchange. Anxious group leaders can prep a lecture, download an articulate sermon or create a handout. A nearly irresistible impulse arises to organize an article review, summarize a book chapter or scrutinize a passage of Scripture to take before the group. A better option would be to seek out a loyal partner not directly engaged in the group, such as a pastoral overseer, informed peer or supervisor. A competent consultant is likely to delve into the leader's feelings first and then use these to encourage group methods that enable members to address concerns over interpersonal hazards. Reach into the fear; then out to others. This is the better strategy.

Education is desirable in helping ventures. It is so important, in fact, that leaders tend to overeducate to the detriment of the group, thus downplaying the grooming of interpersonal possibilities. A small class seems preferable to an awkwardly relating miniature mob. To avoid this pitfall, leaders will find it best to determine in advance the parameters of the educational input. Then they must remain relatively firm on the ratio between the time allotted for content coverage and for interpersonal exchange. Thus a leader is less likely to manage anxiety through increased attention to group content and thereby decrease relational exchange.

A rough rule of thumb would be that helping groups with redemptive purposes have limited instructive material. Adjustment-level group efforts have modest educational objectives. Groups in the advancement category could be moderately weighted toward expanding concepts and competencies. Using terms familiar to counselors, professional therapeutic groups tend to be predominately process or relationally oriented. The psycho-educational groups that are more prevalent in ministry settings need to establish a ratio for informational and interactive activity.

THE WORD IN COMMUNITY

Trekking guides praying toward spiritual formation find the balance in emphasis between education and relational experience to be of great importance. Consider the well-known counsel from 2 Timothy 3:16 refreshed through a contemporary translation:

"Every part of Scripture is God-breathed and useful one way or another—showing us truth, exposing our rebellion, correcting our mistakes, training us to live God's way. Through the Word we are put together and shaped up for the tasks God has for us" *(The Message)*.

Paul directs Timothy on the essential ministry priority of making God's Word known. The passage context reminds us that Timothy has been raised on the Word. Paul's training of Timothy built on the foundation in the Word that Timothy received across generations from a loving family. For the welfare of his children, God himself poured out the Scriptures as instructions revealing the triune God—Father, Son and Holy Spirit. The Word makes clear God's ways and our waywardness, and it tells us how to stay engaged in the efforts he has prepared for us. For Christ-followers it is of the utmost importance to listen to and absorb God's Word. This makes proclamation and application natural for any ministry-oriented small group. While I would affirm this basic assumption, I will still state with conviction that helping groups need not necessarily make increasing Bible knowledge their immediate central purpose. Notice how Paul motivates Timothy to keep the Word of God central in his ministry as he delivers his persuasive charge to "preach the Word" and to "correct, rebuke, and encourage—*with great patience and careful instruction*" (2 Tim 4:2, emphasis mine). Paul weaves his appeal within the relational framework of the integrity of the people in his past and the presence of God who holds the future (see 2 Tim 3:14; 4:1). His devotion to the Word is thus fueled by love and loyalty to those who have shaped him. Timothy trusted the Scriptures because his mother, grandmother, Paul and others in his intimate faith community provided such splendid examples. Timothy had the intense experience of being in the presence of God as manifested in the affirming love of others.

Helping groups may be designed as a catalyst to establish relational bonds displaying this type of integrity. The Holy Spirit may then touch hearts in the midst of a relational encounter to generate a hunger to take in the Word of God. The group experience helps members internalize the value of the Word to the community. Does this suggestion of relational facilitation limit the power of the Word? Not any more than the recognition that God breathed his Word through the lives and hands of human communicators. The social nature of human beings does not surprise the Creator. The transmission of his revelation has been fused with the experience of a community of faith. It is no accident that the Word is preached when the people of God gather for corporate worship, a fact that is not merely pragmatics or convenience. The proclamation of the Word interacts with interpersonal and transpersonal communion. Being with others in an intensive small group may awaken or make available essential intimacy bonds. The Lord utilizes these relationships to draw his children into his presence and to usher them into a consistent walk with him. More will be said about how God's presence can be vitally experienced within groups in the later chapters on weaving meaning into one's internal narrative.

In the book of Acts, immediately following the fulfillment of our Lord's promise to send a Comforter, a striking passage portrays believers functioning in intimate fellowship (Acts 2:42-47; see also Acts 1:8; 2:1-41). Believers observed daily wonders and miraculous signs as evidence of God's blessing. Other than a marvelously large number of conversions, the passage does not offer a detailed record of those dramatic acts of God. Instead, the spotlight shines on the impact of the Holy Spirit stimulating incredible Christian companionship. Believers enjoy togetherness with great gladness, relish the apostles' teaching, share belongings, worship and sacrificially assist those with needs. The love of God in their midst was so brilliant that their numbers were multiplying rapidly. Small group ministry advocates have long utilized this passage to outline four components of healthy Christian fellowship: nurture (teaching the Word), worship (honoring God), community (caring, giving and praying for each other) and mission (tasks, service and outreach).[4] These ingredients suggest a functional meeting model that leaders can use in developing a balanced plan for standard ministry groups. Such groups can advance a Christian worldview with a praxis that corresponds to biblical teaching.

A prototypical discipleship group—whether in a college dorm, coffee shop, church courtyard or family room—dedicates time in approximately equal proportions to activities within each of these four areas. Fellowship groups that complement a worship service with dedicated teaching as a priority might double the portion of time allotted to community. Personal application of the message is thus woven into community communication. The success of this ratio adjustment depends on the supply of nurture to all members outside of the group. A worship team, elder board or service crew justifiably places far more emphasis on mission to plan and pursue its dedicated task. A prayer group naturally allows worship to dominate while a Bible study flows best when nurture takes center stage. The advantage to growth and service groups is that each band can pursue a specific purpose in a customized way. Time can be apportioned in nearly endless variations. The pattern may vary week to week as long as the group maintains its overall target. When one of the components is absent or neglected, the group may flounder, lose focus and, predictably, drop members.[5]

---

[4]Steve Barker et al., *Good Things Come in Small Groups* (Downers Grove, Ill.: InterVarsity Press, 1985).
[5]Ibid., p. 28.

Social scientist Robert Wuthnow coordinated an extensive, multiyear investigation into fourteen different religiously oriented groups representing a wide array of faith traditions.[6] Field researchers monitored trends in home Bible studies, cell groups, social action committees, recovery groups and worship fellowships. This particular undertaking broadly defined *spiritual formation* as the maturing of an individual's faith.[7] Based on a preponderance of evidence from multiple sources, the study concludes that participants do boldly credit small groups as powerful contributors to their spiritual formation. Following this investigation, Wuthnow decisively pinpoints a planning pitfall that must be avoided. Incorporating the leader functions into his insight suggests that when leaders implement their vision, they must avoid structure goals that are "inherently contradictory."[8] What was Wuthnow's prime example of conflicting goals he discovered is his field investigation? He found that when support and study are both targeted as priorities in small groups, tension emerges. When brought into the reality of a session, with people bouncing about in real life, one of these critical functions tends to win out over the other. These ostensibly complementary goals tend in practice to drift until they are eventually positioned as polar opposites. This highlights the pivotal mandate for leaders to establish a realistic educational and community life balance.

Gleaning from the vast wealth of information related to success or struggle gathered from this research, Wuthnow offers three strategies for harmonizing these equally worthwhile demands. First, an assortment of group choices can be made available to participants. The weighting of study and support can be transparent from the outset. Potential members are then able to choose a group that ideally fits their needs and expectations. This would go a long way to reduce later disappointment and discouraging attrition. Second, a group may advocate and organize study outside of its meeting so that support is packed tightly into each gathered assembly. Recovery groups with book tables, readings lists and endorsements offer a fine example of this resolution in operation. Providing separate times for pursuing different goals alleviates the competition between education and social connection. Education is highly honored, while face-to-face meetings are reserved for support. The third approach designates portions of the meeting according to plainly defined purposes. A collective teaching or worship period can be followed by breakout groups heavy on sharing. Planned meal or dessert

---

[6]Robert Wuthnow, ed., *I Come Away Stronger: How Small Groups Are Shaping American Religion* (Grand Rapids: Eerdmans, 1994).
[7]Ibid., p. 6.
[8]Ibid., p. 362.

breaks offer informal community interaction without impinging on nurture activity. Programs with a prearranged worship service or a lecture prior to breakout group sessions exemplify this principle: segregate the portion of time for important but separate priorities. In this way, educational efforts are not forced into competition with edifying encounters.

The support aspect of ministry small groups should never be entirely equated with merely human relationships. Ministry small groups do not necessarily increase their relevance by becoming social gatherings that exclusively provide peer support. In Wuthnow's research, prayer times within small groups were cherished moments. Public prayer modeled for individuals how to pray privately. It was an impetus for spiritual formation. Prayer elevated social community to sacred encounter. Prayer can also serve a therapeutic function for members who share prayer requests with one another.

Making a personal concern public becomes part of the solution for an individual. Words of encouragement from the group help reduce his or her anxiety. Certainly this practice involves dangers as well as benefits—for example, there may be too much emphasis on encouragement from the group and too little on divine resources. Yet the group also draws a tangible link between caring and spirituality. Group prayer occurs in sanctified space. Members feel that God is especially close. The discussion takes on seriousness and reverence. In this context, small expressions of encouragement become more than that. They indicate the group's willingness to take each member's concerns before the most sacred authority in their lives.[9]

Prayer tangibly expresses heartfelt concerns that bond members into a collective community in the presence of God. This is the essence of *koinonia*, that is, Christian-oriented, God-honoring fellowship.

CLARIFYING TREK EXPECTATIONS

So how should nurture, worship, community and mission be packed in different proportions for treks where growth in relational adaptability is the target outcome? In such efforts, leaders intentionally limit educational material. New ideas invade conversations and affect themes to enhance relational connections. This distinction cannot be overstated. Ministry small groups rightly accent study and nurture, particularly seeking to minister the Word. The support component serves to accentuate and accelerate the application of content. Members help each

---

[9]Ibid., p. 355.

other take wisdom from the Word into their lives. In helping groups designed for support, the content goals are substantially reduced and are predominately utilized to nudge forward interpersonal connections. Study of Scripture may not take precedence in these gatherings, yet a leader prays that the Word will make God's presence known through interpersonal encounter (Mt 25:31-46).

Confession to and prayer for one another facilitates an examination of "old self" ways that perpetuate the wandering associated with alienation and isolation (see Rom 7:14-25; Col 3:5-17; Jas 5:19-20). Group members participate in the Holy Spirit's formation and renewal of the *imago Dei* in one another when they have expected from the outset to concentrate their efforts on differentiating between old- and new-self ways of relating.[10] Old-self practices are deeply entrenched in our everyday thinking, feeling and behaving, thus likely hidden from view. The blind spots waiting to be exposed would include habits not easily explored in ordinary conversation. For example, a helping encounter may indeed be the context to address unmanaged sexual desires and behavior or crude remarks. This could be a choice occasion to review compulsions and activities related to greediness, selfishness, impulsivity or undisciplined actions. Troublesome affective states may require taming, such as an extensive range of anger issues from moodiness and irritability to meanness, intimidation and rage. Destructive old-self internal conversations may contain slander, maliciousness and lies. If these surface in a group, they provide an opportunity to recognize the harm and revise the pattern. Ironically, groups provide a comfortable and familiar setting where members may pour out destructive content without even noticing. When people hear truth spoken in love from one seated close by, they are better able to recognize that their inner autopilot has had an unintentional negative impact. This is experiential learning captured in a here-and-now encounter. When the Holy Spirit has prepared someone for renewal, such a realization encourages the person to seek grace and to grow (Eph 4:15). He or she embraces what the Lord has established as the next step in a closer walk with him and with others. The pursuit of compassion, humility, discipline and quiet strength comes about in this manner. In the same way, implementing a psychologically healthy and heaven-honoring practice of forgiveness moves from impossible to plausible to miraculous. Forgiveness empowers people to more accurately form and adjust their relational expectations.

---

[10]It would be useful to read the Colossians 3 passage over several times and pray for discernment regarding its relevance to this section. This paragraph draws phrases and concepts heavily from that passage.

A group trek may convene around a theme such as improving marital communication, parenting challenging children, coping with a chronic health condition, regulating a compulsive behavior or preparing for a new ministry role. As the trek heads off in a specific area, members will receive feedback from fellow travelers about how old practices may be excess baggage holding back their journey toward Christlikeness (Phil 3:12-14). Lightening one's pack by putting off an old-self pattern poses a number of challenges, however. The Holy Spirit enables persons to find the encouragement to put on the new. This old- and new-self application does not place undeserved blame on any sufferer for circumstances, loss or struggle as if the underlying root was directly related to personal sin within their own life. The spiritual formation objective remains a firmer faith and greater cleaving to God. "Consider it pure joy, my brothers, whenever you face trials of many kinds, because you know that the testing of your faith develops perseverance. Perseverance must finish its work so that you may be mature and complete, not lacking anything" (Jas 1:2-3).

EXPANDING SUPPORT AND ESTABLISHING PACE

A helping group expends the thrust of its energy on a subcomponent of community. Such a group does not equally balance the four components of Christian fellowship. More precisely, common-theme groups under the care of an alert leader intend to utilize the group's interior relationships as they form or frustrate. By creating relational experiences inside the group, members can rekindle and refine intimate relationships outside it. These temporary, immediate relational experiences use the heat of group dynamics to teach members how to achieve increased interpersonal synergy. New capacities can improve relational connection and satisfaction in the wider Christian community. While the group may have an attractive theme that creates an immediate sense of homogeneity, the trekking guide knows there will be natural differences in interpersonal motivation, ability and style. Relational communication in the group allows it to serve as an intimacy incubator. Ultimately, these groups do not replace Bible studies, prayer meetings or spiritual formation groups. Rather, these groups provide a means to prepare or return saints to be loyal participants in other fellowship settings. Further, a common-theme group should not substitute for the continuous care of recovery groups or twelve-step meetings. A critical niche remains for extensive offerings of open-ended, self-help support networks. Ideally, such meetings also contribute to the spiritual redemption of struggling people.

My proposal of increasing leader-guided groups within ministry contexts, while distinct from many Christian group ministries, aims to complement the experience of *koinonia* across other ministry offerings. Skilled leaders help members become more receptive to other corporate Christian experiences. My ideas for increasing available group options also follow Wuthnow's counsel to protect intentional study and support ratios. The proposal also unburdens other care ministries, whose efforts often overextend their leadership while participants remain thirsty for deeper support. Again, the value of other ministry groups is not diminished, but elevated. Refining the available alternatives reflects a sharpened focus on formation objectives and provides clarity to potential members who crave relational connection but puzzle over how to obtain it.

One does not need a prophetic gift to confidently predict that participants will display relational raggedness as these treks get underway. These struggles are bound to the social relationships that define the nature of a group. Nearly anyone who has entered into a shared endeavor will attest to observing a variation of a prevailing pattern. Group life tends to move from early cordial contact to conflict to camaraderie or, lamentably, confusion. This progressive movement gives a group its life and tends to surface even when there is an understood and agreed-upon destination. A group's goal may attract members to a core commitment, but this initial draw diminishes as members are forced to function as a collective unit. Each semester, my students colorfully play out this conundrum before my eyes when one of my course syllabi requires a team project in lieu of an individual research paper. Why not share the workload and spread responsibility? Inevitably several students vigorously request to pursue a solo assignment. When teams assemble, they more often consult the instructor about matters related to the establishment of priorities or to resolve discord than they do regarding the underlying academic material. Teamwork compels members to define a social order, navigate differences and negotiate compromise. A team challenge inflicts more insomnia than the extra labor of an unaccompanied effort, and this is actually the point.

The popular and widely circulated group development model of *forming* (orientation), *storming* (conflict), *norming* (structure), *performing* (work) and *adjoining* (dissolution) has gained extensive acceptance and applicability in diverse settings.[11] Having endured for over forty years, there is more to this model's appeal than its rhyming cadence. Camp counselors, business executives and alumni of

---

[11]Bruce Tuckman, "Developmental Sequences in Small Groups," *Psychological Bulletin* 63 (1965): 384-99; Donelson R. Forsyth, *Group Dynamics*, 4th ed. (Belmont, Calif.: Thomson Wadsworth, 2006), pp. 135-68.

any credible social relationship seminar share its insights. Whatever the rationale for inaugurating a group journey in the first place, the external purpose does not mechanically create relational bonds. This is essentially an organic person-to-person and person-to-group process. Each member has to make concerted efforts to enter into a social web. Everyone must take risks. The conditions that convene the group fade into the background. Emotional reactions surface in reference to the task, terms, leaders and fellow constituents. If group members can overcome the inevitable mix of emotional friction, a sense of togetherness or cohesion follows. This unity facilitates positive movement on matters of key interest. Whether the group ending is elective or forced, an emotional upheaval accompanies the loss of this network and stimulates grief, celebration or a unique combination of the two.[12]

Anecdotal and research experiences support this group development model. Stories of how volunteers functioned on a short-term mission trip, how the youth group acted on a recent retreat, or how the tension rose on the elder board after a change in membership give these stage patterns a recurring feel. Nonetheless, trekking guides should not apply this model too forcefully when approaching thematic helping groups in a ministry setting. Leaders must avoid the temptation to measure progress in reference to a stage of cohesion, which may imply that the group has arrived or reached its destination. Groups are generally in constant motion. The whole experience is never about a temporary group reaching an efficiency target.[13] Leaders of thematic helping ministry do better to focus on helping members attain greater intimacy. Members internalize the experience of achieving connection despite tension, an experiential lesson that builds confidence for achieving in other relationships. Moreover, human beings created in the *imago Dei,* even those outside the experience of Christian community, can realistically achieve this relational facility. And even those under grace, who have the resource of the Holy Spirit, must still dispense with entrenched relational patterns that prohibit them from realizing true *koinonia.*

My group dynamic instincts make me averse to following strict stage pro-

---

[12]A similar model of group development stages has a contemporary, refined and detailed description in the work by Marianne Corey and Gerald Corey, *Groups: Process & Practice,* 7th ed. (Belmont, Calif.: Brooks/Cole, 2006). This text also has excellent material on how to design a contemporary helping group and contains numerous examples. Group research has supported the display of group cohesion according to these patterns.

[13]The rationale here for a soft stage view is supported in the descriptions of group development offered by Irvin D. Yalom and Molyn Leszcz in *The Theory and Practice of Group Psychotherapy,* 5th ed. (New York: Basic Books, 2005), pp. 309-43. Yalom prefers phases to stages and points out how easily these cycle. His phrases describe useful dynamics: *in or out, top or bottom,* and *near or far.*

gression within ministry groups for two main reasons. First, events hosted by a church or Christian ministry may influence participant behavior in a host of subtle ways. A Christian context may introduce powerful assumptions about how one should act. The very association of a group within a religious framework sets scripts into motion. Those who identify as Christians may know that a core Christian command is to love others. Yet they may also expect adherence to rigid or idealized norms, the social group rules for relating in their particular setting. An umbrella of faith does not mean that all individual behavior, sin-based attitudes or interpersonal conflict remain entirely inhibited. Rather, the context spells out just how these may be expressed. The stage of group functioning may manifest itself in immediately obvious ways through participant behavior.

Second, my experience with multicultural gatherings and participants with mixed ethnic backgrounds suggests that applying the formerly trustworthy stage model warrants increased caution. Multicultural participation in ministry settings has in my experience rendered obsolete the rhyme model of forming and storming.[14] Cultural and ethnic identity substantially shapes how an individual behaves in a social setting.[15] Thankfully, the ministry scenery I now experience contains a variety of cultural contributors. While I retain the notion of group progression, I try to avoid strict stage language and adopt a modified version that describes progressive trust, or *intimacy pace,* as an indicator of interpersonal closeness. I encourage leaders to monitor degrees of trust—moment by movement by member.

Ideally, leaders cultivate the expression of trust that allows each participant to heal and mature. This requires exposing and then putting aside old ways while experimenting with new relational activity. Leaders gain a sense of a group's intimacy pace by contemplating actions, attitudes and interpersonal engagement. Are participants walking together in light or wandering in darkness (1 Jn 1–2)? Is the group stopped, stalled or stuck? Are members tiptoeing gingerly to avoid interpersonal cracks and personal obstacles? Is there lively and steady movement? Intimacy pace refers to the degree of connectedness evident in the group interactions at the moment. For the sake of convenience, consider these four pace

---

[14]Not long ago, I had the opportunity to teach group counseling in Manila, Philippines, at the doctoral level. The relationship between the individual and groups was discussed extensively in this Asian context. The interpersonal conflict associated with the second stage required extensive rethinking. I do not offer any conclusions, only increased caution about traditional stage models in multicultural work.

[15]For more information see Janice L. Delucia-Waack and Jeremiah Donigian, *The Practice of Multicultural Group Work* (Belmont, Calif.: Brooks-Cole, 2004).

descriptors: cooperation, competition, collaboration and consolidation.

Signs of *cooperation* evidence a basic intimacy pace. These include: sharing background and recent life events; listening with limited interaction; offering low-risk self-disclosure; accepting stories with inconsistencies or ambivalent attitudes; routinely giving advice; and preferring that the leader alone monitors participation. The group engages politely, striving to establish that each member is accepted, respected and approved. Considerable constructive member work does occur at this intimacy pace. One could easily speculate that this may be the most prevalent of the four paces within Christian circles and particularly in helping groups. In settings where membership varies from week to week (open membership) or where the structure of the meeting follows a strict routine (e.g., step meeting or structured educational group) or when leadership responsibilities float (leader rotation), a cooperative pace is ideal and will be productive. Participants empathize with one another, provide insight, and promote support by example. Members give to each other by sharing experiences and describing acquired wisdom. Members might say of a group at this pace, "Each of us strives to encourage each other as we pursue our unique tasks during this time together."

When leaders begin to notice that a group demands more exertion, they are probably observing *competitive* connections arising between participants. If cooperation parallels the exercise of walking, a competitive intimacy pace is stair climbing. Members expend effort to win a position of influence or defend a safety zone around the status quo. Members watch their backs. They invest their energy to win the attention of respected participants or leaders. The following behaviors mark a competitive pace: rehearsed and monitored statements, voiced vague intentions that defy accountability, a reluctance to invest in immediate relationships, a reliance on select members to fill silences, qualifying leader requests and maneuvers that make a bid for power. Leaders note that one of the foremost difficulties when a group has an outward Christian framework is that competitive positioning might be portrayed as personal spirituality preferences. Decisions, behaviors and attitudes might be defended by an appeal to the leading of the Holy Spirit, an insight from a Scripture verse, or credited as a divine answer to a personal prayer. "I sense the Lord's leading in this way" or "I will begin when the Holy Spirit opens a door." Leaders must have spiritual and social discernment when they touch on group dynamics operating at a competitive intimacy pace.

Open membership groups do establish rules of group behavior, or *norms*, which legitimize status and spirituality within the group without directly confronting how these might limit community. As norms stabilize, members learn to relate cooperatively despite any inherent competition. Only when members have intentional goals and a leader cultivates methods to "speak truth in love" can the group examine more objectively any attribution to divine favor for overt behaviors, omissions or other ways of relating. One way a twelve-step group with no formal leader might discourage competitive exchanges is through the prohibition of *cross talk*, which is offering commentary, questions or feedback to each other on material shared.[16] This practice helps maintain an ongoing cooperative pace. In fact, in most support groups, this policy can be an ideal management technique to contain competitive intimacy. Since membership fluctuates, participants learn to have confidence in the program, and building a deeper level of interpersonal trust is not necessary. On the downside, the relational communication left unexamined has incredible potential if addressed in a constructive setting. A step group or support group does not have the structure to host this type of member-to-member work. However, in a group where this is feasible, bringing competitive maneuvers to the surface could assist a member to put off an old pattern that prevents him from walking in greater intimacy with others.

When members speak freely, take risks that may offend, offer multifaceted encouragement and express spontaneous empathy and emotion, they display the intimacy pace of *collaboration*. Typically, this intimacy pace requires that the group achieve a mutual system to move through or beyond any competitive or defensive responses that tend to surface. This intimacy pace is steady, strong and productive. Members would imply this pace when saying, "Now we encourage one another by partnering to reach our desired goals as we benefit through mutual exchange."

Consolidation means that when a member displays mastery of a new skill or perspective, the group does more than notice. The group provides invaluable recognition and genuine respect that is long treasured. Members may even risk offering a few ideas for refinement that reflect the newfound strength of the growing member. The group as a whole experiences the member's genuine gain and affirms the accomplishment. The novel attitude or behavior becomes increasingly permanent as the member seeks to take the new-self action outside of the group for further practice. In general these four intimacy paces are not discrete categories and therefore may overlap. A particular session can commonly be described by stating that intimacy pace was primarily collaborative with signs of sporadic competition that were addressed by group initiatives.

---

[16]Yalom and Leszcz, *Theory and Practice*, p. 441.

A group leader enables members to recognize conditions that contribute to the intimacy pace along with their own particular response patterns. This is the essence of interpersonal learning in a group. It may initially seem disruptive, unkind or discourteous to mention a walking style that perpetuates old-self patterns.

Bethany, did you hear your tone when you spoke to Justin? I felt an edge that seems dangerously sharp.

Bill, run your mind back over what just happened. Have you noticed a recurring protective shield you offer the younger women in this group?

Sharon, have you considered that this may be an example of you turning back our attempts to support you? Each time you reject supportive effort, it gets harder to listen to your struggles and your pain.

In a Christian setting, group participants might be disinclined to use frank feedback as constructive opportunities for investigation and change. After all, this would appear to violate the choice words of our Lord: "Why do you look at the speck of sawdust in your brother's eye and pay no attention to the plank in your own eye? How can you say to your brother, 'Let me take the speck out of your eye,' when all the time there is a plank in your own eye?" (Mt 7:3-4).

However, group interactions display a strong distinction between hypocritical disapproval and constructive feedback. In these helping groups, leaders prepare each prospective member for the trip with an orientation and follow-up reminders about what will be packed into the journey. The group will empower members by discussing crucial common themes (content) and will provide constructive feedback on relational communication (process). Learning in these groups may come through talks, testimonies, readings and teaching. The content will be related to the reasons that each person came. This type of group benefits members because the trekking guide monitors the crucial dimension of interpersonal safety. Leaders apply immediate feedback to aid the member to love self, others and God with greater transparency. Christian fellowship displays characteristics like patience, kindness, rejoicing, truth, protection, trust and hope. Old-self behaviors keep us from this kind of love due to envy, self-seeking, irritability, keeping records of infractions and gaining satisfaction from others' failures (1 Cor 13:4-7). Therefore, as the group explores its central theme through open confession, leaders dedicate their support to considering how each member is walking with others. This cultivates intimate connections within family, colleagues and friendships, and it assists in the attainment of Christian fellowship enhanced by the Holy Spirit. Investing in this type of group is tantamount to inviting the Lord to remove foreign bodies from our eyes by using those who joined in the trek. Raw relational transparency must never be applied to break members down against their will for veiled spiritual purposes or to pressure them to conform to the wishes of the group. Rather, these groups enable members to speak out and work out their goals for healing and growth. Leaders then monitor and encourage interpersonal learning as it is consistent with the individual intentions expressed. This is an expression of speaking the truth in love.

THE WORD APPEARS

The lumpy bag held only a hunk of wood, claw hammer, nails, candy bars and other assorted appealing prizes. It launched a journey with five not-so-ready-to-relate adolescents and two invested, yet untested, leaders. The group for these boys was not going to fix their issues; not even close. I packed into the experience a hand-picked selection of new ideas and choice opportunities to experience each other. I attempted to assist each one to better use the resources around him. Ultimately, this meant making more extensive use of relationships between them.

It was impossible to discern when the competition subsided enough to allow for the few exchanges that might be labeled collaborative. I still carry a collection of replays that tell me, "That made it all worthwhile." For instance, one day the action paused as the small youth with the warm engaging wit was surprisingly stunned into a thick silence. Sure signs of sadness rose to the surface. The exploration exercise involved imaginary time travel, sound bites of past voices and a search for familiar faces once known as *supportive allies*. Usually any emotional surge outside of anger was automatically preempted with a sarcastic jab, a provocative expletive or flying object. Perhaps this stillness was allowed because his voice was the one most likely to fill the room with a lighthearted quip. At this instant, something was caught in his throat. No one ever came close to crying; no norm between these boys would permit it. But I had the distinct impression that a tear was forming in his eye as he strained to recall the sound of his grandmother's too-distant voice. One of the boys who could hardly ever harness his own attention reached over. Instead of making a fist and punching the first boy's arm to knock sense into him, his hand remained open. He placed it on his friend's shoulder. He left it there. "Use my voice," he muttered, "I could be your ally." He smiled. For just a few short blinks, their eyes met. Understanding happened. The blond-haired youth nearby, who avoided eye contact like it contained death, wordlessly entered the exchange. Their eyes met. *Shalom.* Realistically, the whole exchange may have only been seconds by a stopwatch. Yet the intimacy pace of collaboration is outside time. I did not cry at this intersection, but I will confess that I did so later in prayer. My tears expressed joy. Although he was never openly invited, I suspect that the presence of the Lord had been nearby in that rarest exchange of emotional closeness. The Word was present and dwelt among us. He infused love in an instant between boys who had been cheated out of their fair share.

That school group had no explicit kingdom purpose. I have come to accept that the Lord had intentions in it for me. As leader, I learned to back away from vigorous attempts to teach, impress or illustrate. I did better to work at creating openings where group members could taste what working together is all about. They might just develop an appetite for genuine intimacy. The role of a leader in escorting treks toward wholeness is a visionary effort. Leaders pack structuring essentials in wisely so that the interpersonal conditions foster close and change-enhancing relationships. The Lord may just infuse those encounters with love.

Section Three

LEADING TOWARD CARE

7

ALLIANCES FOR THE JOURNEY

LANDMARKS AHEAD

Group treks rely on the deep ways that relational bonds distribute redemptive grace, and the starting point is a leader committed to caring. On the route ahead, we browse material from C. S. Lewis on activating love in relationships; then we link his ideas with the variations of social support. The resulting interpersonal exchanges affect the internal working model (IWM), perhaps best described as our inner relational process- ing hub. Our IWM monitors and mediates close relational attachments. Then I consult the construct of a corrective emotional relationship (CER) to illustrate dynamics for healing that have the potential to produce spiritual refreshment and formation.[1] This chapter tour wraps up by listening in on a startled group leader, Tiana, who refines her perspective through a group with spunk and a client with limited insight. Tiana experiences how the group as a whole can deliver affectionate social support in ways so effective that a single counselor could only imagine!

ALLIANCE RUPTURES

Remember Turkish Delight, a faun named Tumnus, two sons of Adam, two daughters of Eve and of course, a wardrobe? These are fascinating features of the Narnia legacy from the imagination of Clive Staples Lewis.[2] To quote the author directly, "one of the nastiest things in this story" occurs near the outset of the tale just after Edmund has gorged himself on the cunning Queen's enticing Turk- ish Delight. Edmund has shivered through the winter cold, felt the glare of the white witch and been caught by the lure of that strange sweet candy. He knows firsthand that Narnia exists beyond the mysterious wardrobe. Young Lucy is absolutely thrilled that Edmund, too, has visited the fantasyland where winter

---

[1]Stephen P. Greggo, "Biblical Metaphors for Corrective Emotional Relationships in Group Work," *Psychology and Theology*, 35, no. 2 (2007): 153-62. This chapter and the next expand on and make use of material contained in this article.

[2]C. S. Lewis, *The Lion, the Witch and the Wardrobe* (New York: Macmillan, 1950).

never ends, yet Christmas never comes. Now her older siblings will believe her stranger-than-fiction report.

> Up to that moment Edmund had been feeling sick, and sulky, and annoyed with Lucy for being right, but he hadn't made up his mind what to do. When Peter suddenly asked him the question he decided all at once to do the meanest and most spiteful thing he could think of. He decided to let Lucy down.
>
> "Tell us, Ed," said Susan.
>
> And Edmund gave a very superior look as if he were far older than Lucy (there was really only a year's difference) and then a little snigger and said, "Oh, yes, Lucy and I have been playing—pretending that all her story about a country in the wardrobe is true. Just for fun, of course. There's nothing there really."
>
> Poor Lucy gave Edmund one look and rushed out of the room.[3]

In an instant, Edmund reduces Lucy's elation to despair. Suddenly her hope in the one with whom she had shared a unique adventure was turned to betrayal. An alliance born from experience crumbled into alienation. The whole narrative pivots on Edmund's lie and his subsequent actions to justify his jealousy, spite and rivalry. The battle for Narnia unfolds as the four children, displaced by air raids threatening their London home, are forced to face even deeper inner fears. The master storyteller merges each child's unique gifting and accompanying uncertainties within the struggles of that land under siege. The nastiest blow for those who cherish those Chronicles may be that Edmund's failure feels uncomfortably familiar. Or his betrayal may stir a different identification. The wound inflicted on brave little Lucy may correspond to one carried from relational expectations struck down by a stunning act of selfishness. On their voyage through Narnia, the vulnerabilities within the Sons of Adam and Daughters of Eve speak to our insecurities. Lewis's affectionate fairy tale for his godchild, Lucy Barfield, touches many who seek to cope with the perplexing matters of individual identity, loyalty, cruelty, irresponsibility and sacrifice for others.[4]

In *The Lion, the Witch and the Wardrobe*, Lucy discovers Narnia during an innocent game of hide and seek. The ensuing journey exceeds any childish game. In Genesis, Adam and Eve attempted to employ a similar game by hiding from the loving Gardener after their disobedience. They vainly seek to become invisible to

---

[3]Ibid, pp. 35-36.
[4]Ibid., dedication.

the one who had placed every tree and twig in Eden. God calls out, "Where are you?" as if he is entering the charade. Adam and Eve passed their proficiency to hide sin along to all human progeny. Avoiding the Lord, one another and even self to circumvent facing the calculated callousness of our own sin is no game. This perpetual pattern brings loneliness, harm and eventually death. Lewis's fiction resembles real-life stories in that reconciliation of sin-based separations comes only through risk and at a great price. In this chapter, we will ponder this parallel in an effort to grasp the potency of intimate connections. Like the children making their way through the mysterious land of Narnia, adventurous relational trekking brings out the nuances of character, the intricacies of relationship and awareness of "a magic deeper still."[5]

When group leaders exhibit the function of caring, they collaborate with innate *imago Dei* forces for healing, restoration and renewal. Trekking guides demonstrate care through fostering honesty, warmth and compassion. By modeling a consistent respect and receptivity to what members bring into the group, the leader impresses the value of caring into the budding culture of the group. Leaders demonstrate a quality of caring in the vision and structure function through the designing, convening and preparing for the journey.[6] The organization of a group trek in itself communicates commitment to a noble and benevolent cause. Still, that helping mission must become personal. Those who sign on initially wonder if the journey is about caring for a cause, others or them: "Is this group really for me; among so many needs can my soul be refreshed?" The leader's vision and applied structure also indicates that hope is available somewhere out there. As a leader fulfills her caring function, members discover that hope is real and attainable, and that they can carry it home. Through their group, members enter an exchange of genuine give and take in the interest of soul restoration (Ps 23). At such moments, they have confidence in the "deep magic." The One who is the Way, the Truth and the Life is available to convey love through those sitting in that gathered circle. Despite the darkness of resentment, rejection or refusal, a quiet alliance to trek together is born. As this occurs, caring penetrates immediate experience.

Another Lewis treasure enriches the discussion of leader care. Adult readers grasp that Lewis describes the benefits of interpersonal support; namely, mutual

---

[5]Ibid., p. 132. For those not acquainted with the language of Lewis in his Narnia work, the deeper magic is Aslan's way of referencing a law of redemption: "when a willing victim who had committed no treachery was killed in a traitor's stead, the Table would crack and Death itself would start working backwards," pp. 132-33.

[6]Virginia Brabender, *Introduction to Group Therapy* (Hoboken, N.J.: Wiley, 2002).

exchange and emotional nurturance. Lewis's literary gems supply a functional vocabulary for types of care. His words enable us to explore relational exchanges in the community of Jesus Christ where human beings undergo *imago Dei* renewal. In order to place his contributions within the context of group work and broader therapeutic perspectives, we must start with an overview of how love intertwines within casual and close relationships.

ALLIANCE REPAIR BY DESIGN

When Jesus summarizes the law in the great commandment, he reveals how greatly he values human relationships on all levels. "'Love the Lord your God with all your heart and with all your soul and with all your mind and with all your strength" and "love your neighbor as yourself'" (Mk 12:30-31). This expressive command to love refers to ongoing, vibrant relationships between and within the divine and human planes. In these few words, Jesus defines human wholeness and gives a glimpse of *shalom*. Moreover this command implicitly references the reflective relationship a human has with his or her own self. An inner voice, engaging in vivid dialogue within the heart, mind and soul, empowers and guides thinking, feeling and doing. While the phrase "as yourself" does not offer any detailed psychology of self, it does suggest the existence of a self-directed, affect-rich relational bond. This self-relationship tends to be manifest in one's persistent inner narrative. This interior self-view corresponds intricately to one's external worldview, which includes perceived availability of social provisions. *Love* is the New Testament term that encompasses the activities and experiences rendered in the contemporary therapeutic terms "social support" and "closer relational provisions."

Christian psychologist Eric Johnson has described the great commandment's emphasis on loving God and others with recognition of self-love as the "three poles of relational activity."[7] Just as the North and South poles orient observers in world geography, so these three essential human relational polarities generate and sustain love. Thus a three-dimensional perspective is mandatory. The vitality of these poles may be understood as self-love (identity), love of neighbor (intimacy) and love of God (faith).[8] Picture these as reverberating, interactive, dy-

[7]See Eric L. Johnson, "How God Is Good for the Soul," *Journal of Psychology and Christianity* 22 (2003): 78-88. In a closing footnote, Johnson places his discussion within the context of three poles of relational activity: self, God, and others. See also Henri Nouwen, *Reaching Out: The Three Movements of the Spiritual Life* (New York: Image, 1975).

[8]Presenting these poles as complementary relational categories in this dynamic way comes directly from the writing of James Othuis, "With-ing: A Psychotherapy of Love," *Journal of Psychology and*

namic force fields. These are never static but constantly interacting. An intense press toward one must be counterbalanced by an increased pull toward the other two. Helping ventures do well to recognize that self, or to use a more spiritually comprehensive term, *soul*,[9] is not constructed, maintained or transformed outside the framework of dependence on God and others. Each of these relational poles corresponds to targeted enhancement experiences in ministry and spiritual formation groups where the intent is to deepen intrapersonal, interpersonal or transpersonal awareness.[10]

Johnson, in an article titled "How God is Good for the Soul," appealingly portrays the renewing benefits of being in an active love relationship with God.[11] He starts by reviewing what the Scriptures reveal regarding God's nature and characteristics.[12] The God who desires to walk with us has not hidden his qualities. He has spoken and made himself known in the Word, in flesh and throughout creation. When broken and sinful human beings seek to relate intimately with God, his love works at our core as the renewing and reparative force enabling a gradual growth toward holiness. Frequent and deep reflection on the good, personal and benevolent God of the universe redeems, revitalizes and re-creates the human soul. By design, human creatures are incomplete selves unless bound in a loving relationship with their Creator. Within this essential human-divine bond, God's traits address the weaknesses in human souls that require soothing, surgery or strength. Johnson expresses the impact of this bond in this way:

Knowing and being loved by God strangely transforms one's sense of worthlessness and inferiority. The self-importance of narcissism is relativized in God's presence. His sovereignty soothes anxiety and fear. His right-

---

Theology 34, no. 1 (2006): 66-77. His ideas are particularly useful in that he passionately presses healing work that increases mutuality as opposed to mastery of self or increased autonomy.

[9]The self or personality (how one thinks, feels and acts) is a common contemporary term that references individuals as bio-psycho-social entities. These terms tend to fold the spiritual aspect of human beings under bio-psycho-social layers. A more comprehensive or holistic term, soul, includes what we mean by self and personality while placing a much needed accent on bio-psycho-social-*spiritual*.

[10]Thomas C. Oden, *The Intensive Group Experience: The New Pietism* (Philadelphia: Westminster Press, 1972).

[11]Johnson, "Good for the Soul."

[12]This is familiar theological coverage of God's attributes or characteristics. These are derived from Scripture and have at various times been classified in terms of positive and negative, natural and moral, absolute and relative, immanent and eminent, intransitive and transitive, quiescent and operative, antithetical and synthetical, or as is the case in this article, incommunicable and communicable. God has attributes that are not reflected in those made in the *imago Dei* (incommunicable) and traits that are found in human beings (communicable). See Walter A. Elwell and Phillip W. Comfort, *Tyndale Bible Dictionary* (Wheaton, Ill.: Tyndale House, 2001).

eousness and justice helps to put into perspective experiences of injustice and so reduce bitterness. It would seem that whatever one's psychospiritual difficulties, they can be fundamentally improved by looking to God. By focusing increased attention and affection on the beauty of God (and so more and more "bringing" the beauty of God into one's internal world), it would seem likely to lead gradually to a fundamental reconfiguration of one's self-other relational context: one's narrative, one's feelings of security, hope and belongingness, and one's sense of meaning and purpose.[13]

Meditative contemplation on God's essential attributes allows the restorative benefits of relating to the Creator, a being who made humans for his glory. God designed humanity for an intimate faith connection with the One who created them. In essence, this type of transpersonal encounter is the ultimate *corrective emotional relationship* (CER).[14] This phrase acknowledges that as God penetrates one's deep inner emotional template, the Holy Spirit's redemptive work helps balance the three relational polarities. Steadily, the Holy Spirit's re-creative labor allows for more fluidity in the exchange of love within these three polarities.

Loving God blesses people in obvious ways. Followers of Christ have every reason to rejoice. Yet more sober reflection accompanies the second aspect of Jesus' commandment regarding our loving stance toward others (the second pole of relational activity). Relating to others can be marvelously enriching, but we cannot always depend on or predict those results. Others can let us down. We may not know how or when to let them in. A trusted ally might make a decision much like Edmund's in that critical instant when Lucy needed him most. Human interactions affected by the fall and the resulting state of sin may produce distortions within self that have an adverse impact (Jer 17:9-10; Rom 3:10-18). Relating to the Creator nourishes the soul in a way nothing else can. Human relational activity has the dubious reputation of being "for better or for worse."[15] Despite this limitation and the acknowledged hazard, interpersonal relationships

---

[13]Johnson, "Good for the Soul," p. 86.

[14]The choice of this term is an intentional link to the prominent term in psychotherapy, *corrective emotional experience*. See Irvin D. Yalom and Molyn Leszcz, *The Theory and Practice of Group Psychotherapy*, 5th ed. (New York: Basic Books, 2005), pp. 27-31.

[15]The mix of blessings and blows that stem from human relationships is sometimes referred to as the *paradox of close relationships*. This is a reminder that while many positive experiences grow out of human relationships so does the intensity of the pain. Human relationships are a key source of conflict, strain and disappointment. See Barbara R. Sarason and Irwin G. Sarason, "Close Relationships and Social Support: Implications for the Measurement of Social Support," in *The Cambridge Handbook of Personal Relationships*, ed. Anita L. Vangelisti and Daniel Perlman (New York: Cambridge University Press, 2006), pp. 429-44.

can and do contribute to one's well-being and wholeness (see Rom 15:1-7; Gal 6:2; Jas 5:13-16; 1 Jn 4:7-8). Increased or better-integrated relational contact does facilitate re-formation. Sin may hinder, but by grace its pervasive force may be diminished and overcome. For example, in helping groups there are strategic and spontaneous attempts to control the destructive effects of sin. This is the rationale for using explicit purpose statements, facilitated communication and the monitoring of relational communication or process. The structure of any group serves essentially to make the relational experience less influenced by individual and systemic sin.

A construct from developmental psychology known as the *internal working model* (IWM) provides a brief, unifying conceptual explanation of how these three relational poles intersect.[16] This term spotlights an inner, multi-level relational template or cognitive schema. Highly stable sets of expectations regarding how others and self will behave comprise the model within.[17] The IWM governs core processes such as emotional regulation, sense of security, well-being and worth. The IWM is the social mover, shaker, receptor and interpreter. All intimate communication travels in and out through this internal relational hub. Psychologists find it expedient to have a single construct like IWM to reference such an extraordinarily multifaceted operation; defining such terms demystifies the puzzles of human personality. However, the IWM merely helps visualize the centerpiece of vastly complex and intricately layered human activity across thoughts, feelings and actions. Any candid psychologist acknowledges its limitation and complexity. The processes involved in a person's IWM comprise an awesome and wonderful wilderness well worth trekking through. One could follow trails that penetrate deep into the micro functions of brain chemistry or

---

[16]Attachment theory has been making significant contributions to our understanding of human development since John Bowlby first proposed that the quality of early material bonds may have lifelong implications. Today attachment contributions cover the lifespan and are not restricted to discussion of early life experiences. See Robert Karen, *Becoming Attached* (New York: Oxford University Press, 1994); Jeffry A. Simpson and W. Steven Rholes, eds., *Attachment Theory and Close Relationships* (New York: Guilford Press, 1998); or Susan Goldberg, *Attachment and Development* (London: Arnold, 2000).

[17]See John Bowlby, *The Making and Breaking of Affectional Bonds* (London: Routledge, 2005); Mary Dozier and Brandy C. Bates, "Attachment State of Mind and the Treatment Relationship," in *Attachment Issues in Psychopathology and Intervention,* ed. Leslie Atkinson and Susan Goldberg (Mahwah, N.J.: Erlbaum, 2004), pp. 167-80; Roger R. Kobak and Alison Esposito, "Levels of Processing in Parent-Child Relationships: Implications for Clinical Assessment and Intervention," in *Attachment Issues in Psychopathology and Intervention,* ed. Leslie Atkinson and Susan Goldberg (Mahwah, N.J.: Erlbaum, 2004), pp. 139-66; Eva C. Klohnen and Oliver P. John, "Working Models of Attachment: A Theory-Based Prototype Approach," in *Attachment Theory and Close Relationships,* ed. Jeffry A. Simpson and W. Steven Rholes (New York: Guilford Press, 1998).

extend to the cosmic implications of spiritual warfare.

Constructs or psychological terms such as IWM offer convenience. Wisdom would advise that the mystery and beauty of human beings made in the *imago Dei* should remain a matter of awe and wonder, for human beings are indeed "fearfully and wonderfully made" (Ps 139:14). Consider how the psychological concept of IWM mirrors the biblical reference to heart, mind and soul. The Scriptures employ three dense, complex and high-powered concepts to reference a similar relational processing hub within human beings that social science theorists summarize as IWM. A simplistic but useful summation might be: the IWM can be pictured as the interior model governing the balance of the relational polarities of God, others and self. Such a generalization may sufficiently provide a basic conceptual understanding of how ministry groups can focus on accessing relational process.

From a developmental perspective, the IWM is initially constructed in human persons from early encounters with adult caregivers. Once formed on the basis of extensive interaction, the IWM persists as the inner framework for an enduring pattern of relational interactions throughout the lifespan. The IWM remains stable over time. Studies indicate that IWM is not, however, forever fixed. In other words, while the IWM enables one to decide and act with regard to others because its assumptions regarding relational patterns are steady, new experiences do place pressure on the model too, eventually producing processing change. Ongoing relational encounters such as those with crucial caregivers, siblings, peers and romantic partners gradually refine and reshape the IWM. An infant who experiences a caregiver who is responsive, nurturing and consistent develops an internal model of a secure figure as a reliable resource. Fortunately, this secure pattern mostly prevails. Typically children use their attachment figures not only as a secure base to explore the world but also as a source of comfort to absorb blasts stemming from the uncertainties of stimulating social surroundings.

Psychologists apply assorted descriptions to strained, discordant or inadequate parent-child bonding. Most commonly, *insecure attachment style* serves as the global heading for the impact of these experiences on the IWM. A lack of synchrony between child and crucial caregivers commonly results in internal models where human contact sounds an alarm. If the alarm generates an intense reaction to others, the person may resist relationships across a lifespan. Contemporary IWM descriptions tend to reference two continuous dimensions: *anxiety about abandonment* and *avoidance of intimacy*. The first dimension influences the sense of ease and comfort one feels when in a relationship. The more persistent rumination and doubt over the future relationship status, the greater anxiety about abandonment. The second dimension does not reference inner tension over what might happen. Instead, its features include all variants of protective adaptations or motivational inhibitors that restrict receptivity to interpersonal closeness. Those with an IWM characterized by high avoidance of intimacy tend to place barriers between themselves and others. A person low on both the anxiety and avoidance dimensions typically enters relationships readily and has minimal difficulty establishing mutuality. Limited relational readiness, flexibility and fluidity often evidence combinations where there are higher leanings on either one or both dimensions. Overcoming and overriding the filtering effects of the IWM can range from a mild challenge to a nearly impossible feat.

The close or attachment relationships that have the most effect on the IWM are truly reciprocal, even though one member of the attached pair may be dependent on the other for essential resources and protection. This suggests that in the early years the child brings his temperament and will into the formation process. These personality features influence relational communication long before language is on the learning horizon. Significant adult caretakers who respond from their own IWM then act on this communication. In subsequent relationships, the personality along with its established patterns and expectations will guide the resulting reciprocal process. This may affirm or modify the existing attachment schema.

The three poles of relational activity (self, others, God) converge in one's internal working model. Ongoing relational experience within any of the three poles provides maintenance or provokes modification. *Both* transpersonal and interpersonal encounters influence the intrapersonal via the IWM. For emphasis, consider the conversation Jesus had with Nicodemus as well as one of the most quoted and outrageous statements Jesus made: "I tell you the truth, no one can see the kingdom of God unless he is born again" (Jn 3:3). Examination of this passage reveals that Jesus depicts the radical change in personality and relational orientation brought about by a new dependency on a spiritual relationship with God. The faith polarity changes; being "born again" infuses a person with the refreshed relational capacity to converse with God under the nurture of the Holy Spirit. This offers a most reliable secure base, ready accessibility to divine resources and a safe source for emotional grounding. While empirical research should be used to fortify and shed light on this claim, there is a growing recognition that a spiritual attachment affects the IWM and vice versa. The term *corrective emotional relationship* (CER) attempts here to reference any redemptive relational encounter that draws one to a closer, more transparent faith walk with God. In this way, the IWM is steadily shaped, moment by moment, as the Lord utilizes relational encounters to accomplish sanctification and reconfigure the *imago Dei*. Succinctly stated, *corrective emotional relationship* is a phrase offered to indicate a grace-based, positive influence on the sin-tainted internal working model. A steady supply of CER encounters may increase one's fluidity for moving in and out of meaningful interpersonal relationships. Such relationships touch the intensity and balance between the three relational polarities.

This brief attempt to bring complex theoretical constructs into a conversation about relational alliances leaves much unaddressed. It serves as a starting point for trekking guides, suggestions for tying the pragmatics of helping others to the broader theoretical and empirical literature. The summary may be carried further in conjunction with the leader's caring function. All ministry helping groups offer soul care as solace for sojourners through providing encouragement, accountability and resources. Self-help and support groups have leaders who coordinate and facilitate while the emphasis remains on structured sharing, reporting and the mutual exchange of insight into useful discoveries. People are assisted in their transition from points of need to positions of relative security. Common theme groups with a designed trekking guide serve similar purposes but intentionally add the opportunity (in varying degrees) for communication about relational patterns. This style of caravan does move loosely linked travelers though hostile or tough terrain. In addition, they intentionally consider the formation of alliances along the road. All of these group options assist in facilitating movement from places of threat to the most peaceful pathways possible. Groups with trekking guides use the caravan experience itself to increase awareness, ability and attitudes regarding alliances within the group so that relationships beyond it are enriched.

Are group ventures launched in ministry settings designed to restructure and reform the formidable IWM through the use of CERs? Are these time-limited ministry groups an alternative to long-term intensive psychotherapy or deep spiritual formation work? No. Professional therapists, pastoral leadership, group members and group guides alike should recognize this as a significant overstatement of the benefit of these short-term, focused journeys. This serious misconception could be extremely discouraging to trekking guides and participants. Such overstatements are not and cannot become the mission for these groups. This limitation applies even to groups with exclusively redemptive destinations. *It is our lifelong heavenward journey by faith with an ever-deepening love of God, others and self that accomplishes the Spirit's mission of making us new creations in Jesus*

Christ. This formative trek alone modifies in what way, who and how generously we love.

Instead, these pages describe a modest venture designed to enable increased caring exchanges and fulfilling alliances along the great journey that gives purpose to our lives. This eschatological vision acknowledges that the only sure fulfillment comes on the day of Christ Jesus. Only in a far more limited manner can these groups contribute to eventual progress in spiritual maturity. However, the community experience of the group can nonetheless assist members to recognize, receive and return love. This allows the redemptive relationships the Lord supplies to accomplish recreation by grace. With this honest and realistic intent stated plainly, we can consider how redemptive relationships move us to love others better.

ALLIANCE AS LOVE IN ACTION

The term *social support* generically refers to people interactively deriving help from others.[18] Numerous professional disciplines—such as social psychology, behavioral medicine, social work and group therapy—have a vested interest in this topic. No one disputes the benefits of social support on a variety of levels; it corresponds to health, productivity and relational satisfaction. A recent review of the literature reported that nearly eleven hundred research and clinical articles per year attest to the power of social support, while still fine-tuning the comprehension of the variables that tend to make specified social exchanges valuable.[19] In general, however, the literature refers to three common types of interpersonal support.[20] *Informational support* is communication offering guidance, direction, perspective and/or useful resources. *Emotional support* is any behavior that communicates care and love for another. *Instrumental support* refers to any behavior that offers assistance in task completion or increases coping skills and/ or resources. Not coincidentally, these broad external support areas parallel the everyday depictions for one's internal personality, namely, how one thinks, feels and acts. External social support nurtures the cognitive, affective and behavioral

---

[18]A related term that could also be introduced into this discussion is *social capital*. This is used more by sociologists to reference definite outcomes resulting from social interactions where goodwill, neighborly exchanges and emotional energy are shared. Individuals within social units and communities are thus able to accomplish together what they cannot do alone. Social capital carries the idea of both public and private good while social support tends to describe what the individual is pulling from and providing to the surrounding social world. See Robert Putnam, *Bowling Alone: The Collapse and Revival of American Community* (New York: Simon & Schuster, 2001).

[19]Shelly Taylor, "Social Support," in *Foundations of Health Psychology*, ed. Howard S. Friedman and Roxane Cohen Silver (New York: Oxford University Press, 2007), pp. 145-71.

[20]Barbara R. Sarason and Steve Duck, eds., *Personal Relationships: Implications for Clinical and Community Psychology* (New York: John Wiley, 2001).

domains central to the individual's internal world.

When it comes to social support, problems arise when people adopt a naive view that adding help is always justified and advantageous. A commonsense version of this premise starts with a pluck on the heartstrings and automatic pop-up that says, "Need plus support equals relief." The logical prediction follows that any style or amount of social support will be constructive. The additive support view has good intentions, but is likely to be short-sighted. A quick illustration helps assess the veracity of this appealing premise. Consider one typical support resource: in-laws. Would it be reasonable to assert that an ever-increasing amount of in-law assistance will automatically reduce stress and reliably improve the smooth running of the receiving household? In order to develop a fair response, more detailed information would be requested. One might seek to obtain an in-law interaction history with a survey of favored intervention methods. There are numerous complexities and competing factors at work when messages regarding competency and control are communicated. What core beliefs, patterns, expectations, heritage or loyalties would be under pressure? How would chemistry between the personalities be described? The additive support formula needs refinement to weigh pros and cons, risks, unintended implications and actual results. Plain addition is not enough; an algebraic equation is necessary. Ample research findings indicate that an erroneous mixture of support in dose, form and intensity may result in decreased self-efficacy, reduced personal investment and a lower level of adaptive functioning. Well-intended support can actually foster passivity or inhibit growth. When it comes to social support, basic math has limits.

A second viewpoint assumes that social support supplies a stress buffer or insulating factor protecting the health and functioning of the individual personality. People who have a protective layer of relational support generally exhibit increased resiliency in difficult issues of life. However, further queries may reveal a fatal chink in this "armor" view of social support. Would a shiny, one-size-fits-all protective metal covering afford safety in battle for every knight? The answer could only be yes if all knights were identical in terms of size, build, favored battle implements and style of movement. Unfortunately, medieval jousting and social support both have more precise requirements. The protective presumption does not account well for individual differences in personality, cultural values, context or the particulars of the stress phenomenon. Social support is certainly a dynamic helping variable. Still, only tailored applications can address the actual strain posed by a stressor and an existing social network, as well as the condition, preferences and perspectives of the recipient. Will the beneficiary welcome the assistance as applicable and useful? Nobody disputes that activating social support holds potential gain, yet individuals require a unique blend of interpersonal support to ease demands and alleviate need. Therefore a trekking guide gathers as much reliable information as possible about a group's target population to fulfill two leader functions: (1) to inform the best vision and structure, and (2) to offer care that can be effectively assimilated. In an earlier chapter, group leaders Randy and Erin attended to this kind of relational support assessment when designing their treks. Once a group is assembled, the leader monitors members to discern how they might best experience and internalize support.

Many types of social contacts and networks foster resiliency, recovery and nurture. The intricate maze of these support routes has been the subject of considerable investigation. This work contributes to an appreciation of how core alliances interface with our wider array of associates.[21] For example, support that is *grafted,* or introduced, operates differently from *indigenous,* or preexisting, ongoing relationships. Such insights highlight the distinctions between support experienced through general social networks and through one's intimate circle. Factors beyond what, when and how much interpersonal help is available must enter the equation. Who does support come from? What degree of closeness is experienced in the transmission of this assistance? Close allies and objective acquaintances may offer a blend of support that fits with the unique features of the individual to influence health, wellness and overall quality of life (see figure 7.1).

A number of years ago social psychologist Robert Weiss described six provisions of relationships in categories useful for theoretical understanding, measurement and research.[22] The following list, adapted from Weiss, summarizes these things relationships provide:

1. Relationships offer an *attachment* bond that yields a palpable sense of security, stability and closeness. More than mere fleeting feelings, these bonds are the actual footings for the foundation of trust and hope.

---

[21]See Hoda Badr, Linda Acitelli, Steve Duck and Walter J. Carl, "Weaving Social Support and Relationships Together," in *Personal Relationships: Implications for Clinical and Community Psychology,* ed. Barbara R. Sarason and Steve Duck (New York: John Wiley, 2001), pp. 1-14; Kenneth Heller and Karen S. Rook, "Distinguishing the Theoretical Functions of Social Ties: Implications for Support Interventions," in *Personal Relationships: Implications for Clinical and Community Psychology,* ed. Barbara R. Sarason and Steve Duck (New York: John Wiley, 2001), 119-40; Robert Weiss, "The Provisions of Social Relationships," in *Doing Unto Others,* ed. Zick Rubin (Englewood Cliffs, N.J.: Prentice-Hall, 1974).

[22]See Robert Weiss, "The Provisions of Social Relationships"; Heller and Rook, "Distinguishing the Theoretical Functions"; and Nelly Vanzetti and Steve Duck, *A Lifetime of Relationships* (Pacific Grove, Calif.: Brooks/Cole, 1996).

2. *Social integration* is the provision of belonging to a network of like-minded others. Class photos, family portraits, sport team t-shirts, simple bows of pink ribbon and bumper stickers may signify an identifying brand of social connection. These symbols say, "I belong with them."

3. *Altruism* is the activity of serving and nursing others that also returns a premium to self. This does not reference an economic exchange where the receiver reimburses the giver. Rather, the caring activity itself yields inherent positives for the one doing the caring.

4. The *reassurance of worth* fortifies feelings of esteem, value, and affirmation. This provides an important lifeline.

5. *Reliable alliances* suggest the availability of dependable resources for mutual support and assistance. Help is regularly available on matters that maintain routine, such as a lift when the car is in the shop, relief when one absolutely needs to be in two places simultaneously or a cup of tea when the pace is pushing one beyond capacity.

6. *Guidance* is a means for obtaining advice, direction and strategic help when addressing stressful events or threats.

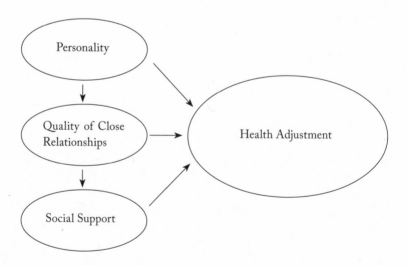

Figure 7.1. Relationships and health adjustment. (From Barbara R. Sarason, Irwin G. Sarason and Regan A. R. Gurung, "Close Personal Relationships and Health Outcomes: A Key to the Role of Social Support," in *Personal Relationships: Implications for Clinical and Community Psychology*, ed. Barbara R. Sarason and Steve Duck [New York: John Wiley, 2001], pp. 15-42.)

Note that while guidance is tied most to the cognitive (thinking) domain, the other five provisions identified here are associated with the affective (feeling) domain—even if the assistance is tangible and action-oriented.

Group guides benefit from an awareness of these categories. Recognizing these underlying relational contributions adds breadth to the generic term *social support*. Leaders can listen for cues expressed by group members regarding social integration to understand the extent and concentration of existing alliances. They can ponder references to sources rich in the nutrients that supply worth, hope and sanctuary. As participants reveal the important "who's who" in their lives, hearers are quietly prompted to survey and review their own relational ties. Ambivalence regarding the trustworthiness or reliability of available support because of their imperfections, irresponsibility or inconsistencies provides other relational clues. Leaders must cautiously consider a trend to discount care from less than ideal personalities. Severe black-and-white reasoning can result in neglecting or refusing scarce but available provisions. Are there areas of a group member's life where the social provisions are low, have recently shifted or have gradually dried up? This may offer clues to where natural relational support is weak, weary or faltering.

A leader can regularly use the above six provisions to summarize session themes. If discoveries regarding the effects of changes in close alliances contributed to recent discussion, it may be productive to name the provision or its absence directly.

> Looking over our time, several have recently changed neighborhoods or employment. Seems like figuring out where you belong is a recurring theme . . .

> The twists and turns in the close relationships discussed today are important in a way that goes beyond the immediate hurt or frustration. Awareness may be dawning that your basic security has been drastically shaken . . .

> Recalling our conversations over the past hour, one theme has been conducting an inventory of who fills our confidence tank. Several here have friends and family who offer generous fill-ups.

Participants may be so engrossed in coping with life events that they have lost a sense of the ebb and flow of social provisions.

These descriptions place the focus on how human relationships are shaped and sustained. For those who are open to the relational polarity with the Lord of the universe, it is uplifting to share how the Lord himself supplies these same provisions. Consider how echoes of old melodies and phrases from traditional hymns give testimony to his generous supply:

He hideth my soul in the cleft of the rock, Where rivers of pleasure I see.

A mighty fortress is our God, A bulwark never failing; Our helper He amid the flood, Of mortal ills prevailing.

O God, our help in ages past, Our hope for years to come, Our shelter from the stormy blast, And our eternal home.

When peace like a river, attendeth my way, When sorrows like the sea billows roll; Whatever my lot, Thou hast taught me to say, "It is well with my soul."[23]

Each provisional category captures a source of human stability, service, satisfaction, purpose and place. Christians marvel over how the Lord furnishes himself to supply these benefits in open relationship. He may show up and offer these provisions through his Word. Sometimes He makes companionship and contribution memorably near in the midst of worship. Often, he ministers via a fellow trekker, a process made possible by the ministry of the Comforter, the person of the Trinity who comes alongside to allow enjoyment of the presence of the Father and the Son this side of heaven (see Jn 14:16-17, 26; 15:26; 16:7-11, 13-15; 1 Cor 2:12-16; 12:12-26; Eph 4:3-16). This raises a key question: might these social provisions reflect spiritual priorities and processes? This is entirely reasonable considering the priorities Jesus Christ himself established.

A wonderful nonfiction work by C. S. Lewis, *The Four Loves*, illuminates the function and benefits of close human relationships.[24] He unpacks four Greek words for love that are found in the New Testament, though not for the purpose of an exegetical study to uncover precise textual meaning.[25] Rather, he offers a

---

[23]*Logos Hymnal*, 1st ed. (Oak Harbor: Logos Research Systems, 1995).

[24]C. S. Lewis, *The Four Loves* (New York: Harcourt, Brace & World, 1960).

[25]These four loves provide a useful typology for describing categories of relationships. There are numerous alternative systems to separate relational types. See C. Arthur VanLear, Ascan Koerner and Donna M. Allen, "Relational Typologies," in *The Cambridge Handbook of Personal Relationships*, ed. Anita L. Vangelisti and Daniel Perlman (New York: Cambridge University Press, 2006), pp. 91-110. One reasonable alternative would be to adopt the two-tier proposal by R. Weiss where there are *attachments* relationships with an imbedded security and *affiliation* with an emphasis on mutual interest, support and resources. This system would fit well with what has been presented here, for social support is tied to relationships of affiliation and close relationships are variations of attachment relationships. See Robert Weiss, "A Taxonomy of Relationships," *Journal of Social*

literary, rich, passionate reminder that people experience love at a variety of levels and in a number of contexts; and that love pours purest when people submit themselves to the Lord's care. Lewis's study reflects the necessity of relational experiences to make sense of the journey of our lives. These loves outline the community of support that not only fortifies human beings through severe crisis, but also instills strength to pursue daily chores and rewards. In Lewis's work it is clear that these four variations of love can soften the blows of life, provide deep satisfaction or reveal the sharp edges of sin. Is this not what occurred when Edmund sought to bolster his personal sense of importance by trampling on the trust of his younger sister?

Affection *(storge)* captures the general warmth and goodwill of familiar faces and acquaintances. These are the kindnesses passed along by the regular folks in our lives with whom we grumble about the weather, share smiles and exchange encouragement in the little things. Affection is the humblest love; it is never glamorous and is often barely even noticeable. "Affection almost slinks or seeps through our lives."[26] People may notice it most when it is surprisingly lost or disturbed. Affection has the feature of being able to mix and mingle with other loves. Affection can help or harm. It shows its dark side when provision contains conditions and pressures for control. Lewis displays his wit and wisdom as he works his way through this complexity.

Take for example his picture of affection as "an affair of old clothes."[27] He conveys the local social world as the fine place where one is recognized, known by name and valued. This setting provides a steady source of snug security, ease, cozy feelings and a royal freedom to be expressive. In this way, affection is like putting on a favorite shirt and melting into a sense of homey bliss. On the other hand, he goes on to insist that enjoying old clothes is not identical to wearing the same shirt until it stinks. Similarly, it would not be right to show up at a formal gathering with garments that make you feel right but convey utter disrespect for your host and his guests. Affection may be comfortable but must never be neglected, taken for granted or presumed upon.

The next more intensive type of love is found in a person's inner circle of close relationships. In friendships *(philia)*, humans work side by side to pursue and support communal interests. People make friendship ties completely by choice

---

and Personal Relationships 15 (1998): 671-83. Connecting Lewis's system with that of Weiss also does not require much of a stretch. Affection and friendships fit Weiss's relationships of affiliation while Eros and Charity could indeed represent attachment relationships.

[26]Lewis, *Four Loves*, p. 36.

[27]Ibid., p. 67.

and deepen them through voluntary commitment; this is the fantastic feature of this type of love. Blood ties or convenient proximity do not force friendship.

> It is an affair of disentangled, or stripped, minds, Eros will have naked bodies; Friendship naked personalities. Hence (if you will not misunderstand me) the exquisite arbitrariness and irresponsibility of this love. I have no duty to be anyone's Friend and no man in the world has a duty to be mine. No claims, no shadow of necessity. Friendship is unnecessary, like philosophy, like art, like the universe itself (for God did not need to create). It has no survival value; rather it is one of those things which give value to survival.[28]

Brotherly love grows between those who share no DNA in common, only uncommon commitment to the welfare of the other. The freely bestowed gift of fidelity and kindness elevates the beauty of friendship. Lewis intentionally stirs reflection on the state of friendship bonds within the contemporary social scene and in the fabric of our lives. When people consider the important value of friendship, the result will likely be an increase in their esteem and the energy poured into maintenance. A treasured Friendship love will not be treated as disposable.

Love between the sexes *(eros)* yields a special return. This is a unique and intense bond. Some wonder if there is an inherent danger of turning "being in love" into a sort of religion or form of idolatry. Lewis insists that since Eros in marriage is woven into the ordinary by the humble love of affection, there is no risk of ever turning love for each other into an idol. It is softened and made real by "private things; soft slippers, old clothes, old jokes, the thump of a sleepy dog's tail."[29] "The real danger seems to me not that the lovers will idolize each other but that they will idolize Eros himself."[30] Lewis prophetically reverberates with the words of Dietrich Bonhoeffer, who warned that "he who loves his dream of a community more than the Christian community itself becomes a destroyer of the latter, even though his personal intentions may be ever so honest and earnest and sacrificial."[31] Any of the loves could be abstracted and stereotyped to the extent that the extracted ideal becomes a useless idol. When separated from imperfect alliances with those who are here in the flesh, these loves turn to lust for picture or projection, not for a genuine person. This undermines any rejoicing in the

---

[28]Ibid., p. 103.
[29]Ibid., pp. 56-57.
[30]Ibid., p. 155.
[31]Dietrich Bonhoeffer, *Life Together* (New York: Harper & Row, 1954), p. 27.

blessing of the ordinary because endless expectations are built on surreal expectations of an illusive ideal. Thus Eros itself is a good gift and poses no threat to our devotional state, as long as it remains rooted in reality.

This brings us finally to Charity or self-giving love *(agape)*. Charity moves beyond the previous three natural loves in the same way a tended garden exceeds the wonder of a wilderness or a meadow. Similar live elements are present, but in *agape*, a gardener directs the form and balance. The other three loves are transformed by *agape* as the Divine Gardener steps in to attend fondly to the essential details of daily care. Love within Christian community is earthy, yet it still takes on a heavenly outlook as the Lord himself infuses his gracious care.

We must not ignore the corollary regarding the way God bestows undeserved favor on those who become his adopted children. No bond or necessity compels him. Through the good news of the gospel, he routinely blesses his beloved with sustenance and intensity. Recall this reminder from Isaiah:

Why would you ever complain, O Jacob,
   or, whine, Israel, saying,
"God has lost track of me.
   He doesn't care what happens to me"?
Don't you know anything? Haven't you been listening?
God doesn't come and go. God *lasts.*
   He's Creator of all you can see or imagine.
He doesn't get tired out, doesn't pause to catch his breath.
   And he knows *everything*, inside and out.
He energizes those who get tired,
   gives fresh strength to dropouts.
For even young people tire and drop out,
   young folk in their prime stumble and fall.
But those who wait upon God get fresh strength.
   They spread their wings and soar like eagles,
They run and don't get tired,
   they walk and don't lag behind.
(Is 40:27-31 *The Message*)

Many on a small group trek desperately require this very renewal. Why not seek this refreshment directly from our loving Father? By all means, seek him in worship, prayer and in the Word. His answer may be the blessing of Charity or *agape* love. The Lord is ready to give fresh strength. And here is the predictable surprise: people commonly realize this provision through human alliances acting on God's behalf as loving agents.

The rich insights offered by Lewis capture how these types of love sustain a person's self-identity while giving life purpose and depth. For relational trekking, leaders do well to grasp a simple yet key application from Lewis's study: how might leaders conceptualize kingdom-oriented intimacy treks using Lewis's exploration of love from the world of language? Like a tended garden, what occurs in these encounters certainly can and does occur normally elsewhere. The four loves are natural social relationships. However, the relational component within these groups receives divine tending in order to produce insight and motivation to pursue these four loves outside the group. The Lord uses these earthy occasions, where people share stories that reveal strategic information, supply direct encouragement and curtail actions that thwart the experience of these love types. As each trek begins, participants ideally open the gate and welcome in the Divine Gardener to cultivate, prune and nurture relational patterns. These natural loves are watered in groups to flourish under supernatural care.

In addition to identifying love types, Lewis distinguishes between "gift" love and "need" love. He argues gently but persuasively that God himself is the decisive example of gift love. The assumption may follow that humans love most purely when imitating God—that is, in the expression of love not motivated by the expectation of receiving anything in return. But Lewis teases out the critical flaw in this logic. A man's love for God is at its best always a need love. Are not people most open to a spiritual quest to unite with the Creator when need is painfully overwhelming? Therefore as creatures, human beings will never be able to return to the Creator a pure gift love since our entire existence is dependent on him. "Man approaches God most nearly when he is in one sense least like God. For what can be more unlike than fullness and need, sovereignty and humility, righteousness and penitence, limitless power and a cry for help."[32] Lewis's insights regarding the underlying motivations for these loves suggest that relationships can be both functional and healthy when mutual but asymmetrical. When a human bond involves a combination of gift and need love, it can be healthy and rich even if it appears one-sided to the unenlightened human eye. There are provisions being exchanged that flow both ways. Lewis's gifts to us bring out the complexity of human-to-human and human-to-divine poles of relational activity.

Lewis's work provides one further application for group work. In individual

---

[32]Lewis, *Four Loves*, p. 12.

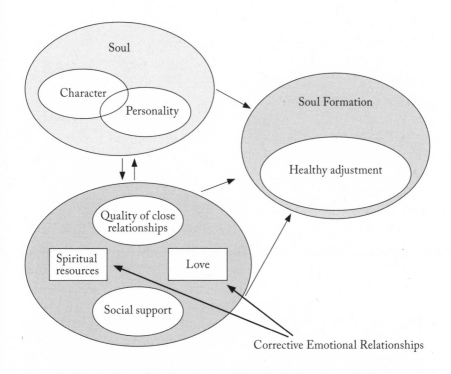

Figure 7.2. Relationships and soul formation. (Adopted from Sarason, Sarason & Gurung, "Close Personal Relationships.")

counseling, therapy or pastoral care, helpers who are congruent, objective, knowledgeable and/or strong will offer relational stability through the therapeutic alliance to a client who is experiencing incongruence or lacks necessary relational supports. This may reflect the provision of gift love with its countless benefits. If the mutual exchanges of gift love and need love provide potential benefits to all involved, then perhaps the group format optimally facilitates nurturance. Groups contain multiple prospects for a variety of reciprocal relationships. These designated travels bring about a surge in transparent mutuality. Activating the unique relational pathways a group can provide via affectionate love may stimulate waves of change through the loves of friendship, marital love and Christian fellowship (see figure 7.2).

No one has fully charted the territory of ways that the three relational polarities form, sustain and reform our soul. No GPS system can allow for navigating these paths with no wrong turns or disappointing detours. Yet an old-fashioned compass can point out the necessary direction. Look for ways to explore the three relational polarities—self, others and God—and welcome the corrective emotional relationships that redeem and release our *imago Dei* capacity to love others. Relational encounters can refresh our souls.

Trekkers receive guidance in developing a deeper appreciation for the dynamic polarities of relationships from the level of the ordinary to the heights of the extraordinary. Not only does their awareness of social support (affection) and close provision (friendship and eros) increase, but they also learn to appropriate each through charity. *Agape* applies the love-of-God polarity to the relational activity of self-identity and intimacy. Two dimensions are transformed into three. "Behold, I will create new heavens and a new earth. The former things will not be remembered, nor will they come to mind" (Is 65:17).

THE WONDER OF CARING ALLIANCES

Tiana spoke with church and civic leaders about her concept for a parent support initiative for those frazzled by the experience of living with an emerging adolescent. Their reception was enthusiastic. Each week local residents reeled from one tragedy or another involving a teenager engaged in violence, vandalism or victimizing others. Local parents needed all sorts of help. It did not take long for Safe Passage to gain funding, a prime meeting place, referrals and recognition.[33] Tiana designed the group to assist parents in guiding their children in a protected transition from dependency to greater autonomy.[34] Screening out twelve participants for a three-month run demanded more and more time as nominations grew daily. After week four, the waitlist was high enough that Tiana considered setting aside a second evening for another cohort. After all, each session had been nearly running itself as members clamored for attention. Several of their kids had officially only recently hit their teen years, but the only way

---

[33]One detail from this fictional composite requires qualification, namely, the statement about rapid funding. Great helping ideas are often *not* easily funded. Start-up funds may be obtained as one-time gifts or grants while ongoing endowments are rare. Participants may have the means to pay for services directly. Private health insurance may cover group therapy if deemed medically necessary. In either case, participants tend to choose individual services if their own or third-party funding is available. Group efforts thrive when external funding provides assistance. One of my own prayers as I write *Trekking Toward Wholeness* is that ministries will be encouraged to take on this type of helping venture. Cooperative and creative thinking could result in sponsoring trained leaders to offer such groups for the mutual benefit of all invested parties.

[34]Stephen P. Greggo and Helen Messick, "Autonomy, Attachment, and Adolescent-Parent Relational Strain in Christian Families: Assessment as Treatment," *Marriage and Family: A Christian Journal* 6, no. 3 (2005): 317-30.

to call their actions *juvenile* would be to insert the word *delinquent*. Her assembly represented every combination of married, single, blended, cohabitating or stage of separation parent that one might imagine. One mom, Miranda, lived with her fiancé on the first floor, while her mother lived on the second and the father of her oldest son inhabited the basement. It was hard to figure out which level was actually home for the four children.

As Tiana debriefed one night's session with her astute coleader, the passage ahead was not looking too definite, let alone safe. Her topics were solid, but that was not a concern; attendance fluctuated, but she had anticipated that. What gnawed at her was that less than a handful of these parents could readily recollect or relay caring qualities from a consistent parent during their own adolescent years. Last night the group voted, without actually consulting her, that any new group should be devoted to their adolescents, not other parents! After a strong start, success was far from certain.

As Tiana faces these parents in her genuine attempt to assist, she can sense that they respect her leading and expertise. The members hold her position of leadership in such high regard that they would like for her to deal directly with their teens. But this might result in both an increased dependency on her and a corresponding decline in parenting poise. Must all meaningful support stem from the position and personality of the leader? How can she foster cooperation and trust between members so that the ingredients of social support are tasted and savored? Can she offer support that is customized to fit unique care needs and member experience? Will the group as a whole provide nurture? These are a few of the questions that social support literature would suggest that Tiana consider.

When the eighth meeting of Safe Passages arrived, Tiana was fully prepared. Still, a phone conversation with her sister had formed an uneasy sensation within that she was not ready. Her discomfort was nothing heavy; it just persistently nudged her to pay attention or be on alert. Her sister had reported that the biopsy of the small shadow found during her routine breast exam required additional attention. A consultation was pending. It all sounded so sterile and routine. No one denied the underlying threat, they merely delayed it until necessity demanded that it be faced. The sisters had lingered on this call longer than usual. Neither wanted to be the first to say "gotta run." Tiana had taught classes, run meetings and done intensive counseling with far weightier matters on her mind. The evening's theme was "Making Memories," and she intended to stimulate creativity on how to get into decent, non-confrontational conversations with a young adolescent. Those fun exchanges, though usually short, could leave a positive lasting impression.

Only two chairs were empty and it was an insignificant ten minutes past starting time. She kicked the session into motion. Not bad. First an upbeat concise welcome, then a reminder that the group was into its second half and heading toward home, and finally a three-sentence capsule review of the last meeting. Tiana was on a roll and her best three tales of teen dialogues-to-die-for were ready for the retelling. She momentarily tuned into what might represent a somber mood in the room. Her polished approach dissolved into a puzzled look. Out popped an unplanned yet entirely honest question: "Is everything alright?" Miranda's eyes turned glossy and her face reddened as several sets of eyes looked right at her. Tiana's instantaneous inner response was a tinge of anger. Something is up with Miranda! She doesn't keep order in her own household and now the group is going to veer off track. For several weeks, Tiana had been wondering when and how to challenge Miranda over the chaotic conditions in her home life, with an alcoholic mother upstairs and an ex-alcoholic ex-boyfriend downstairs. No wonder her fourteen-year-old was showing signs of moving heavily into the party scene. Maybe this would yield the optimal opening for Miranda to recognize that she needed to obtain distance from the drunks in her life for the sake of her kids. These thoughts remained silent blips on Tiana's inner screen.

It was not Miranda, but the woman in the next seat that spoke. Usually a quiet, steady voice in the room, that mother of three did not appear to need these sessions. Tiana admired her and she was aware that others did as well. "Miranda's daughter was in the hospital for two days. They found her passed out in a snow bank real early Saturday morning. She didn't come home after the basketball game at school. The police say she may have been taken advantage of; but she's getting stronger and should be perfectly fine. Was that all right, Miranda?" Miranda was letting the tears flow and she nodded approval. Tiana scanned faces and realized that most everyone in the room must have already heard about this. Several directive probes moved into launch position on the tip of her tongue, but surprisingly, she felt her own eyes getting wet and she simply said, "I'm so sorry." There was a brief silence. Tiana couldn't exactly describe who said what and when, but the following messages were stunning and easy to recall.

One member told about a cousin who was raped as a teenager who grew up to be a type of social worker. These days she runs meetings for young women twice a week. The office was not far and several members offered Miranda consistent transportation. Burton hesitantly spoke up that he knew he wasn't supposed to say, but it was a real comfort to know that the teen's father, Miranda's ex, was doing meetings and getting to work every single day. Two members each gave testimony about how much they appreciated Miranda's tireless dedication at the daycare center at the Stonehall Church for so many years even though the pay was pitiful. Folks recalled seeing Miranda walk preschoolers down the block holding onto a thick rope. There was laughter about other potential uses for that heavy rope. "You always love those little ones and it's gonna come back to you." Tiana took this in as she wondered if any of her discussion questions would be needed. This was not the kind of confrontation she thought Miranda deserved. In a series of roundabout ways the group discussed school events, how to get kids there, keep them there, let them have fun and get them back home again without big trouble. One nearby church opens its gym and community center after school sporting events for supervised hanging out. A local superstore supplies snacks. Miranda was mostly silent. She did stutter thanks and her awareness that the Lord was giving her a second chance. She was praying for the courage to use it. Several voices told Miranda that her girl and family had been prayed for in services on Sunday. When the session was nearing its end, Tiana found these words: "I need to thank all of you for your kindness tonight. You each gave memorable words in this session and our dialogue won't soon be forgotten. That was our theme, 'Making Memories.' These words may have been for Miranda but there is much here that we can each take home to use with our families. Good work and I'm looking forward to our next gathering."

The session was chock-full of informational, emotional and instrumental support. The love of affection was felt. Hints of the flow of other social provisions were everywhere. Basic caring showed up, consisting of respect, recognition and empathetic embrace. The Divine Gardener may have even visited. As Miranda left, she took Tiana's hand. "Thank you for being there for me. I saw you crying for my girl." Tiana wasn't sure this was true. She let the words stand and gave Miranda a hug. The group had done its thing. A deeper magic beyond any of Tiana's plans was plainly at work.

A LAST WORD

C. S. Lewis took us through the intriguing world of Narnia. We encountered strange creatures, watched as battles were fought, all while two Sons of Adam and two Daughters of Eve discovered new identities and how to get along with each other. Aslan the Lion redeemed Edmund's nasty betrayal. Aslan's grand act of gift love was worthy of great recognition. He demonstrated even grander humility. In the midst of the concluding celebrations and festivities, Aslan, the warrior and redeemer, quietly slipped away. It was Mr. Beaver who explained by warning everyone about the actions of Aslan:

"He'll be coming and going" he had said. "One day you'll see him and another you won't. He doesn't like being tied down—and of course he has other countries to attend to. It's quite all right. He'll often drop in. Only you mustn't press him. He's wild, you know. Not like a *tame* lion."[35]

It is reassuring to know that, like Aslan, God will be coming and going. Experience has granted me more comfort regarding the uncontrollable aspects of group work. The unpredictability of it all is no longer as disturbing or confusing. To soothe those inner pricks to gain control, I just recall the words of Mr. Beaver and wait for Aslan to drop in.

---

[35]C. S. Lewis, *The Chronicles of Narnia: The Lion, the Witch and the Wardrobe* (New York: Harper-Collins, 1994), p. 149.

8

HOSPITALITY ON TREK

LANDMARKS AHEAD

In this chapter, we continue to explore the leader's care function with the spotting scope set on caring as hospitality. The true advantage of this age-old courtesy for weary travelers does not end when members recognize that the leader cares. Hospitality finds its fulfillment when recipients turn and extend an ongoing welcome to others. This particular trail reaches its high point when we visit the healing benefits of groups as gleaned from therapeutic literature. The concept of leaders as authentic chameleons provides an unusual explanation for how to get trekkers comfortably engaged. And we address the question, how can leaders blend in without compromising character and values? A three-installment narrative reflects this chapter's major lessons; they tell a story about Devin, who launches a trek for men seeking to practice purity. We track the shaky start to this trek toward wholeness: Surfing True.

ADVANCING CARE

Christian guides must be intuitively aware of this common sense principle: caring follows no formula; compassion, no program. Genuine concern does not spontaneously arise from a set of techniques or a meticulously designed meeting agenda. Session activities, strategic conversations and stories are useful, but other conditions are vital for care to flourish. Leaders discover creative methods of using their own presence to communicate a warm welcome that inspires contagious caring between participants. Lord willing, leaders can escort the group through the novelty of bearing with strangers, beyond superficial Sunday-morning-style compliments and into a multifaceted exchange where each passes along intimate blessings. Charity and *koinonia* can then move from the theoretical to the experiential.

The themes explored in this chapter form an odd couple. One concept might be called plain, down-home ordinary. Its partner may strike the reader as out of character for Christian praxis. First, a leader's thorough dedication to exhibit *hospitality* fulfils the care function. This basic posture deserves respect for its critical role in helping participants realize the journey's ultimate purpose. Hospitality links the pursuit of a Christian ministry calling with a set of well-established therapeutic factors from group counseling literature. The second construct for exploration evokes a strange image: an *authentic chameleon*. It might initially seem counterproductive to the transparent demonstration of God's love, but in fact we will see otherwise. Representing a leader as an authentic chameleon demonstrates how to expand and make use of one's relational repertoire for the advancement of care.

Leaders must create an atmosphere of close connection and expectancy within trekkers, encouraging them in the areas where change is plausible. When such care becomes palpable, the great Comforter has room to roam freely within these relational encounters.

SURFING TRUE

The executive pastor approached Devin about a matter that weighed heavy on his heart.[1] Spiritually open young men within the college fellowship were repeatedly caught in the tidal wave of pornographic material flooding the Internet. For nearly a decade the church had made the nearby sprawling state university a dedicated ministry priority. This was their field, "ripe for the harvest" (Jn 4:35). The Lord had blessed their efforts bountifully. This privilege brought with it intricate responsibilities of pastoral care that the leadership team humbly accepted. The psalmist did get it right over two millennia ago: "How can a young man keep his way pure? / By living according to your word" (Ps 119:9). They found that this instruction revealed a resource not to be dismissed as mere spiritual rhetoric. Infusing this principle into daily lifestyle choices and purity practices constituted a miraculous feat within their contemporary culture.

Living on a college campus meant lightning-fast Internet, the fascination of fraternity row, advertisement blitzes that persistently pushed past the edge of decency and conversations everywhere to stimulate decadent fantasy. The pressure of temptation could reach a painful pitch. Among the college fellowship, there were some for whom sincere conversion and dedication to Christian service motivated an urgency to curtail indulging in these mind-polluting inputs. For others, the presence of a serious relationship or pending engagement

---

[1]Surfing True is once again a fictional composite based on actual leader and group experiences. For those former students who guide purity treks and share their hearts, I am most grateful.

raised questions about customary practices. For a critical few, the preferences aroused by the explicit material brought powerful sexual identity issues into sharp relief. Ministry leadership knew that even marriage offered no instant fix. Special lectures, training sessions and retreats provided a positive step. Preachers and discipleship mentors admitted that they did not have the time and resources necessary to travel the required distance with willing trekkers to help them establish an alternative route toward holy living. An astounding number of private confessions and requests for prayer alerted the church leadership to the magnitude of the matter. Devin's training in pastoral counseling made him the point person for issues like these, so this difficult concern was tossed his direction. He felt like he'd caught a burning coal with his bare hands. He already had intense conversations with several guys to explore their persistent purity lapses. Then an idea surfaced: why not sponsor and establish a supportive accountability group? This would be a dynamite merger of counseling and pastoral care. Surfing True caught its first wave. An announcement was crafted to gather participants.

Surfing True

Seeking to steer clear of the dangerous current of Internet pornography? This short-term care group is designed for any male desiring integrity in the area of sexual purity. Now is the time to take preventative measures against permanent consequences from the unchecked progression of sexual sin. Surfing True will enable members, with support, to achieve freedom over sexual sin. Surfing True calls men to seek accountability with fellow strugglers and to increase their love for God by practicing holy living in community. Contact Devin for information and a confidential interview.

Devin gathered stories, discussion topics and tips for curbing a host of ugly habits. He crafted questions for use during the upcoming orientation and screening interviews:

Surfing True Screening Questions

1. How does the description of Surfing True fit with what you were hoping for in a helping experience? Do you have any questions regarding the purpose or nature of this care group?

2. What brought you to realize that you might be heading into rough water with Internet pornography and sexual sin? What is your estimate on when this started?

3. Have there been any recent circumstances that gave you a sense that this behavior might prove to be troublesome in the future?

4. From your vantage point, describe what has made this a temptation for you.

5. What frightens you most about these behaviors in your life?

6. Are you currently seeing a counselor about your behavior on the Internet, sexual sin, or other matter? If so, how do you picture this group contributing to that one-on-one work?

7. How do you anticipate that this experience might be of help to you specifically? What do you expect to gain?

8. On a low to high scale of 1 to 5, how would you honestly rank your willingness to participate in this group to get what you need?

9. Do you have any expectations regarding the leaders in this group? How do you feel about the possibility of a female coleader in the group?

10. In what ways if any do you see this commitment as affecting your overall spiritual growth?

11. Surfing True will run with a simple covenant: what others say in the group stays in the group. Does this bring up any questions or concerns?

Surfing True would be a closed group. This meant it would have a screened and consistent membership. It would run on a twelve-week cycle and participants would be invited to come back through for a second round. New members would be brought in as each new cycle began. This way, Devin could possibly work with select men for nearly six months. Over the long-term, Devin could envision Surfing True alumni eventually forming a step-style, self-help, stop-in-as-needed group for ongoing follow-up. At the outset, this would be a common-theme, adjustment-level group with redemptive features. Due to the need to establish limitations, this group would not likely be suitable for married men recently involved in affairs, those who had unusual sexual fetishes or men who sought activities that crossed legal limits. Yet if Internet-related sexual behaviors were becoming troublesome, unacceptable habits were forming, thoughts were interrupting activities with a forceful compulsive press or finances were being tapped out, Surfing True would be an ideal match. Having developed his approach based on the recent stories he heard, Devin felt prepared for the requests that would soon pour in.

Devin unquestionably stretched his skill set in the planning stage. Nonetheless he had discerned that this trek must address immediate concerns and have a lasting discipleship impact for guys who committed. He also understood this premise as his overarching mission: *a leader fulfils the care function as the relational nourishment members experience within a group becomes the catalyst for increased intimacy in naturally occurring relationships.* The leader will commence conversation and spark caring initiatives that spread well beyond the prominent concern.

In Devin's effort, the content areas were repentance, diminishing sexual sin, and termination of wandering in forbidden territory. Beyond this, the design emphasized an improved capacity to love others. Devin knew the importance of this objective for those in Surfing True as the practices being shed amounted to an entrenched idolatry of false intimacy. A taste for bona fide relating was the replacement feature to put on. Phrases from seminary coursework bounced around in Devin's mind. Care of souls, *cura animarum,* traditionally contains elements of both cure and care.[2] Where sin once had dominion and caused extensive damage, this objective requires repair and healing. Cure restores well-being. Beyond disease treatment, people must embrace good health. Care promotes *ongoing* well-being. In Surfing True, Devin resolutely maintained that the group must have a cure component in terms of curtailing destructive and sinful behavior. Its care element would seek to activate authentic connections and practices with men, women, and one's heavenly Father. With this keen sense of purpose and sharp planning, what could possibly delay an appreciative crew from hitting the beach to enjoy this adventure?

SPIRITUAL CONDITIONING FOR HOSPITALITY

Well-known author Henri J. M. Nouwen primarily dedicated his over forty books to discussing spiritual formation. A Catholic priest with roots deeply planted in pastoral care, Nouwen was keenly alert to psychological matters.[3] Christians perhaps know him best as a professor and spiritual director. Prior to his death in 1996, he spent the last ten years of his earthly life living with and ministering to

---

[2]Gary W. Moon and David G. Benner, eds., *Spiritual Direction and the Care of Souls: A Guide to Christian Approaches and Practices* (Downers Grove, Ill.: InterVarsity Press, 2004), p. 11. See also David Benner, *Care of Souls: Revisioning Christian Nurture and Counsel* (Grand Rapids: Baker, 1998).

[3] See <www.HenriNouwen.org>.

developmentally disabled adults.[4] Daily he provided personal care to others as he sought to grow in his own spiritual walk. Such life choices lend credibility to his insights. Selected works apply remarkably well to group treks. Within Nouwen's framework for the cultivation of a deeper spiritual life, this study introduces the important biblical practice of hospitality.

In his classic work *Reaching Out*, Nouwen affirms the centrality of the three relational poles for spiritual growth (self, others and God). He adds considerable depth to these relational resources by describing each area as containing a distinct continuum running from problematic to positive. Spiritual formation work does not involve randomly reaching into each of these dimensions blindly hoping for good outcomes. Instead, formative efforts involve the strategic and humble pursuit of God-honoring attitudes within each of these areas. Consider how each of these intertwined dimensions brings out a vital relational stance. In the polarity of self, the attitudinal dimension is *loneliness vs. solitude;* regarding others, the dimension is *hostility vs. hospitality;* and in reference to relating to God, the dimension is labeled *illusion vs. prayer.*

In the middle of all our worries and concerns, often disturbingly similar over the years, we can become more aware of the different poles between which our lives vacillate and are held in tension. These poles offer the context in which we can speak about the spiritual life, because they can be recognized by anyone who is striving to live a life in the Holy Spirit.

Consider how Nouwen's categories so aptly describe human experience. During our life we become more aware not only of our crying loneliness but also of our real desire for a solitude of the heart; we come to the painful realization not only of our cruel hostilities but also of our hope to receive our fellow humans with unconditional hospitality, and underneath all of this we discover not only the illusions under which we act as masters of our fate but also the precarious gift of prayer hidden in the depth of our innermost self. Thus the spiritual life is a constant movement between the poles of loneliness and solitude, hostility and hospitality, illusion and prayer.[5] A group leader's caring function most specifically relates to the polarity of hostility and hospitality, and provides the bulk of our investigation into Nouwen's thought. The group applications from the first and third polarity, however, warrant a short trip into Nouwen's helpful categories.

Technological advances steadily endow human beings with unfathomable

---

[4]Nouwen joined a L'Arche community called Daybreak in Richmond Hill, north of Toronto, Canada. The developmentally disabled man he cared for was named Adam. Nouwen described him as "friend, teacher and guide."
[5]Henri J. M. Nouwen, *Reaching Out* (Garden City, N.Y.: Doubleday, 1975), pp. 12-13.

opportunities for instant contact within a global community. These widespread means for communication make it all the more stunning that the acute ache of loneliness remains vividly familiar and nearly universal. While the group treks advanced in this work provide significant benefits to participants, no one should assume that such connections with others offer the necessary antidote to loneliness. Nouwen stated that merely seeking out others to ease loneliness, in and of itself, is misleading, shortsighted and spiritually void. Community will not advance us toward wholeness. His words are worth pondering steadily and grasping gradually.[6] The remedy to loneliness lies in the recognition that rushing in and recklessly relying on others can never quench it. Only gentle courage and persistent effort to comprehend the joy found in solitude will soothe the dark cry of loneliness. Consider this synopsis, which weaves together Nouwen's worthy explanations.

Solitude begins with a realistic appraisal of a flawed and needy self. It ends with a self-acceptance not based on shallow self-satisfaction. Instead, with a faith-based hope for future restoration, people develop a patient willingness to sort through their internal world of brokenness, need and desire. Loneliness transforms into an acknowledged solitude. Entering reflection in a state of loneliness produces desperation. Solitude yields a dedication to enjoy God and others. Then and only then do affirmation, support and compassion derive from the encounter with others. "The movement from loneliness to solitude, however, is the beginning of any spiritual life because it is the movement from the restless senses to the restful spirit, from the outward-reaching cravings to the inward-reaching search, from the fearful clinging to the fearless play."[7] Thus a growing steadiness in accepting solitude facilitates a readiness to engage with others.

So how does the dimension of loneliness and solitude affect group trekking? When members expect the group experience to offer a remedy to loneliness but see no need for the soul searching that cultivates a readiness to enjoy solitude, their craving for others will hinder the enjoyment of others.

Remaining in solitude is never the ultimate objective. Nouwen wholeheartedly contends that we do not exist for ourselves or for others, but for God.[8] This explains his title choice, *Reaching Out*. God's work of grace in modifying loneliness into an attitude of solitude still leaves a healthy appetite for the other two polarities. One can rest in the confidence that both God and others are available for relationship. This security breathes wonder into solitude.

---

[6]Nouwen's *Reaching Out* is quite accessible and only slightly over 100 pages. The publication date should not discourage a worthwhile read.
[7]Nouwen, *Reaching Out*, p. 23.
[8]Ibid., p. 110.

With respect to our basic themes of walking, wandering and wisdom, loneliness may be likened to a profound sense of shame accompanied by the rapid-fire impulse to hide. Those sensations subside with the reminder that God's voice is already calling out "where are you?" We are enabled to walk with him when we apply the wisdom that our wholeness and journey depends on him. This enables us to accept solitude and hold back the urge to wander. Solitude draws us to better understand our need and grow in our desire to be with others. The inner rumblings of aloneness can become frightening. They reside within as motivation to assist those made in the *imago Dei* to join a community where God is present.

The pursuit of unadulterated Christian spirituality fundamentally exposes spiritual idols of illusion and calls all to release such idols in favor of following the God of Scripture. The quest for a transpersonal experience—in Christian belief, an encounter with the personal Creator of the universe as revealed in the Scriptures—is never about mastering spirituality procedures or stoically pursuing empty mechanical steps. Christians do not practice mysterious or mystical magic. Nor can spiritual intimacy consist of grasping the infinite realities of the Almighty with our finite minds. Attempts to control or contain the Alpha and Omega are vain, useless shadows of spiritual peace. In order to experience tranquility within the third relational pole, we must surrender these illusions and instead enter into a constant dialogue with God in humble prayer. Wisdom leads those on a spiritual quest to simple, dependent prayer. No one attains success in the spiritual life by an increase in control or autonomy. There are no right steps to take, techniques to exercise or knowledge to obtain; instead, to "pray continually" characterizes a mature spiritual life (1 Thess 5:17). Nouwen references this as moving from a continuum of desperate illusions to a posture of prayer. Within group treks, as participants share stories, reveal hurts and expose dreams, they usually expose deep-seated beliefs which include false notions of how God will act, intervene or answer. A group offers a redeeming service by helping the seeker to release those illusions in favor of *conversational prayer*, that is, truly relating to God rather than investing in ridiculously vain attempts to force him to conform to human wishes. Groups offer the ideal venue to sort through relational expectations. Replacing faulty demands with flexible openness powerfully moves people toward the experience of *shalom*.

From these crucial attitudes of solitude and prayer, we turn to the dimension leaders can thoughtfully adjust when approaching an experience of guided care: hospitality and hostility.

HOSPITALITY VS. HOSTILITY

How often we humans either force or constrict our feeble attempt to exhibit hospitality! Nouwen contends that shifting from a hostile stance to genuine hospitality actually requires difficult interpersonal work. Contemporary social conditions, he explains, generate "fearful, defensive, aggressive people anxiously clinging to their property and inclined to look at their surrounding world with suspicion, always expecting an enemy to suddenly appear, intrude and do harm."[9] It takes deliberate, determined and faith-based activity to notice and shed prejudice, jealousy and worry. Such decisive action enables us to "convert the *hostis* into a *hospes*, the enemy into a guest and to create the free and fearless space where brotherhood and sisterhood can be formed and fully experienced." Hospitality is not passive tolerance. Rather, we actively and intentionally open ourselves to others, creating a refreshing space for ministry.

In C. S. Lewis's terms, the act of hospitality surges more from gift love than need love. Within the encounter itself, both sides do benefit. At the outset, one member is offering love from a position of security while the other is vulnerable and seeking. This version of intentional welcoming challenges another modern cultural trend. Hospitality in the current day functions more as a recreational activity or an entertainment sideline. In Christian circles, hospitality may be portrayed as a spiritual gift. This designation can make hospitality seem applicable only to an inspired few—responsibility shifts only to those whom God has commissioned. But according to Nouwen, God charges all believers with the practice of hospitality as a way of expressing love. It is a way of welcoming others that reflects the direction, devotion, maturity and quality of our spiritual lives.

Nouwen's call for hospitality finds roots in a rich biblical context. Scripture recognizes this practice as a solemn social requirement with spiritual repercussions. The Old Testament stage is set, we recall, within a nomadic world amid desert terrain and perilous political alliances.[10] Any sojourner exiting one's homeland to enter foreign territory consciously engaged in a life-endangering undertaking. Traveling through the rugged and arid landscape made reliance on established locals a necessity. The code known as the *love of strangers* evolved into the dominant rule of the land. Granting hospitality to a traveler was an essential, non-negotiable social and political responsibility. The culture deemed this practice so imperative that the traveler could assume traveling mercies as an established right.

---

[9]Ibid., p. 46.
[10]Paul J. Achtemeier, *Society of Biblical Literature: Harper's Bible Dictionary*, 1st ed. (San Francisco: HarperCollins, 1985), p. 408.

A prime example of the extensive effort ancient Near Eastern culture dedicated to showing hospitality to the traveler occurs when Abraham entertains three unknown men (Gen 18). In the passage, Abraham interrupts a dramatic period of prayer to plead with these passers-by to pause and allow him the privilege to host. His actions display his intense investment to transform these strangers into guests and guests into friends. This demonstrates the aim of these important customs: to build loyalty and establish an alliance. He brings water for washing, has his wife Sarah bake bread from the finest flour, handpicks a choice calf and has it prepared for a gourmet meal, and stands by a tree while these strangers reap the benefits of his hospitality. The passage moves back and forth between how Abraham entertains these guests to the messages delivered from God regarding his unique plans for Abraham and Sarah. The modern reader would miss the point of the passage by attributing Abraham's attentiveness to his awareness that the Lord was revealing his plans in these conversations. Instead, Abraham honors the Lord through the routine but earnest expression of social etiquette. And God returns that favor by adding blessing after blessing.

Given our modern modes of travel, comprehension of these hospitality practices requires a substantial crosscultural mental adjustment. In the Old Testament, the host would willingly assume the status of a servant in his own surroundings to grant esteem and honor to the one being entertained. A host offered protective freedom. His home was to be a secure, friendly space to rest, refresh and refuel. The host made a serious commitment to produce all the necessities for the sake of the traveler's journey. Hospitality extended so far within the nomadic setting that a host would place the benefits of his human possessions at a guest's disposal. Further, to accent the nearly total reversal of roles, the host would express thanks to the traveler for the honor of granting hospitality! Finally, the host offered shelter and nurture in blind faith based on a cultural understanding that the stranger would never attempt to violate the trust willingly granted.[11] This expression of hospitality was a decisive action designed to turn stranger into ally. This strategic motivation behind hospitality clashes with common sense and everyday practice in our contemporary cultural setting. Commercial enterprises or social service systems exist to assist strangers. Etiquette insists on steady trust-building through prescribed exchanges. Only a fool would extend hospitality without ample evidence that an outsider can sensibly be merged within our intimate circle.

---

[11]B. S. Easton, "Hospitality," in *The International Standard Bible Encyclopaedia*, ed. James Orr (Grand Rapids: Eerdmans, 1939), pp. 1432-33.

Jesus understood the cultural importance and function of hospitality when he sent out his disciples to "heal the sick, raise the dead, cleanse those who have leprosy, [and] drive out demons" (Mt 10:8). The disciples were to "take no bag for the journey" (Mt 10:10). They could expect to be granted hospitality as they made their way doing the bidding of their Lord. One might mistakenly assume that the disciples would anticipate this basic care out of respect for Jesus as Rabbi or to honor their service to the Lord of the universe. This was not likely at this stage of Jesus' ministry. Hospitality would primarily have been bestowed on those novice disciples due to the cultural mandate of the historical period and geographic region.

Customs related to hospitality evolved as cities matured, roads were constructed and shipping routes became conventional. Commercial establishments rose to accommodate the steady comings and goings of caravans. Despite the availability of a developing travel industry, New Testament believers were sternly admonished to engage in the practice of granting hospitality to strangers. This was particularly applicable to those in need. Acts of hospitality for the distressed testified to one's love of Jesus Christ. "Do not forget to entertain strangers, for by so doing some people have entertained angels without knowing it" (Heb 13:2). Such practice fulfilled what Jesus referenced when he encouraged kindness to the unfortunate, rejected and thirsty stranger. He suggested that the grace of hospitality be extended as if he himself were the guest to be refreshed by the "cup of cold water" provided to the victim or outsider in dire circumstances (Mt 10:42; 25:34-45).

The biblical roots of hospitality set the platform for exploring how the hostility to hospitality continuum contributes to caring within group work. Any application must maintain three points regarding Nouwen's framework. First, the three relational dimensions are inseparable and without sequential order. Any segregation of these polarities reduces complex relational territory to a mere cognitive map. Second, these attitudes are deeply imbedded within our internal working model. Our entire bio-psycho-social-spiritual nature maintains them. The narratives that fill our constant thought flow guide our activities. Achieving a God-honoring attitude on any of these polarities will require dedication, grace, novel relational experience and opportunity for practice. Last, these relational positions apply to all believers and therefore are applicable to all group members, not only leaders. Granting these points, hospitality practices that change people from strangers to allies reflect a group's progression from basic polite cooperation to a more advanced consolidation of relational learning.

Thus those in formal helping relationships must determine boldly to cultivate a climate of hospitality. This applies to counselors, medical specialists, spiritual directors, pastors and for our purposes, group shepherds. Appropriating the term *hospitality* to ministry-oriented relating implies a correspondence between those engaged in fostering corrective emotional relationships and the practice of hospitality. In our day, the therapeutic setting of a clinic or the care of souls in pastoral ministry establishes a defined space to offer the weary sojourner encouragement for renewal, growth and healing. Christian helpers share hospitality out of their love for Christ. This requires an active realignment of any and all of a guide's defensive postures. The love and grace of God is expressed toward the stranger, who in this case is a person in need. Nouwen observed the following difficulty in constructing warm interpersonal hospitality within today's professional ethos:

> In our society technocratic streamlining has depersonalized the interpersonal aspect of the healing professions to a high degree and increasing demands often force the healer to keep some emotional distance to prevent overinvolvement with his patient.[12]

Professional helpers face the challenge of how to practice hospitality in an active, relationship-enhancing manner while still remaining true to the boundaries necessary for both ethical and empirically supported practice. In Christian ministry, leaders puzzle over how to institute a caring ambiance without compromising the gospel and the message of Scripture. Neither scenario can sustain blanket acceptance of all client perceptions, values and choices. Confrontation may be necessary while the hospitality-building process continues. Correcting or redirecting a wanderer is an act of mercy, not offense. The Christian shepherd does not give up truth or witness when welcoming a stranger with different views.

Nonetheless, since the Lord is leading, the hostility of our private fears, worries or prejudices must not energize occasions for challenge. Admonitions will be spoken and shared in love. A pervasive effort to demonstrate loyalty frames all communications of correction. The challenge has a greater likelihood of being received as the entire endeavor establishes an alliance for the welfare of the other. This demands that the leader's self be grounded in solitude and groomed by dependent prayer. Such an alliance fosters readiness to enter into refreshing relationship. It requires that the helper instill graciousness and genuineness within the encounter. Picture Abraham serving the needs of those strangers as he en-

---

[12]Nouwen, *Reaching Out,* p. 85.

tertained the Lord's representatives. He bowed down before them, made himself a servant and implored those wayfarers to become visitors by resting under his attentive watch. Abraham created the atmosphere of welcoming through every intentional gesture of refreshment and promotion of the guest's welfare. Leaders expend this level of passion when extending Christian hospitality.

This notion applied to a group demands more than the guide simply adopting a non-defensive stance. Extending a welcome compels an inner attitude adjustment and outward deliberate labor, both of which promote productive peace and acceptance. Helpers assertively move to bring visitors into the experiential warmth of their love for strangers. Cordial hosts modify their interpersonal style to ease the sense of distance, to reduce the tension of unfamiliarity and to bridge the gap resulting from the lack of shared experience. The Holy Spirit can use this active yet unpretentious outreach advocated by Nouwen as a sign of a Christ connection in order to melt hostility and promote relational connection.

When believers extend biblical hospitality using contemporary approaches, they bring soul concerns within the healing reach of the church community. A trekking guide stimulates such activity by infusing care into everything from the group's mission to the screening interviews, from themes introduced to conversations encouraged. Following the guide's lead, trekkers themselves are motivated through modeling to become a conduit for God's redemptive and restorative love.

HOSPITALITY FOR HEALING

So, what does modeling hospitality really look like? More to the point, what do participants notice when a group leader demonstrates care that stimulates hospitality within a ministry group? After all, Abraham's precise actions cannot be replicated in current common-theme groups. Providing refreshing beverages, homemade bread, cheeses and rest time could be an enticement to participate. Butchering and roasting fresh veal right off the hoof would take the parallel far too literally. Rather than the social expectations of the ancient Near East, Abraham's persistence, energy and service posture in demonstrating hospitality provides an exemplary model for group leaders. Such persistence, energy and posture provide an inclusive ministry to transform strangers into guests, then guests into allies.

Fortunately, extensive group counseling literature details a variety of experiences that participants identify as valuable, refreshing and memorable for facilitating closeness and change. In order to explore how hospitality fosters healing,

Irvin D. Yalom, one of the most prominent group therapy figures over the past thirty years, once again makes important contributions.[13] His experience, extensive research and review of considerable empirical material coalesced into a refined set of pivotal therapeutic factors in group success.[14] A selection of these will flesh out my response to the question of what hospitality generates and actually looks like within groups.[15]

The four healing elements that display hospitality tend to be important early in the trek: hope, universality, imparting information and altruism. These apply nicely to the common-theme style of group advanced in this study. Hospitality has its desired impact when participants witness any combination of these elements. First, *hope* makes a quiet but definitive entrance. The very possibility of involvement in an activity that holds promise for a desirable outcome contributes to a light atmosphere. Hope is like a soft breeze cutting through stifling humidity on a hot muggy night. This little four-letter word conveys an expectation of fulfillment, a simple idea with incredible potential for good. Hope awakens the imagination even with limited fanfare and no obvious celebration. Leaders do well to blow tenderly on each slight spark that hope ignites. For example, a leader may describe the mission of the trek with a sense of confidence that the journey will actually make a difference. This rekindles hope. Or a leader may preserve hope by conducting a care-filled screening procedure. Excluding a potential participant can be an act of care. Leaders protect the other participants when some possible members are directed elsewhere for help because their current characteristics, level of motivation or circumstances make it unlikely that they will

---

[13]Irvin D. Yalom and Molyn Leszcz, *The Theory and Practice of Group Psychotherapy,* 5th ed. (New York: Basic Books, 2005), pp. 1-18.

[14]These identified elements of group work were for many years referenced by Yalom as "curative" factors. This is the rubric that I both learned and taught. Yalom explains that the decline in positivistic assumptions has resulted in a humbler view of the impact of these critical factors. This explains the change in terminology from curative to therapeutic. In bringing these into this discussion of brief groups within Christian settings, the newer label is appropriate and provides an even better fit. Ibid., p. xiii.

[15]These factors were initially distilled from extensive interviews with both group leaders and participants. As objective research tools and methods developed, extensive validation research followed. Yalom and Leszcz explain in their most recent review that it is now possible to discuss which features are more prominent in what type of groups at particular stages of development. This demonstrates considerable progress. See ibid., pp. 77-115. Two points should be noted. Yalom holds that while these elements provide useful insights, the entire process of group counseling is extremely complex. Therefore it would be a serious mistake to reduce the benefits of group work to any single or simple combination of these factors as if they occurred in isolation. Second, my review of published studies in Christian-oriented journals did not uncovered research that has addressed these factors. My application to ministry settings must be viewed as both speculative and tentative.

eventually form helping alliances within the group. Screening and interviews send a message of care to those who join. Such actions are leader moves, but ultimately the leader does not provide the therapeutic hope. Rather, members communicate shared hope with other members; their very decision to join the trek reaches out toward hope. When this anticipation can be infused into early conversations between participants, it is contagious and has an instantaneous benefit. Participants in successful groups report the powerful ingredient of hope as a critical beneficial factor of the shared experience.

Second and closely related, relief stems for the experience of *universality*.[16] Each life dilemma, obstacle or challenge perpetuates an internal myth of absolute uniqueness: "Why me?" This breeds isolation. Our inner subjectivity can feed a frenzy of inadequacy, separation and unproductive distinctiveness. When a group convenes, others bring their personal stories, dreams and perhaps, parallel experiences. The infusion of companions who face similar hurdles breaks the loneliness barrier and begins movement toward a bearable solitude. A leader can initially deliver the message that trekkers are not alone in their journey, and its comfort may be heard. But when members experience hospitality between one another, the relief of community drives that encouragement into the sojourner's heart. Shared hospitality induces people to abandon the familiar but isolated hiding place and walk openly beside others with increased confidence.

Third, when people come together, they immediately fill a resource pool for *imparting information*. A leader may promise to teach, make referrals to useful resources and shed light on matters formerly misunderstood or mysterious. But members multiply this healing phenomenon tenfold. As the group gets underway, members confirm the very real potential for informational support. The leader can prime the pump with a reference list, a presentation of basic facts or predictions about what lies ahead. It does not take much to swell the informational pool. But most participants thrive on exposing their own discoveries and lessons from the school of hard knocks. Each participant has collected pieces of wisdom along life's pathway that take on renewed freshness when they are passed along to another who finds the idea novel and innovative.

Finally, *altruism* or giving to others while attending to one's own issues surely signifies that hospitality has taken hold. Openhanded generosity, not merely soaking in nourishment exclusively for their own needs, refreshes group members. The naive notion that people with issues will have little to offer others can be a frontline objection to committing to a group. How can someone present

---

[16]Ibid., p. 6.

assistance or perspective when personal issues are so prominent? Can the over-whelmed have anything to offer? The leader steadily introduces members to the fundamentals of group work and each one learns how to be a resource for others. The uninformed slander of group therapy as "blind leading the blind" soon fades away. Trekkers receive renewed energy and encouragement by kindheartedly giving to fellow travelers.

These four factors of hope, universality, imparting information and altruism represent only a portion of a group's therapeutic factors.[17] When considering these elements, leaders do best not to treat these constructs as the discrete build-ing blocks of group experience. Instead they supply words to some of the various factors that combine to make the group welcoming to participants. These factors capture the complexity of human beings relating intensely and intentionally with one another. Awareness of these phenomena enables a group leader to discern the moods, moments and movements within the subtle process that unfolds within a relational encounter. Group members experience the tension and relief that flows from interpersonal relating through some unique combination of hope, univer-sality, exchanging information and expressions of altruism.

A trekking guide performs a fundamental service by summoning the group into existence, preparing the proposal, setting the conditions, and screening through the selection and matching of members with careful attention. Defin-ing parameters, clarifying expectations and ensuring a reasonable commitment to participation protect the integrity of the group through its early unstable ex-istence. These priorities are not self-serving. Careful activities promote the wel-fare of all those willing to take the journey. The leader then performs a second necessary service by giving hospitality a tone, rhythm and melody. The opening strains begin to rise as the leader exhibits concern for members by recollect-ing details, recalling requests and expressing empathy. Members are accepted as participants even with their mixtures of motives, layers of resistance and unique impossible scenarios. Most important, the leader conveys the one quality that is impracticable for any other to demonstrate: a vision for what the group can become. The leader's conviction regarding the group's soul-care possibilities re-freshes and gives life to hospitality. To illustrate hospitality's importance further, let's return to Devin's efforts on Surfing True.

---

[17]While the number and exact titles have changed over the years, Yalom and Leszcz place the list of therapeutic factors at eleven: instillation of hope, universality, imparting information, altru-ism, corrective recapitulation of the primary family group, development of socializing techniques, imitative behavior, interpersonal learning, group cohesiveness, catharsis and existential factors. Ibid., p. 2.

It was the appointed meeting for Devin to update the church leadership in general terms on the status of pastoral care initiatives related to sexual purity. Devin could hear an echo in his head as he spoke to the elders and fellow pastors. His explanations felt shaky even to him. "The motivation to change isn't out there." The bottom line was that Surfing True was dead in the water. He had exchanged messages with eight men and one woman. After interviewing two, only one was ready to proceed. If the need was so great, it was not reflected in the responses he'd heard over the past month. Devin heard statements like: "Now that I've made my decision, change will be no big deal." "This is a real personal thing, so I've got to handle it myself." "Knowing that you will pray for me is all the help I need." Such rugged words resounded as hollow to Devin. Yet what could he say? The ministry team who heard Devin's status report was not nearly as discouraged as he. This area was a stronghold and they had recognized that right from the start. This spiritual battleground warranted dedicated prayer. Contacts would continue to be referred to Devin. Per standard practice, the particulars of appropriate pastoral care in these cases were left entirely for him to determine. After the meeting a veteran elder, respected for both spiritual maturity and success in the business world, pulled Devin aside to share his point of view. Devin had been nicely affirmed by the support of his fellow caregivers. Now he was about to be stunned by the gut-wrenching words of this trusted elder.

"Devin, my sense is that your instincts are on target. Surfing True has promise. I would like to share two areas of trepidation." This personal style of candid feedback was not a regular occurrence. This gentleman spoke with kindness and astute insight. Devin was intrigued and had ears to hear. The elder began with vague references to former career duties, being worn down as a "road warrior" and being uncomfortably accustomed with moral failure. Details were hidden yet Devin sensed resolve regarding the anguish beneath. Then the elder spoke directly to Devin. "When you speak about sexual sin, there's anger in you at the insidious nature of the problem. Your concern for the person who's been crushed gets lost." Devin felt the weight of the challenge as a few worn-out old phrases were tossed back and forth. Was there any chance that he was coming across as hating both the sin and the sinner? Was hostility in his heart driving those with needs further away? Then the elder spoke very softly: "Devin, come to terms with what makes this a supercharged matter for you." There was no rancor or ill will in his tone, only empathy. They exchanged a few critical observations and the elder committed to pray. Then he made an offer. "When Surfing True is ready, consider using the conference room in my building. It's extremely private, the parking is conveniently in the rear, it's only a few blocks from the church, and the coffee will be on me." Devin caught the central concern regarding a secure and neutral meeting place; it had been hard even for him to grasp the intensity of the shame that cripples spiritually sensitive men when it came to behavior related to sexual purity. Devin determined to proceed differently. He would prepare, speak and anticipate from a heart ready to minister to the density of such shame. Perhaps the Lord was already answering prayer and working on the stronghold.

LEADERS AS AUTHENTIC CHAMELEONS

The phrase *authentic chameleon* may appear an oxymoron. The core meaning of authenticity is sincerity and truthfulness. Authenticity implies being the real thing on the inside that one portrays on the outside. On the other hand, a chameleon is a small, weird lizard whose skin changes color according to the shade of the surroundings. Doesn't this make a chameleon the polar opposite of authenticity? What is a chameleon's real color and why doesn't it consistently show its true skin? These questions indicate why this adaptable lizard has become synonymous with superficiality and a lack of inner conviction. Even the dictionary provides a secondary definition of the term *chameleon* as "a person given to often expedient or facile change in ideas or character."[18] Based on this usage, *chameleon* could be a favored insult for fickle people or Christians who lack courage in their faith commitment.

In Philippians 3:2, perhaps one could imagine substituting *chameleons* for Paul's *dogs:* "Watch out for those chameleons, those men who do evil, those mutilators of the flesh." Paul was making reference to those who wanted converts to Christianity to blend into Judaism by following Jewish rules and customs. In this context, he uses a culturally demeaning term by equating these false teachers with dogs. Dogs in Paul's world were barely domestic scavengers; they were not the pampered pets of today. Paul interjects the term *dogs* to categorize and condemn the insincere, manipulative behavior of those who would make those newly freed from sin through Christ into slaves of Jewish law. Access to the grace of the gospel was not restricted to the circumcised. In this example, Scripture guides believers away from conformity for convenience. In the vernacular, acting like a chameleon suggests behavior that is expedient to please the person or group in a dominant position. The follower of Jesus Christ who seeks to help others heal, grow and mature may frantically avoid behavior associated with a lack of

---

[18]Merriam-Webster, Inc. *Merriam-Webster's Collegiate Dictionary,* 11th ed. (Springfield, Mass.: Merriam-Webster, 2003).

backbone and conviction. Who would aspire to become like a creepy lizard that absorbs its identity from the environment? There is no honor in fearfully hiding by blending into the background. What quality of life could there be in fading into the immediate decor? Last, something about a chameleon seems profoundly un-American too. True individuals show themselves for who they really are and don't blend quietly into background obscurity. A philosophy of rugged individualism does not esteem the chameleon.

But consider possible motives for this type of adaptation. For the little lizard, such change is a matter of survival. Disciples of Jesus Christ see a matter of how best to serve the Master. For example, Paul clearly took the position that there are indeed times and circumstances to blend with the surrounding culture or immediate company in order to gain a listening ear. "To the weak I became weak, to win the weak. I have become all things to all men so that by all possible means I might save some. I do all this for the sake of the gospel, that I may share in its blessings" (1 Cor 9:22-23). Paul insists that adaptation and adjustment are not forbidden. Rather, it is a matter of who and what is motivating such behavior. Christians maintain convictions for the sake of Christ and his kingdom. Voluntary submission to the needs of others to bring them into that very kingdom glorifies the Lord. Paul addresses this principle at length regarding the correctness of consuming meat previously offered to idols (see 1 Cor 8:13; 10:23-33). To eat or not to eat is a wisdom matter involving how to inspire conversions and extend an effective Christian testimony. On this practice, there were no absolute behavioral prescriptions. From this perspective, perhaps a chameleon need not have such a negative image. The mission and ministry of Jesus Christ himself gives the most potent argument in defense of adaptation for the sake of the gospel. The Son of God took on real human flesh and pitched a tent among plain, ordinary people (Jn 1:14; Phil 2:6-8). He humbled himself by blending into humanity to bring glory to the Father and to provide for our salvation. The physical appearance of Jesus Christ camouflaged from many the true nature of his person, both fully human and fully divine.

Even the origin of the term *chameleon* speaks to the potential of wise adaptation. Chameleon is carried over from the French *chamai*, literally meaning "on the ground" and *leon* translated as "lion." So a chameleon is a "lion on the ground." That word picture, in the present discussion, emerges as an image of a firmly grounded, flexible and finely attuned wonder of our Creator. A chameleon avoids center stage to accomplish its ultimate purpose. Perhaps a creature that is purposeful, patient and effective in adjusting to its environment does not conflict with the idea of authenticity, consistency and honesty, after all.

A clinician with behaviorist leanings named Arnold Lazarus first applied the term *authentic chameleon* to counselors more than a decade ago.[19] The upside to his staunch theoretical orientation was that the therapist universally performed as a detached scientist, meticulously collecting data regarding all aspects of the person-environment interaction. Lazarus himself is best known for devising a clinical assessment grid that systematically examined multiple domains and jointly guided the counselor and client toward a corrective plan.[20] But Lazarus also identified the downside to a systematic model. He noted that drive toward research-level objectivity drove therapists to operate as sterile mechanics. Behaviorally oriented clinicians viewed themselves as scientists first, perhaps displaying greater concern for flawless technique than for the actual patient. His solution to the modern quest for a universal helping style was the imagery of the helper as authentic chameleon. In order to facilitate treatment, increase compliance and reduce resistance, the helper applies a "flexible repertoire of relational styles and stances to suit the clients' needs and expectations."[21] True to his behaviorist leanings, Lazarus avoids jargon and labels in favor of straightforward descriptions. Implementation requires a sincere effort to construct a collaborative alliance by making strategic choices that match client need. For Lazarus, a modification in relational style or stance had pragmatic meaning:

> Whether and when to be cold, warm or tepid; when and when not to be confrontational; when and whether to be earthy, chummy, casual, and informal rather than "professional;" when to self-disclose or remain enigmatic; when to be soft-nosed, gentle and tender, and when to come on like a tough army sergeant; and how to adjust my levels of supportiveness and directiveness.[22]

Remember that Lazarus made this application to helping efforts with individual clients and was not addressing group interventions. Is there any realistic possibility of bringing a relational style by choice into group work? When among differing needs, to whom does the leader adjust? An instance in my own group work comes to mind.

---

[19]Arnold Lazarus, "Authentic Chameleons: Tailoring the Therapeutic Relationship," *Psychotherapy: Theory, Research, Practice, Training* 30 (1993): 404-7.

[20]The approach was called "multimodal" therapy and followed a sequence called the BASIC ID or Behavior, Affect, Sensation, Imagery, Cognition, Interpersonal, Drugs/biology. Arnold Lazarus, *The Practice of Multimodal Therapy* (Baltimore: John Hopkins University Press, 1989).

[21]Lazarus, "Authentic Chameleons," p. 405.

[22]Ibid.

The group session had come to an end and the room was nearly empty. A smiling participant threw a parting comment toward me that rode the fence between compliment and condemnation. Her perception was that my leader behavior over the past hour had been markedly different. When I invited her to explain her observation, she rehashed several instances when my words endorsed the direction, but my pace "applied the brakes." Her conclusion was that over the past few weeks, my efforts had generally heightened intensity. Today, there was more tranquility in my leadership. The session had been dynamic and lively with considerable collaborate interaction. She specifically cited the juncture where the group had steadily raised the force of therapeutic pressure on a reserved member, shy by temperament, who frequently stayed well within safe territory. This was primetime. The pressure was on target and the opportunity ripe. The group was prepared to assist the member to engage in risk beyond previous willingness. The summary I offered at that precise instant essentially granted that quiet member a reprieve and afforded her the opportunity to consider her options further. According to this observer, my face had dropped its more typical intense presence and even my voice turned mellow. The term *chameleon* was never evoked. Nonetheless, she'd caught me in the act of exhibiting flexibility in relational style. A thrilling trekking memory occurred not two weeks later. The introverted member was once again fully engaged with her peers as my previous inquisitor coached tentatively, quietly and effectively. Those strangers formed an alliance with a steady and reassuring message of "move when ready." The coach, who had once noted the variation in my approach, now adjusted her own. This enabled her timid ally to respond.

A group leader increases therapeutic mobility by pondering the wonder of those little lions on the ground. Drawing attention to oneself by any surprising action, provocative words or unpredictable intervention does not belong. Instead, leaders operate by the dominant principle of consistency in demonstrating care. They do not compromise themselves or their values to increase their prestige or popularity. Leader behavior does not conform to the pressures of the group, the expectations of the majority or the will of the influential. As an authentic chameleon, a group leader demonstrates an extraordinary sensitivity to participant relational needs and then instinctively adjusts when this would best communicate hospitality. This may involve altering the degree of emotional closeness, the stance of subjective vs. objective involvement or the overt demonstration of investment level in the change process. By attending to client readiness, member-to-member interactions and group cohesiveness, the leader can apply a flexible repertoire of relational styles in the interest of initiating hospitality. It does not matter if anyone notices. Rejoice when strangers are made to feel like guests and guests form alliances. Each functioning group has a distinct relational mix. Through this diversity, members learn to adjust to others within this stimulating blend of unique persons.

A CHANGE OF HEART

A number of months had flipped over on the calendar. Devin faced the ministry leadership team and offered a marvelous update. Surfing True was now up. This was no stunning success story with big numbers. Each week, six guys were plugging along with one another to honor the Lord in the pursuit of sexual integrity in thought and behavior. A central event had assisted in bringing the group into reality. Another major scandal had hit the nightly news a few months back. This exposed a recognized evangelical leader caught in a flagrant moral failure related to sexual sin. Devin thought this had brought his current crew forward by pressing their readiness to enter the group. This was pure speculation. He did not mention that a barrier had broken down within him even though he knew this invisible shift had silently played a part.

What he did know for sure was that in each session, he was increasingly blessed. The experience appeared mutual. Devin kept his comments in his report to the leadership global. Inwardly, he held a vivid recollection in his recent memory and this allowed passion to escape. A great joy flooded his senses when he recalled one member, beset with shame, finally telling his story. Rather than receiving condemnation, a hardy sense of "we're there" had surfaced. The teller was accepted despite his failings. In one of the rarest of moments, this man grappled up close and personal with the concept of grace as a paralyzing burden lifted. Devin knew that what he and others had witnessed that evening was truly and unspeakably beautiful. He finished with an invitation to spread the word that the second round of Surfing True would be starting up before too long. The group would be honored to interview and welcome others into this journey. The surface was rough, but the water was fine. Devin returned the smile as he caught the gaze of the elder who'd helped infuse hospitality into this ministry. An issue that previously stirred hostility now invited strangers to a community colored with compassion. There was a distinct possibility that this renewed hope for change would spread.

Section Four

LEADING TOWARD
AFFECT AND ATTACHMENT

9

ENTERTAINING TREKKERS UNAWARE

LANDMARKS AHEAD

This chapter and the next examine the function that enables leaders to find sure footing when negotiating awkward trails. Guides direct trekkers to face emotional material that regulates connectivity in relationships; in other words, they stimulate affect. Recognizing emotion and relational risk taking strengthens all interactive human process. God works by his Spirit to redeem human beings, remedy the broken relationship with himself and instigate a consecrated walk with him. Jesus Christ accomplishes his good work in the midst of critical human interactions. The chapter draws on the Gospel of John and his vital portrayals of Jesus Christ. The excursion conceptualizes the stirring and shaping of spiritual growth in groups. John's vivid word pictures offer a means to pursue wisdom within small group work.[1] Jesus Christ becomes the life-infusing essence of intimate relational exchanges. Our initial path surveys literature about the third leader function, leading toward affect and attachment. We find applications to this important goal when we consider a wedding that Jesus rescued. The trail concludes by unpacking rich metaphors that describe Jesus' provision of abundant life.

CAUTIOUS CONNECTIVITY

Group therapeutic literature uses the term *emotional stimulation* to mean activities that intensify the "experience and expression of affect in the group."[2] The concept is the same as the leader function introduced earlier as *affect*. This function uniquely contributes to establishing a climate where participants can recognize relational process and experience decisive growth. Earlier the concept of corrective emotional relationship (CER) described affect-laden, personal en-

---

[1]The ideas contained in this chapter are general enough to be applicable to a wide range of helping groups utilized in ministry. These reflect matters central to the functioning of the priesthood of believers and thus are not limited for exclusive use in common-theme groups. The same blessings may occur in any gathering of believers as Jesus Christ instills abundant life.

[2]Virginia Brabender, *Introduction to Group Therapy* (Hoboken, N.J.: Wiley, 2002), p. 154.

counters that result in redemptive shifts in relational adaptability. The ultimate CER is a joyful exchange with the Creator, who loves to walk with his children as we worship, pray and allow his Word to permeate our hearts. The Lord revises the relational dimensions within us involving self, others and God. This overtly Christian, simplified explanation of a vastly intricate process does not promote emotional outpouring purely for the rush or cathartic effect. Catharsis may release repressed or held-down, intense feelings, but merely diminishing internal pressure cannot serve as the goal of bringing affect to the surface. Rather, I wish to emphasize the relational benefit of affective expression when people dismantle their barriers to interpersonal connection. I recast the leader function of emotional stimulation in conjunction with the formation of bonds with others, thus revising the function's label from *emotional stimulation* to *leading toward affect and attachment*. The function involves contributing to interpersonal exchange by directly promoting commonly avoided affective states, and in so doing, demonstrating how safe expression can facilitate intimacy. When leaders give attention to emotional states and guide constructive communication, they help group members turn into a community. Exposure of affect enables participants to establish new supportive affiliations and deepen existing attachments.

Communication within a working, collaborative group conveys a force exceeding that of routine, casual conversation. Leaders influence group norms that regulate the acceptable intensity level. Those who fulfill this particular function will open opportunities for the entry of affect that is not customary in everyday Christian study sessions or gatherings. This should not imply an anything-goes atmosphere or a reckless let-it-all-out standard; emotional nudity is never the objective. Instead, modest emotional arousal and engagement maintains the steady press to address concerns and pursue change within the group as a whole. Leader behavior associated with this function generally conveys these characteristics: revealing affect in self, others and the communication between; fostering direct conversation and confrontation; challenging inconsistencies; and exposing limiting assumptions or beliefs.[3] A prepared leader models risk taking through the vulnerable expression of both tough and tender emotions. Ideally, these disclosures contain enough differentiation to allow for vibrant descriptions of the color combinations of coexisting emotional states. For example, in real life, anger and admiration, joy and sorrow, disappointment and happiness coexist.[4] Leaders

---

[3]Morton Lieberman, Irvin D. Yalom and Matthew B. Miles, *Encounter Groups: First Facts* (New York: Basic Books, 1973), pp. 238-48.
[4]For a recent treatment of the intersection of cognition and emotions from a New Testament perspective, see Matthew A. Elliott, *Faithful Feelings: Rethinking Emotion in the New Testament*

stimulate emotional expression within the group by displaying transparency and modeling self-disclosure with discretion. Revealing current reactions related to being together (here and now) is considered more productive than retrospection (there and then). Shorter statements that exchange and clarify affect can be more potent than long stories. Demonstration done well inspires participants toward deeper, free-flowing transparency.[5] It does not attract undue attention to the leader, but instead equips members to delve into currents within their own inner emotional states.[6]

Relational patterns, beliefs and automatic assumptions revealed by emotional reactivity identify a participant's optimal zone for interpersonal learning. Leaders do not mine emotion in a blind search for cathartic expression, nor do they merely engender an informed response to the ever-popular counseling query, "How do you feel about that?" The discovery, definition and expression of one's immediate emotional state all contribute to a broader pursuit. The effort is intended to produce a shift in the prevailing focus from content to process, from topical- to relational-level communication. Attunement to emotional cues may raise awareness of automatic or intuitive reactions and reveal the hierarchy of inner values. Identifying discrepancies between verbal and non-verbal communication reveals inconsistencies between intent and impact. When emotion and cognition intersect, they yield insight into relational bonds, barriers and friction. A leader grants permission and gives voice to the affective layer, thereby making sense of the communication hits and misses in the immediate fledgling friendships.

The leader affect-stimulation behavior described above can indeed activate closer relational bonds, but three qualifications are in order. First, the assembly of a group in itself generates mild to moderate anxiety within participants.[7] For certain

---

(Grand Rapids: Kregel, 2006).

[5]See Irvin D. Yalom and Molyn Leszcz, *The Theory and Practice of Group Psychotherapy*, 5th ed. (New York: Basic Books, 2005), pp. 136, 374-81.

[6]Might the leader function of emotional stimulation be another way of characterizing a leader's charismatic qualities? Barbender offers her conclusion based on the Lieberman, Yalom and Miles (1973) study. A charismatic leader in the sense of an extraverted or engaging personality (not 'spirit-filled') may be viewed by members as exhibiting high levels of emotional stimulating behavior. It does not follow that members flourish under such a dramatic leader who may be entertaining or who draws attention to himself. This function does not point to a particular personality type as the most effective group leader.

[7]It is with only mild hesitation that I include anxiety within this discussion of emotional stimulation without extensive explanation. My assumptions regarding anxiety have been influenced by dynamically oriented therapists thanks to my longtime friend and practice partner Brian Fast, Psy.D. This perspective views anxiety as a sign that more primitive emotional impulses are threatening existing superego defenses and may surface. If the ego is afforded reasonable support and less threatening conditions, the emotional impulse may safely surface and be tolerated. See Habib

potential members, the whole idea of sharing private dilemmas and dreams with mysterious others churns up so much inner fervor that the resulting panic prohibits dedication to the entire enterprise. This fear is one of the foremost reasons for the pervasive resistance to group helping interventions. The prevailing preference for individually oriented, expert-seeker dyads over the joint mutual assistance of a group reflects the gripping apprehension of going public. Take for example a frequent occurrence in orientation sessions. An interested candidate will express eagerness to observe a group but will avoid the threatening commitment to actively participate. Before forging bonds of trust and visualizing behavioral norms, participation feels ominous. The imagination strangely escalates this social anxiety to the point that sharing aloud carries the momentous weight of speaking to a menacing mob. The leader must sensitively monitor this tendency. Take to heart this essential guiding premise: emotional arousal facilitates participation; undue anxiety cripples openness to establish trust. In a sense, anticipatory stress in groups runs parallel to performance anxiety in sports, academia and the arts. Moderate levels are deemed useful for optimal investment, mental acuity and alertness. Whether running onto the playing field, writing an examination or stepping on stage, the right measure of angst—with its accompanying physiological counterparts—can bring out one's best contribution. Thus a leader fosters a reasonable dose of baseline anxiety for both the particular group and the unique individual participants. Ongoing assessment of anxiety levels allows for optimal regulation of the degree of emotionally oriented challenge introduced.

Second, the successful group session cannot be characterized by chaos or affective bedlam. Leaders don't take on the task of inciting maximum emotional expression, thinking that an adrenaline rush accompanied by demonstrative meltdowns will produce therapeutic growth. If this were the ideal, then all collective helping ventures would be converted into a contrived and contorted survival game. The interpersonal quarrels that inevitably surface under extremely competitive or adverse conditions spark the predictably tumultuous drama suited to the unending stream of reality entertainment shows. What emerges from eccentric individual personalities, odd alliances and group conduct in the presence of conflict is indeed fascinating. Human beings are drawn to watch others

---

Davanloo, *Unlocking the Unconscious: Selected Papers of Habib Davanloo* (New York: Wiley, 1990), or Diane Fosha, *The Transforming Power of Affect: A Model for Accelerated Change* (New York: Basic Books, 2000). In group sessions, I am likely to explain that anxiety is a complex fear fueled by a mixture of other intense emotions. This may be overly simplistic, yet it points to emotional material beneath or hidden by anxiety. It is important to associate anxiety in groups with the relational issues such as trust, acceptance, value and worth. Empathy is key to any productive response.

struggle under intense emotional and social pressure with a voracious, voyeuristic appetite. Unusual and potentially threatening environmental conditions produce waves of stress, awaken flight or fight responses, and stir interpersonal turmoil in a raw and rowdy form.

By contrast, when considering leader activity in terms of stimulating and using affect, it may be useful to remember the old childhood story of Goldilocks. When Goldilocks raided the home of the three bears, she avoided soup that was too hot or too cold, chairs that were overly large or small, and beds that were painfully hard or annoyingly soft. Her comfort zone was in the mid-range and that was "just right." Goldilocks's preferences can guide the leader in the application of an experience-based technique or conversational challenge to open up vulnerable material. The use of emotional material in groups is not irresponsible provocation but a matter that requires discerning members' readiness for risk. The promise of affective expression for realizing change warrants no reckless or random behavior. In stimulating affect, leaders inspire productivity within the group and progress toward members' self-selected goals.[8]

Contemporary, empirically based literature on helping groups offers considerable insight into the skills and tools that leaders utilize to regulate the intensity level and clarify communication patterns within groups. Close scrutiny and systematic investigation into the intrigue of interactions within therapeutic clusters has produced a high yield of cogent material. These resources translate into practice principles, which should be useful to ministry leaders simply by building awareness of available interventions (see Foundational Group Leader Skills on page 188). The information on group interaction validates objective analysis of leader moves and group responses. Leaders who make advanced use of these skills are in a superb position to manage the intensity level of the group's communication and tap into affective material to help members reach their goals. Through the application of these maneuvers, members receive coaching that enables them to wander less in isolation and instead walk in consistent mutuality, intensity, reciprocity and love. When this occurs, emotion will ascend from deep within our souls and illuminate conditions in the bonds between persons.

---

[8]Lieberman, Yalom and Miles, *Encounter Groups*, p. 240. In this study, both the executive and emotional stimulation functions yielded correlations that were curvilinear. The functions of caring and meaning attribution were linear. This indicates that when it comes to the executive and emotional stimulation functions, either too little or too much is likely to inhibit positive learning outcomes for group members. These functions are logically connected via the mechanism of operating structure. Generally, more defined structure yields more specific expectations and lowers the member's anxiety. Remove or reduce structure and group anxiety will likely rise. Modification of structure is thus one leader method of managing emotional stimulation.

Foundational Group Leader Skills

(Adopted from Marianne Schneider Corey and Gerald Corey's *Groups: Process and Practice*, 7th ed. [Belmont, Calif.: Brooks/Cole, 2006], pp. 33-40.)

Active listening: Attending to the full range of surface and subtle, verbal and non-verbal messages in order to receive and comprehend. The communicating loop is then completed, meaning that the source is assured that the message has been heard correctly.

Reflecting: Catching the message's depth and restating it to the group or member without rigid parroting. A key to reflection is highlighting value and message.

Clarifying: Bringing concerns, conflicts and themes to the forefront in a way that helps others gain a sharper focus and deepen understanding.

Summarizing: Shifting and selecting central themes, gains and direction in the session.

Facilitating: Guiding members with encouragement to make use of the group experience via sharing, risking, focusing and making progress toward attainable goals.

Empathizing: Communicating that one comprehends the internal world and subjective experience of the other.

Interpreting: Providing compassionate and balanced explanations for behavior patterns so that these have meaning in reference to the big picture or broader framework.

Questioning: Open-ended, potent, well-formed and properly timed questions stimulate creative thought and move the responder toward action. Too numerous or overly dull questions suppress group interaction.

Linking: Sensing connection and prompting productive member-to-member interaction.

Confronting: Within a climate of care and respect, members are artfully challenged to seriously review, evaluate or reconsider behaviors and beliefs to accelerate growth.

Supporting: By noticing strengths, effort and step-by-step progress, members are encouraged to remain consistent and on target in the pursuit of change.

Blocking: The discernment of counterproductive communication contributes to active management of disruptive or distracting behavior. This may protect an individual, subgroup or the entire group from harm or needless detour.

Assessing: Detecting personality, relational or behavior patterns that contribute to the member's issues or goals. Beyond diagnosis or negative labeling, this is the perceptive recognition of individual resources to overcome liabilities.

Modeling: Demonstration of effective behavior or patterns for members to use inside and outside of the group.

Suggesting: This is discrete and strategic idea sharing that enables members to take independent and productive action.

Initiating: Breaking new ground, raising novel material, "priming the pump" or getting a session started are examples of leader-assertive effort to set the pace and establish a climate conducive to the mission of the group.

Evaluating: Based on the group purpose and member goals, the leader points out progress markers and benchmark criteria to demonstrate process and existing group dynamics. Communication with members is crucial to maintain motivation and investment.

Terminating: In order to maximize the allotted time, leaders prepare members and guide the group to end well. Members leave with clear plans on how to continue to grow and an understanding of what they have gained from the group experience.

Third, general counseling and mental health settings recognize value in using affective expression and clarification to build interpersonal connection. Unfortunately, this leader practice can appear out of place in Christian community. In a Christian context, perhaps it would be better to explain this function in this way: pursuing emotional material stirred by relating in order to bring about transparent community not only within the group, but also in the lifelong journey of fellowship in the body of Christ.

In brief groups, a homogeneous population assembles to address the announced common focus. The identified concern may itself already be stoking emotional distress to the extent of interfering with healthy functioning and relating, such as coming to grips with a loss, finding stability in the aftermath of a crisis, and accepting unwelcome change, disability or divorce. Such participants have ample reason to believe that they are living on a frightening emotional roller coaster. In such groups, the leader fulfills the function of drawing affect to the surface by designating the group session as a specially reserved and supportive opportunity for meaningful emotional expression. The prescribed time, set place and consistent fellow trekkers enable participants to deescalate the harsh reverberations of affectively loaded events. The leader assists by empowering affective expression in a safe setting with compassionate peers where emotional communication is permissible, protected, facilitated and productive. It would be a severe misunderstanding to view this function simplistically by equating stimulation exclusively with a relentless increase in pressure. Further, a good leader raises awareness of a full range of emotions, not only those with negative overtones. A beautiful comfort exists in laugher in the midst of grief, refreshment from the touch of kindnesses when recalling abuse, and hope in freedom following the recognition of rage. Wise trekking guides craft and coach emotional exchanges so that the group and its members can observe, directly experience and strategically make use of relational communication.

Last but not least, leaders facilitate preliminary dialogue to establish a credible platform for, and foster collaboration in, expressing affect in ways that move toward wholeness. During orientation, leaders state that communication within sessions is bound to become emotionally intense when addressing crucial concerns. While temporarily uncomfortable, this feature separates a working group from a social gathering. It does not indicate a problem or misdirection. On the contrary, gritty emotional discussion may suggest that the group is moving forward on its intended course. Leaders assist members in setting personal goals for growth throughout the trek. Recalling these goals at critical junctures will tie the difficult work of affective exploration to previously verbalized and personally desired outcomes.[9] It may be productive to conduct a brief check-in procedure at the outset of the session. Participants can establish an agenda or expectation regarding a relational skill that they intend to practice.[10] If a member has announced how she would like to use this gathering for interpersonal exercise, taking a risk displays intentionality. Such plausible links can maintain motivation when the pursuit of an emotional trail enters uncharted and rocky terrain.

Helping groups in a Christian framework reflect Christ-honoring priorities, values and ultimately wisdom. Therefore, when working with such groups, two questions persistently drive my introspection and intercessory prayer: "Lord Jesus, will my leading in this session reflect your wishes? Will our communication and connections invite you to visit and permeate our interactions?" Our efforts are surely intended to bring emotional relief. Yet ultimately, the mission is to present our Lord with a community where he can infuse his love. He may even join the trek.

A QUIET MIRACLE

Quality group ventures with guided interpersonal exchange can open the way for Jesus to work his ministry of spiritual formation. Jesus Christ breathes life into relational bonds, and in doing so his presence becomes the central factor in experiencing the wonder of a helping group and the attainment of positive outcomes for individuals. When interpersonal connections become a means to realize kingdom purposes, intimacy transforms into communion.[11] Social support becomes a sacred gathering. Members expose their once private, personal matters and patterns. Participants embrace the experience in ways that promote inclusive fellowship with the triune God and other Christ followers. This *imago Dei* restoration demonstrates that Jesus Christ has visited and blessed a reciprocal

---

[9]The suggestion of linking goals to assist in facing emotionally challenging communication points reinforces the notion that all four leader functions are closely related. A willingness to face risk is facilitated by guiding the process with meaning.

[10]Mei-whei Chen and Christopher J. Rybak, *Group Leadership Skills: Interpersonal Process in Group Counseling and Therapy* (Belmont, Calif.: Brooks-Cole, 2004), pp. 136-84.

[11]The word *intimacy* connotes sharing one's innermost and private areas with another or others. Intimacy therefore communicates a rich sense of caring, warmth, familiarity and friendship. Communion outside of any reference to a sacrament or church ordinance indicates sharing, intimate fellowship, enjoying common ground and rapport. While these terms both reference similar human experience, communion is the one that conveys a spiritual overtone. Therefore communion is the choice term when human encounter involves relating to Jesus Christ.

human encounter to join gift and need love. To appreciate how quietly Jesus can accomplish remarkable transformations with no fanfare or fireworks, let's recollect his first miracle. Recall these familiar phrases that convene the traditional Christian wedding service:

> Dearly beloved, we are gathered together here in the sight of God, and in the face of this company, to join together this man and this woman in holy matrimony; which is an honorable estate, instituted of God, signifying unto us the mystical union that is betwixt Christ and his church: *which holy estate Christ adorned and beautified with his presence and first miracle that he wrought in Cana of Galilee.*[12]

This opening announcement of the consecrated nature of the gathering concludes with a perpetual reminder of Jesus' personal participation in a wedding celebration (Jn 2:1-11). On the threshold of his public ministry, he immortalized that special occasion via an undisputable sign of his divine nature. Jesus transformed six stone jars of ordinary water into extraordinary wine. Best estimates are that this inaugural demonstration of his divine power resulted in the immediate production of over one hundred gallons of fine fruit of the vine![13] This is an impressive feat. Thus it is not surprising that clergy formally and boldly recount such a miracle each time witnesses gather to hear marital vows exchanged. Stunningly, Jesus himself underplayed his first sign. Only a select few were aware of this awe-inspiring act. Very likely, the majority of those fortunate guests concluded that festive week and returned home without ever realizing how Jesus had so powerfully revealed his divine presence. In like manner, many who participate in helping groups have observed the effects of his gracious touch without recognizing that our Lord was the unnoticed guest who quietly met essential needs.

Beyond recording miracle basics, John as Gospel writer includes details within the narrative both to fortify the conviction that Jesus Christ is exactly who he claimed to be and to convey the manner by which Jesus progressively revealed himself. John intentionally uses this event to mark the initiation of Jesus' ministry. Several points may prove instructive for exploration, so let's pause over Eugene Peterson's telling of the text.

> Three days later there was a wedding in the village of Cana in Galilee. Jesus' mother was there. Jesus and his disciples were guests also. When they

---

[12]Edward Thurston Hiscox and Frank T. Hoadley, *The Star Book for Ministers,* 2nd ed. (Willow Grove, Penn.: Woodlawn Electronic Publishing, 1998), electronic version. Emphasis mine.
[13]Donald A. Carson, *The Gospel According to John* (Grand Rapids: Eerdmans, 1991), p. 173.

started running low on wine at the wedding banquet, Jesus' mother told him, "They're just about out of wine."

Jesus said, "Is that any of our business, Mother—yours or mine? This isn't my time. Don't push me."

She went ahead anyway, telling the servants, "Whatever he tells you, do it."

Six stoneware water pots were there, used by the Jews for ritual washings. Each held twenty to thirty gallons. Jesus ordered the servants, "Fill the pots with water." And they filled them to the brim.

"Now fill your pitchers and take them to the host," Jesus said, and they did.

When the host tasted the water that had become wine (he didn't know what had just happened but the servants, of course, knew), he called out to the bridegroom, "Everybody I know begins with their finest wines and after the guests have had their fill brings in the cheap stuff. But you've saved the best till now!"

This act in Cana of Galilee was the first sign Jesus gave, the first glimpse of his glory. And his disciples believed in him. (Jn 2:1-11 *The Message*)

Notice the communication between mother and Son. Mary brings the concern over the depleted supply of wine to Jesus' attention. The content of their exchange focuses on a circumstance that will soon disrupt the surrounding celebration. A wedding feast within the culture typically lasted for a week. A lack of wine would reflect badly on the groom. His poor planning and management would constitute ample justification for later social ridicule that could unfavorably brand the couple for a lifetime. In a culture where shame was a dominant social force, avoiding this embarrassment would be a critical priority. Therefore Mary's attentiveness to the wine problem was justified and not an obscure, trivial distraction. Jesus' direct reply to his mother turns the conversation away from this mini social crisis. His respectful rebuke and reference to their immediate relationship is an excellent example of process exploration. In counseling terminology, this is an example of *immediacy* or you-me talk.[14] Such dialogue moves the conversation from the base level of informational exchange to the more intense level aimed at relationship adjustment or explication. In an open and firm manner Jesus redefines this central maternal bond from this point forward. His ministry will yield only to the sequence and parameters ordained by his heavenly

---

[14]Gerard Egan, *The Skilled Helper*, 8th ed. (Belmont, Calif.: Thomson Wadsworth, 2006), pp. 209-13.

Father; it will not be subject to human wishes, even the will of his own mother. This is not his hour. When his time does arrive three years later for betrayal, Passion and crucifixion, Jesus himself submits even his own will to the bidding of the Father. "Father, if you are willing, take this cup from me; yet not my will, but yours be done" (Lk 22:42). This complete submission and obedience was already familiar to Mary, who could recall her conversation years earlier with the angel Gabriel (Lk 1:26-38). Jesus' words may have been painfully blunt as he affirmed the utmost importance of his divine mission. His message contained no surprise, disappointment or reason for embarrassment. This relational communication between Jesus and Mary is of course secondary to the main purpose of the narrative. But it is meaningful enough for John to record for our edification (see Jn 20:30-31). This critical conversation defines the relational priorities and establishes the context for the sign that follows. From this point forward, Jesus commences his journey to the cross. Human relations will not deter this divinely ordained purpose.

Second, notice the exclusive observers of this sign. Only the wedding servants were involved in the filling of the ceremonial jars to the absolute limit of their capacity. It was the servants who then drew the water, served it to the master of the banquet, and heard his praise regarding the late appearance of such a quality wine (Jn 2:7-8). The disciples who had accompanied Jesus to this feast were also in the inner circle. The text declares their faith response to the revelation of Jesus' glory. Thus it is evident that they were privy to the proceedings (Jn 2:11). Perhaps neither the host nor the honored guests were ever aware of the wine shortage or of their divine benefactor. As the wedding celebration proceeds in traditional fashion, only those close to Jesus or those who directly followed his commands observed the work of our Lord. Jesus avoided dramatic, attention-getting tactics. He never performed a grandiose stunt on demand. He softly and surely provided signs to those whose eyes were open to see the wonder of his divine hand.

Herein lies the parallel to modern therapeutic groups. I contend that many helping groups move members into substantial interpersonal encounters by resolving a crisis, clarifying relational roles or challenging ingrained behavioral patterns. The contemporary technology of group dynamics supplies reasonable explanations for occurrences and gains. Results are attributed to natural social forces and human effort. This may be an accurate account of the interaction as captured in the language of content and process. But those seeking to cultivate formation work by our Lord may be blessed with a glimpse of a supernatural intervention. The same interpersonal event may be explained via insight that flows from a different plane.

There is one last illustrative point from the Cana wedding passage. Significantly, the stone water jars were designated for a Jewish ritual of purification. Wine would make such containers unclean.[15] Therefore using water from those vessels for this sign may have had symbolic meaning: Jesus as Messiah will replace former rituals with a New Covenant. The Gospels reveal more about symbolic meanings associated with both water and wine. In particular, John shows how Jesus uses down-to-earth words to convey messages with important theological meaning. Within this event, Jesus not only redefines his relationship with his mother but reveals his willingness to place divine purpose over religious traditions and rituals. Such an observation receives additional legitimacy from observing the passage with what immediately follows it: Jesus' cleansing of the temple and his incredible conversation with Nicodemus. Within this section of John's gospel (Jn 2:1–3:35), the actions and words of Jesus reveal that the former religious rules and routines are of little importance to his mission. They have no authority over his divine presence. While highlighting the potential symbolic meaning woven into this miraculous sign may have no overt bearing on group trekking, it does serve as a dramatic reminder that our Lord has his own methods to solidify his purposes. Jesus habitually transforms the ordinary into the extraordinary. When addressing an obvious need, Jesus can instill into that blessing a profound encounter with the gospel and his own glorious nature. This multi-layered flow of earthly and kingdom-oriented activity is what Christian guides are honored to observe in helping groups. Emotional arousal may signal the way toward heart matters and indicate that the wind of the Spirit is on the move.

WORD PICTURES FOR LIFE

The gospel message boldly calls for radical conversion, recognition of eternity and living life fully under the authority of Jesus' name (Jn 20:30-31). Courageous change can follow audacious conversations. For example, a prestigious religious leader, Nicodemus, breaks rank with his fellow Pharisees. He privately conveys the compliment that Jesus' activities imply divine sanction. Jesus instantly escalates the conversation's intensity from tame intellectual ruminations to daring contemplation of core beliefs, regeneration and rebirth (Jn 3:1-16). A social outcast fetching well water expresses interest in a remark that alleges a renewable supply. Jesus counters with a full commentary on her lifestyle, social status and

---

[15]Craig S. Keener, *The IVP Bible Background Commentary: New Testament* (Downers Grove, Ill.: InterVarsity Press, 1993), p. 268 (see Jn 2:7).

religious background (Jn 4:1-26). Sisters send word to a traveling rabbi that Lazarus, their brother and his friend, is extremely ill. Jesus responds on a timeframe
that raises emotions to explosive heights, then he demonstrates his power over
death (Jn 11:1-43). In striking words and stunning activity, Jesus evokes intense
affect as he reveals himself.

The disciple whom Jesus loved selected a sample of signs and memorable
pronouncements to introduce Jesus Christ as the source of everlasting life.
His evangelistic thrust invites belief that is simultaneously rational and relational (Jn 20:30-31). Here the Gospel author records the spiritual reality of
the universe and divine redemptive activity. *Belief* in gospel terms demands a
persistent, intimate encounter with the God-man, Jesus Christ, who is Truth.
Once belief is born, a living truth emerges in a continuous encounter with Jesus
Christ that nurtures followers wholly into abundant life. John's phrase "life to
the full" suggests that the sheep under the care of the Great Shepherd are fat,
flourishing and astonishingly content.[16] Jesus redeems the relational rupture
triggered by the rebellion of sin and restores creatures' bond with the Creator.
This relationship perfectly complements creatures made in the *imago Dei*. Jesus
Christ provides the sustenance necessary for eternal life.[17]

Theological tradition and the doctrinal creeds since the Council of Chalce-
don hold that Jesus Christ is complete in deity and humanity without separation, division, confusion or change.[18] Therefore he purely exemplifies what the
imago Dei would be like without any destructive taint of sin.[19] Not only is the
Creator's original design evident, so is the future destiny of those who are new
creatures in Christ.[20] The Incarnation displays the full benefits of human relationality. Recall at this juncture the component relational provisions suggested
by social scientist Robert Weiss (i.e., attachment, reliable alliance, belonging,

---

[16]Carson, *John*, p. 385.

[17]Michael Card, *The Parable of Joy: Reflections on the Wisdom of the Book of John* (Nashville: Thomas
Nelson, 1995); Craig S. Keener, *The Gospel of John: A Commentary*, 2 vols. (Peabody, Mass.: Hen-
drickson Publishers, 2003).

[18]Wayne Grudem, *Systematic Theology* (Grand Rapids: Zondervan, 1994); B. B. Warfield, "Person
of Christ," in *The International Standard Bible Encyclopaedia*, ed. James Orr (Grand Rapids: Eerdmans, 1939), pp. 2337-48.

[19]Since Jesus is fully God in human flesh, it would not be accurate to apply the term imago Dei
directly for he does not reflect God. He is God.

[20]Wolfhart Pannenberg, *Anthropology in Theological Perspective*, trans. Matthew J. O'Connell (Philadelphia: Westminster Press, 1985), as cited in Kevin Vanhoozer, "Human Being, Individual
and Social," in *The Cambridge Companion to Christian Doctrine*, ed. Colin Gunton (Cambridge:
Cambridge University Press, 1997), pp. 158-88.

worth, altruism, guidance).[21] Does not Jesus Christ fulfill each of these human needs through his divine gift love? Weiss's social psychology constructs deserve consideration alongside the person of Jesus. The gospel paints its own portraits of how Jesus Christ sustains human beings in relationship with himself. Words from our Lord recorded in Scripture can serve as the ideal descriptors for these life-supporting demonstrations of gift love in action.

The Gospel of John contains a theologically rich account of Jesus Christ. Through metaphors, potent one-word parables and phrases with double meaning, the apostle John depicts how the God-man offers life (e.g., Word, Light, Bread, True Vine, etc.). The reality corresponding to these vivid word pictures shows the fullness of relational experience, reflects interpersonal provisions and exemplifies authentic relating. John clearly uses metaphors that are intended to surpass the selected imagery. The idea under consideration is too vast to be contained adequately by even the best tools that human language has to offer. No single word or phrase can contain the theological concepts referenced by these literary forms. In rousing the imagination of his readers, John instills appreciation for the sustaining and transforming resources available in the Word become flesh. Many of these metaphors have Old Testament roots or had persuasive meaning within the divergent cultures in the New Testament world; some even had extensive usage in secular philosophy. John records how Jesus Christ spoke to all these diverse domains, revealing himself and offering relationship. Instead of reducing these word pictures to bland descriptive traits, guides should meditate on these ideas in their biblical context to absorb their full relational implication. The Word of God provides informational support in its content and message. These metaphors are active and living declarations regarding the emotional and instrumental support that Jesus Christ offers. Through these provisions, he nurtures his followers via ongoing relationship.[22] Five samples will display how these metaphors capture the way Jesus himself fills and enhances life.

Word. The Word, *logos*, captures numerous relationships simultaneously (Jn 1:1, 14; 1 Jn 1:1). By weaving *Word* into phrases that mirror the opening of Genesis, the Holy Spirit through John's Gospel fuses a collection of astonishing con-

---

[21]See chapter 5; Robert Weiss, "The Provisions of Social Relationships," in *Doing Unto Others*, ed. Zick Rubin (Englewood Cliffs, N.J.: Prentice-Hall, 1974), pp. 17-26.

[22]A number of commentaries contributed to my grasp of the power of these metaphors with substantial relational meaning. Two authors significantly formed my thinking and the reader is referred to consult these works directly. Any misrepresentation of the biblical text reflects my own weaknesses and I look forward to continued growth in "handl[ing] the word of truth" (2 Tim 2:15). See Carson, *John*, and Keener, *John*.

cepts. The gift of God's law to the Jews, or *Torah*, merges with wisdom, deity and humanity. This is a stunning synthesis of Creator with creation, eternal with temporal, and transcendent mind with corporal form. John binds the Greek concept of a grand universal rationality with the Jewish God of the Scriptures. Trinitarian implications also exist for distinctive persons and intimate union within the Godhead. This incredible Word became flesh. By grace, an enfleshed tabernacle was established to communicate the glory of God to humanity. The Incarnation exhibits the value God places on direct relating for the purpose of revelation.

How does this intensely packed *logos* word picture then speak to human relationships? The creative force that structured, unified and continuously holds together the universe flows from God into human form so that he can be known and relate to humanity. Rationality within the *imago Dei* reflects *logos*, for it fuels and governs how human beings construe and construct reality. The rationality of the human mind unites and organizes the entire narrative of life. Thus this constructive agency displays a defining feature of the *imago Dei*. Nonetheless, rationality is not a self-generated, internal or autonomous quality. This capacity emerges from *within* and is elicited by being *in* relationship with others. The Word was there when the chaos of the universe was tamed and transformed into a world good for life. The Word supplies wisdom, conceptual categories and the clarity necessary to empower the human mind through relational experience. The Word returns and restores rationality within the *imago Dei*. Ponder these implications for people-helping ventures!

Dwelling in community is a mind-energizing and equipping encounter. Minds lost in a mixture of reality distortions and chaotic contradictions, mired in repetitive thoughts and confusion, or mesmerized by racing ideas and endless possibilities must experience renewal. Others offer relief through the dynamic process of drawing on their rationality and wisdom to add cohesiveness to one's grasp of reality. When relational process strengthens human agency by sharpening rationality and redirecting will, the Word, *logos*, has ministered. A coherent perception penetrates chaos.

Light. Jesus Christ entered the chronology of creation as the "light of the world" (Jn 1:4-5, 7-9; 3:19-21; 8:12; 9:5; 11:9-10; 12:35-36, 46). John joins this motif with the theme of life. He infuses the Jewish view of light as Wisdom and Torah into a metaphor that declares power over darkness, evil and death. John the Baptist bears witness to this light (Jn 1:7-9). Elsewhere in Scripture, believers are instructed to provide light in a dark world (Mt 5:14-16). John directs believers to share this light: "But if we walk in the light, as he is in the light, we have fellowship with one another, and the blood of Jesus, his Son, purifies us from all sin" (1 Jn 1:7). Fellowship facilitates sanctification by bringing light to life through the power of the cross. The experience of human connection and communication under grace opens our eyes to righteous living and energizes the affective motivation to pursue it. Fellowship provides a sharing of light that dispels fears, illuminates moral actions and displaces shadows of depression.

Gate. Jesus declared himself to be the gate for the sheep (Jn 10:7). In the first century, the gate to a city served the same purpose as security checkpoints in the twenty-first. For this metaphor, our picture of airport security screening or a border crossing conveys the ancient connotation. The doorway into the walled portion of a city served as a place where government authorities could assert control, search for known criminals, enforce regulations or collect fees. The security of the gate symbolized the safety and strength of the city as a place where the ruling authority was asserting its power. These gateways served as meeting places, so markets were often clustered close by. Those who heard Jesus speaking about sheep pens and doorways would hear *gate* as a meaningful and reassuring image. A secure gate meant safe living and peaceful rest. Jesus is the sentry, security system, fortification and power establishing eternal safety for his people. A relationship with Jesus Christ provides the comfort basic to a

Table 9.1. Relational Word Pictures from John's Gospel

Poetic Description	Relational Component	Implication
Word (1:1, 14)	Wisdom/deity within humanity	Support social self/mind
Light (1:4-5; 8:12; 9:5)	Wisdom/righteousness displayed	Inspire hope for holy living
Lamb of God (1:35)	Sacrificial burden bearer	Prevent or bear others' pain
Living water (4:10; 7:37)	Refreshment resource	Encourage and refresh
Messiah (4:25-26)	Redeemer and healer	Intercede and cure
Bread of life (6:35, 48)	Nurturance source	Nurture and support
Gate (10:7)	Watchman/security system	Provide safety
Good Shepherd (10:11)	Attendant, protector, provider	Selflessly serve
Resurrection (11:25-26)	Guide through death	Affirm life and hope
Eternity's pioneer (14:3)	Caretaker for an eternal home	Foster role and place
Way (14:6)	Pathway and guide to eternal life	Inspire wisdom
Truth (14:6)	Ultimate authority for reality	Speak truth in love
True Vine (15:1, 5)	Supply connection and lifeline	Establish life in community
Advocate (16:23)	Intercessor and ally	Communicate alliance

good and happy life. Genuine security begins with our relationship with him, the ultimate secure base.

Living water. Jeremiah once assured self-confident Jews that man-made cisterns leak, stagnate and become polluted, but that living water is found in the Lord God alone (Jer 2:13; 17:13). In a similar manner, Jesus offers himself as a renewable resource that refreshes from the inside out. A parched soul requires a permanent spiritual solution to the lifelong struggle for refreshment. Living water is that intimate relationship with the One who satisfies those inner thirsts that defy description and are impossible to quench with any earthly liquid. Jesus offers to take up residence in lonely, empty hearts and becomes an eternal source of soothing. Is this not what occurs as reassuring words from supportive others seep inside? When those phrases gently begin to flow within, the words become the living water, quenching the emotional effects of fiery darts that have pieced the soul. In this way, the human system can manifest Living Water.

Bread. "I am the bread of life" (Jn 6:35). In this statement, Jesus evokes a word that has both an extensive faith history, multiple levels of meaning and universal appeal. When Jesus himself spoke this phrase, tongues were still blazing about a recent meal at which Jesus had given thanks for a small portion of bread and fish and then fed thousands. There may have been listeners within earshot who had actually tasted that literal bread Jesus had blessed. The provision of manna in the desert was old news. This more recent sign brought its awe-inspiring spiritual significance into intense focus. Bread was a prevalent symbol for wisdom and Torah. Jesus shifts the emphasis from a provided item that will satisfy only temporarily to the true Provider who is ready to relate and satisfy perpetually. Believers were taught to pray, "give us today our daily bread" (Mt 6:11; see also Lk 11:3). The stomach may seek its day-to-day ration; the soul hungers for nurturing alliances that supply lasting bread.

A selected list of word pictures from the Gospel of John along with plausible relational implications is found in table 9.1 on page 197. The list is *not* comprehensive. The richness of these pictures must not be reduced into mere operational definitions or a simplistic checklist. Doing so could threaten to restrict the power of this Scriptural language that speaks throughout the progression history, between the diversity of cultures and across the divine-human divide.

These word pictures suggest and stimulate further contemplation regarding relational dynamics. Investigate the other terms and contemplate their implications. Take for example the True Vine. The chart suggests that the True Vine imagery may depict the sustenance for and consistent supply of necessary interpersonal resources as summarized by the phrase "life in community." There is so much more to consider. The Scriptural context suggests the vinedresser's care, correction and pruning. Thus important aspects of the Vine picture are not immediately apparent in the brief summaries given. The True Vine also links connection, support, accountability, and social as well as divine control. The Vine metaphor also suggests the tension between the freedom of the individual and life together in Christ. Unfathomable depth and richness come from these portraits of how Jesus Christ as the ideal human being demonstrates restored *imago Dei*. He continues to transcend the divide between heaven and earth—his holiness and our sinfulness, the infinite and the finite—to provide his followers with abundant life.

These relational provisions belong uniquely to the One who was without sin. Nonetheless, they do indeed speak to ways that every human being returns support to those growing or in need. The Fall darkened but did not eliminate the *imago Dei* in humanity. Society, family and friendships continue to transfer these relational resources to their members. People can and do bear each other's pain and hurt. They serve as safe retreats from the wider competitive world by expressing love and concern for others, particularly to those within their immediate family and social context. When the community surrounding the individual is in Christ, people have special hope for substantial change and re-creation due to Christ's presence experienced in the operative work of the Holy Spirit (see Eph 4:22-24; Col 3:9-11). In this Spirit-driven context, Scripture admonishes believers to love patiently, kindly, without envy or excessive self-interest in a manner that protects and produces trust and hope that results in renewed ability to persevere (1 Cor 13:4-8).

Thus love as relationship in action supplies essential social resources. By describing *imago Dei* nurture, these biblical metaphors expand our ability to conceive of how such love is transmitted to others. One may experience these provisions through transpersonal encounter with the Lord Jesus Christ *and* within interpersonal exchange as he makes his presence known through the supply of Bread, Light, Truth, etc. Biblical word pictures do not have the linguistic precision of the related psychological terms such as *social support* or Weiss's list of relational provisions. If these living words could be pinned down with exactitude they would no longer be metaphors! However, these terms do represent in a parallel language the underlying interpersonal process while directly referencing their divine source.

QUIET MIRACLES ON THE TRAIL TO WHOLENESS

Leaders instigate greater transparency in members through modeling it themselves and coaching the group to allow emotional expression to build bonds with others. In this way, they fulfill the function of moving members toward affect for attachment purposes. A leader provides the most noticeable type of direct expression by bringing attention to an experience that has just occurred within the group. The leader may disclose a sensation from within and share an explanation of what has recently occurred. Here are two examples for illustration.

> Right now, let's step back from our conversation. I would like us to consider an observation. For several minutes my heart has been beating rapidly, I feel warm, stirred up, and detect tension in my throat. I am aware that many of you have been investing much into this exchange seeking to convince Tyrone to take certain steps. Are you having similar reactions? Let's take a moment to check our emotional temperature and consider its message.

> Run an instant replay and look at what just took place in our group. I suspect we witnessed an important happening. If I'm right, this is actually pretty exciting. I acknowledge that what I am saying is not a certainty. So, I am relying on the group as a whole to think out loud with me to get it right. Having been together for six sessions, this is worth considering.

This type of intervention is not venting, impulsive or random. These are critical moments, opportunities to consolidate learning, and occasions to celebrate.

Techniques for stimulating affect lend themselves best to person-to-person encounters, but the concept is so important that I wish to try a version of it in the paragraphs that follow. The role of group leader requires one to take risks and verbalize hunches for community consideration and member reflection. Leaders anticipate an outcome of consensual validation, additional group clarification or outright rejection. Consensual validation is rightly prized as a unique tool that a group offers members and leaders. A leader respects and values the small gathered community enough to solicit its commentary. In print, author and reader do not interact in real time as a leader and participants do in a group. Therefore the technique is not perfectly transferable by example. Nonetheless, the following narrative can apply to the leader function of stimulating affect. The essential value in my transparency resides in the ensuing discussion, not in the revelation itself. Hopefully, reader-to-reader consideration of my sharing will generate reasonable results. Input and exchange from other group guides can eventually be collected, consolidated and refined. In the interest of promoting intimacy on this trek, please allow room for this personal musing. Here are my hesitations and observations for validation, refinement or dismissal.

I'm having a hard time committing to conclude this chapter. From the outset, one central message ignited my passion to communicate. The moment to state that message with clarity has arrived. Unfortunately, I am noticing a personal struggle to keep words on the computer screen. How can a core message about leading ministry-oriented group treks coexist with hesitation? The principles and applications incorporated into the previous chapters have considerable support in sturdy group counseling theory and in the corresponding empirical literature. Other points rest on biblical passages, theological material or respected Christian sources. What I now put into words has a prominent subjective quality. This is the amalgamation of direct and borrowed group moments, filtered through my own spiritual lens. An unusual and ancient personal life episode will set the stage.

As an adolescent, I wore torn jeans with symbolic patches. I honored the first official Earth Day with a sewn-on green ecology flag merged with a peace sign. During that youthful period of my life I also performed folk music with a close cohort of friends. When we played together, our collective identity went under the name *TimePeace*. This reflected our grasp of urgent purpose, an uninformed but intense ideology that once took us to a large psychiatric facility known as Pilgrim State Hospital.[23] We did so near the end of the era of immense institutions that housed, or perhaps better stated, warehoused, extremely large numbers of those deemed mentally ill. The buildings were brick and the windows barred. The customary derogatory term for Pilgrim was *the funny farm*. Diagnostic categories were not precise and medication options were limited. Thus the patient population was colorful and unpredictable. At Pilgrim State, *TimePeace* sang at a series of Christmas parties. After singing

---

[23]Pilgrim State Hospital in Brentwood, New York was commissioned by the New York State legislature in 1927 and named after Dr. Charles W. Pilgrim, a former state mental health commissioner. It was designed to provide self-contained community where work was an aspect of care. After opening in 1931 on 825 acres, it had 2018 patients in its initial year. It grew to be the world's largest farm-focused mental health facility with its own railroad station, post office, police department, court system, food production facilities, electricity plant, cemetery and physician/staff residences. At its peak in 1954, it housed 13,875 patients and had thousands of employees. Deinstitutionalization and downsizing occurred as community-based care and modern psychiatric approaches become available. My visits were during the days when farm-focused care was past its prime and Pilgrim's momentum was grinding to a halt. Retrieved from <http://www.omh.state.ny.us/omhweb/facilities/pgpc/facility.htm>. Last modified March 6, 2008.

all the verses of Bob Dylan's "Blowin' in the Wind," it was time to mingle with the audience.[24] I will never really know how much those conversations influenced my later interest in psychology. The lasting impression that follows, however, testifies to their partial impact. The halls we visited were like large caverns, and strange-looking people wandered about. I cannot forget a choice meeting with one individual. My memory suggests that he was a patient, but the lines of separation were never clear. There are three details I can recall: His eyes were large and hollow. His dark hair was messy. When he introduced himself, he said firmly "I am Jesus" and then mumbled something about the birthday party. This brief episode had no elaboration. This was not a religious revelation. Still, could Jesus have been living on an outdated funny farm? One deemed insane said "yes" on that December Saturday afternoon. This adolescent was there to hang with friends under the pretense of changing the world. After all, the answer was "blowin' in the wind."

Let's leave that odd story from my past floating for a moment and turn again to the present context. Groups can address emotionally charged material to foster greater relational adaptability, and in doing so they promote corrective emotional relationships. The interpersonal support serves as the means for emotional release and reconfiguration of relational expectations. This occurs on an interpersonal level, yet it reflects God's re-interjecting divine community in the midst of human companionship.[25]

The ultimate corrective emotional relationship is the redemptive embrace of the Creator. By granting prayerful attention and affection to God, the resulting relationship steadily reconfigures one's self-other relational template, or internal working model. This occurs as (1) the gospel story infiltrates one's inner narrative; (2) the foundation for one's feeling of security, hope and belonging is fortified; and (3) the destination of one's future of being face-to-face with Jesus Christ instills meaning into the present.[26] A human relationship, by grace, becomes a corrective emotional relationship when that connection increases relational adaptability or, to use an alternative phrase, one's capacity to love.

Intensive groups use corrective emotional relationships by taking opportune moments to turn the subject matter from the unifying topic to relational communication. This strategic attempt strives toward authenticity, intimacy and

---

[24]Bob Dylan, *The Freewheelin' Bob Dylan*, Columbia Records (1963).
[25]Gareth Weldon Icenogle, *Biblical Foundations of Small Group Ministry: An Integrational Approach* (Downers Grove, Ill.: InterVarsity Press, 1994), p. 372.
[26]These points are adopted from the quote by Eric Johnson listed in chapter seven. See Eric Johnson, "How God Is Good for the Soul," *Journal of Psychology and Christianity* 22 (2003): 78-88.

love. Empathy ignites loving connections where truth is spoken and received. Jesus Christ is incognito in this entire empathic process, supplying the critical ingredients that bring life—ingredients like rationality, moral direction, affirmation, protection and hope for the future.[27] These relational provisions are illustrated in John's word pictures in conjunction with the incarnation. I contend that when these redemptive and sanctifying relational provisions are present, the Holy Spirit has moved as a breeze through the human encounter and has raised the impact of the interpersonal to the level of the incarnational. Jesus Christ takes residence in the space between sin-stricken human beings. Making use of flesh-and-blood human beings created in his image, Jesus Christ enables broken persons to experience the freedom to bear failure, release pain, lessen hurt, let go of automatic and addictive behaviors, and put on the fruits of the Spirit such as love, joy, peace, patience, kindness, goodness, faithfulness, gentleness and self-control (Gal 5:22-23).[28] I am convinced that the Holy Spirit has been quietly active in small groups and communities I have known. The Spirit made the presence of Jesus Christ a reconciling reality to honor the Father. This is the Holy Spirit moving as the wind; touching and refreshing souls.

Leaders should avoid thinking that a specific technique derives from this explanation, however. No formula exists for Christ-honoring success; no method truly harnesses the power of Jesus under the discretion of human will. There are no promises or assured outcomes, and no procedure dictates that Jesus Christ will quietly attend a small group gathering. Yet a leader does exert effort to invite Jesus' entrance, and this doesn't mean just stepping back and waiting for Jesus to speak or intervene. I encourage leaders in these groups to cultivate a deeper level of intimacy between members than what conversational content customarily allows. This demands earnest and dedicated effort to assess and alter critical relational polarities. An experiential encounter with any of these variations of embodied wisdom is bound to renovate affective, cognitive and relational categories. Leaders can wisely use themselves, effective group strategies and moments of reflection on relational communication in service to the King. In this way, leaders promote mutual corrective emotional relationships, and Jesus can use them to accomplish his kingdom work at a time, rate and method of his own choosing. Trekking guides who have much to overcome in moving toward this destination find profound encouragement in these words.

---

[27]Thomas C. Oden, *The Intensive Group Experience: The New Pietism* (Philadelphia: Westminster Press, 1972), p. 136.
[28]Icenogle, *Biblical Foundations*, p. 373.

Two questions then remain open to contemplate, discuss and research.

• Does the experience and explanation of effective group process as defined here resonate with your own group leadership experience?

• When reflecting on episodes of change within small communities, have you recognized moments that Jesus quietly supplied resources that resemble the metaphors noted from John's Gospel?

Now that these questions have been exposed for consideration, the opportunity is ripe for consensual validation, refinement or restatement. In the same way that group members would discuss a reflection or question about their own lives, readers may also interact with this material.

In conclusion, I will return to the story of that strange incident in a community hall at Pilgrim State.[29] What made that absurd claim by one mental patient so memorable? What was provoked by my experience of his delusion? The incident has served as a thread in the cord that unites a lifelong story of people-helping endeavors. In Matthew 25:31-46, Jesus tells a story with severe criteria for separating sheep and goats. He makes crucial statements about service to those who are prisoners, strangers, sick, thirsty and hungry. The text makes an absurd assertion: Jesus himself may actually be represented among those who are hurting, helpless and in need. "The King will reply, 'I tell you the truth, whatever you did for one of the least of these brothers of mine, you did for me.'" (Mt 25:40). As a teen, I made a Saturday excursion to that mental hospital to perform folk songs with friends because it seemed a cool thing to do. One mental patient seized the moment and gave me a refrain that has echoed over a lifetime of ministry. The lesson: no matter what the mission, location or population, Jesus may be in the midst. Jesus can make his redemptive presence real on a funny farm in a chance conversation or in a guided relational trek designed to restore and nurture. Groups are hosted to entertain him, even if we remain unaware of his presence (Heb 13:2).

---

[29]At the time of my adolescent visits to Pilgrim State, I had absolutely no awareness what the institution itself represented across its history as a mental health facility. At particular times and in certain ways, this was the frontier of compassionate mental health treatment where structured community was the means to promote healing. At other junctures, good intentions may have given way to efforts that perpetrated the horrors of experimental procedures on human subjects and inhuman institutional neglect. Myths abound. Today my awareness of its controversial past is a vivid reminder that there is much to learn about the mysteries of mental illness and what constitutes effective treatment. For an important read on the long-term effects of deinstitutionalization and the continuing insanity in mental health service systems, I strongly recommend Pete Earley, *Crazy: A Father's Search Through America's Mental Health Madness* (New York: G. P. Putman, 2006).

Our trekking-toward-wholeness experiences may parallel those of the wedding guests and servants from Cana nearly two thousand years ago. For most attendees, that social occasion was an ideal break in routine, a chance to catch up on town gossip and swap stories. Those guests did enjoy a pleasant surprise. The host broke into the deep recesses of the cellar, bucked tradition and raised the caliber of the entire event by serving a premium vintage for the conclusion of the festivities. A crisis was averted by the introduction of a fresh beverage supply. Those guests went home refreshed with positive memories. A pleasant, thirst-quenching social experience is a worthwhile outcome for a wedding celebration. Similarly, when a participant leaves a group trek revitalized, success criteria have been achieved.

Others who joined that neighborhood wedding left thrilled by a close look at a remarkable new rabbi. Beyond enjoying the ceremony, rejoicing in community and being introduced to a fine wine, these blessed few were granted a surprising revelation. A special guest quietly shook their assumptions of reality and faith. This unexpected encounter sealed a fervent commitment to submit to extensive discipleship. The same outcome may stir a select few to be astounded when Jesus ministers powerfully in a helping group. In some cases only the guide alone will recognize the signs that Jesus has visited.

I offer this perspective as encouragement. Group leaders pledge to use all available skills and resources to assist participants in reaching their goals. We all pray that Jesus Christ may take ordinary interpersonal interactions and transform them by his gracious presence into an extraordinary redemptive experience. Perhaps these words of paraphrase will place our treks toward wholeness in perspective.

Dearly beloved, we gather together for this trek in the sight of God, and in the face of this company, to join together in a mutual process of edification, sanctification and spiritual formation. This is an honorable venture, dedicated to God, and submitted to him to accomplish his purposes. As we give the Holy Spirit freedom to minister through our conversations, may we actually witness the mystical way that Christ blesses his church. Our time to journey together is temporary, yet being a participant in Christian fellowship anticipates eternity. May these guided experiences thus affect other relational commitments and opportunities. Just as Christ adorned and beautified with his presence and first miracle that wedding feast in Cana of Galilee, may his ministry here transform our ordinary interactions into lifelong blessings.

10

COURSE CORRECTIONS

LANDMARKS AHEAD

Helper multitasking may seem like an extreme sport in this chapter. I charge leaders with attending sufficiently to individuals, coaching changes productively, managing community and apportioning aid to each participant. Placing our sights on wisdom and growth toward shalom, groups become a unique conditioning route to Christian maturity. Vigilant leaders constantly work on central group attachments; they catalog inherent participant strengths, routine pitfalls and pressing needs. Discernment of decisive individual events contributes to a leader's ability to swiftly shift attention, catch pivotal action and make the most of critical junctures. Temperament distinctions alert leaders to the trekker's subjective world. This chapter appropriates a framework for assessing individual personality differences known as the Five-Factor Model (FFM). This flexible grid unites change agendas to the Christian character choices that ultimately foster formation. To close, Rachael and Maria, coleaders of Bad Break; Better You, display how personality patterns are as relevant for guides as they are for trekkers.

THRILLS AND WILLS

Guiding a group trek requires considerable adeptness at monitoring compound layers of communication and connection. For illustration, picture an enormous circus known for its collection of novel acts. Jugglers, prancing horses, death defying daredevils, colorful comics reenacting battles, acrobatics and exotic animals all amaze crowds with heart-pumping performances across multiple rings. How does a spectator take it all in? In one ring, a trapeze artist flies through the air, in another elephants dance, and in a third, clowns with huge flowers frolic. The viewer's attention is divided among an assortment of fascinating feats occurring either concurrently or in rapid succession. Adults often find marveling at the circus menagerie an acquired taste. The thrills can overwhelm. Children enjoy the feverish excitement of the non-stop show as they freely let their eyes wander at whim across the spectrum of dazzling options. Where's the resemblance to group trekking? Leaders will do well to maintain a childish sense of wonder regarding the exhilaration of the group experience as a whole. Further, they serve best when they apply a mature and attentive vision to the details of the performers. The action flows quickly as multiple lives play out their unique stories right before our eyes! The astute viewer takes in the thrill of the human drama without missing the subtle demonstration of the human will. A group displays constant performance of human wills invested in constructive work, stalled at cross-purposes or stuck in a rut.

A leader absorbs complex activity emanating from the intrapersonal, interpersonal and collective. Add to these human levels the silent push and pull of the Holy Spirit. The leader scrutinizes the various exchanges intent on making beneficial use of any critical interactions between members, between leader and members, and within the group as a whole. Fostering a trek that utilizes intimacy as a healing force means getting comfortable watching more than three rings! And then trekking guides must be prepared to join in, guide action and coax diverse wills to dare joining their resources.

For a group to make use of relational-level communication, leaders operate according to a fundamental assumption.[1] Namely, they trust that the perspectives and behaviors participants display are consistent with the typical patterns and unmonitored responses that dominate the participants' actual lives. Given the opportunity to relate spontaneously *in* a group, people engage others as they customarily do *outside* of the group. Learning about the influence of one's immediate relational behavior potentially bears on the concern that brought the participant to the group. Professionals who lead therapeutic groups find this premise so imperative that they may apply it exclusively or extensively, paying minimal attention to specific content. Common-theme groups in a ministry context will incorporate content-level communication and typically will have a narrow focus. Thus these helping ventures make only limited use of process observations to encourage greater relational adaptability. Experienced guides do seek to make such moments potent, redemptive and consistent with the movement of the Holy Spirit. In broad terms, each member exposes a portion of personality—a sample slice of one's characteristic manner of thinking, feeling and acting. The slice publicly introduced into the immediate interpersonal activity could indeed be a contributing factor to the issue that the member wishes to address. If so, the

---

[1]Irvin D. Yalom and Molyn Leszcz, *The Theory and Practice of Group Psychotherapy*, 5th ed. (New York: Basic Books, 2005).

Figure 10.1. Journey toward client change

group submits both feedback and encouragement to cultivate alternative, effective and biblically consistent responses. The diagram Journey Toward Client Change summarizes this progression.[2]

A group member who comes across as having a sharp edge could carefully watch how she makes contact as well as when she drives others away. The member who remains steadfastly agreeable yet avoids making waves could be coached to use his voice more effectively. Exploring observed behavior and communication introduces reflection about inner assumptions, expectations and automatic reactions. One's internal pattern for relating presents itself for investigation through the here-and-now relational experience. This requires candid communication regarding actions and attitudes that are normally left unaddressed,

---

[2]Mei-whei Chen and Christopher J. Rybak, *Group Leadership Skills: Interpersonal Process in Group Counseling and Therapy* (Belmont, Calif.: Brooks/Cole, 2004), p. 280.

politely ignored or never questioned. Sometimes, a person's standard response has a familiar echo: "That is not what I meant by that." "The words didn't come out right." "That's how I share when I get upset; I don't mean anything by it." These explanations could be what they seem at first, a denial or defense. However, leaders can pose a neutral approach simply by accenting any disconnect between repeated communication efforts with unintended or null effects. This critical clue would genuinely acknowledge that the exposed piece of the self is comfortable, natural and practiced. Without extensive digging for roots, the leader builds acceptance that the relating pattern is activated with no or only limited mediating conscious thought. Members realize that the overall outcome of the combined non-verbal cues, voice tone, intensity and selected words are communicating more or less than what they wished. Once they recognize this discrepancy, dialogue can help them make new choices. The net result is a set of deliberate responses consistent with actual intentions. Participants can use such a choice opportunity to take risks to relate more authentically. From another angle, group members present a naked vulnerability. Leaders must handle the exchange graciously and infuse hope into the change process. Wise leaders understand that any default mode of operating is deeply embedded and will not yield to impulse for alteration. Redirection can be costly, but change can be realized under the direction of the Holy Spirit.

The leader assists the group to address emotionally charged issues so participants can expose underlying beliefs, habits and patterns in light of their interpersonal impact. Leaders also simultaneously groom group norms so that immediate meta-communication dialogue is productive. Groups use process—direct relational communication—to increase awareness of what works when forming effective connections. For example, members share their own experience of the other without blaming, pejorative labeling, scapegoating, dull advising, attributing motivation, sarcastic blasting or fatalistic predicting. Ideal confrontations emerge from multiple sources, have a direct bearing on what has brought the participant to the group, harmonize with desired outcomes and invigorate hope. These are ripe opportunities to bring scriptural charges and word pictures into the vocabulary of the group, which leaders can do when the direct use of biblical terms fits with the group mission. The characteristics of love (1 Cor 13:4-7); qualities that are to be put on and put off (Eph 4:25, 31-32; Col 3:5-10); or the fruits of the Spirit (Gal 5:16-26) make handy illustrations. A relational metaphor from the Gospel of John as mentioned in the previous chapter is also an option.

The leader and fellow members assist in identifying emotional states. In this way, groups consistently teach about personal affect. Similarly the leader provides succinct, strategic commentary on interpersonal and personality styles. This contributes to an ever-increasing awareness of tendencies, strengths, governing schemas and relational behavior that may be ineffective at the moment or have adverse consequences. The Five-Factor Model (FFM) reasonably allows leaders to assess these specific personality patterns in a constructive manner. The contemporary version associated with Paul T. Costa and Robert R. McCrae is only one of multiple options and methods to depict personality tendencies.[3] I've selected this particular approach because of its linguistic roots, ample empirical support, crosscultural validation, and potential for use across the spectrum of redemptive, adjustment or advancement groups.

The FFM model is nothing new, though over time it has become increasingly refined and simplified. An early ancestor appeared in preliminary form in 1933 when Louis Thurston gave a presidential address to the American Psychological Association. At that early stage, his personality research had identified sixty popular, prevalent and pointed adjectives from the vernacular that referenced key qualities of human uniqueness. In research, Thurston's subjects were directed to apply these terms to familiar acquaintances. The resulting data was reviewed using factor analysis to ascertain how these adjectives clustered together to produce comprehensive personality descriptions. Surprisingly, in spite of the intricate and sophisticated psychological theories, this populist approach yielded a stingy five factors that pulled together various diverse phrases and terms.[4] Proponents of FFM have difficulty explaining why such a parsimonious and practical finding was virtually set aside for nearly fifty years, but some think that the appeal to folk wisdom inherent in ordinary language inhibited its popularity within the academic world. This commonsense approach built with lay language eliminated the necessity for more grandiose psychological theories. Thurston's study was one of the first to apply a lexical method to describing personality.[5] This vein of research capitalizes on the premise that accurate communication regarding variations in personality is a crucial, everyday social function: "She is the sweetest person, real sincere; you can tell or ask her anything." "Catch him on a good day. He has a crotchety and cantankerous side." "Get her as a babysitter. She's

[3]Paul T. Costa and Robert R. McCrae, *Revised NEO Personality Inventory and NEO Five-Factor Inventory: Professional Manual* (Odessa, Fla.: Psychological Assessment Resources, 1992).
[4]John Digman, "The Curious History of the Five-Factor Model," in *The Five-Factor Model of Personality: Theoretical Perspectives*, ed. Jerry S. Wiggins (New York: Guilford Press, 1996), pp. 1-20.
[5]Raymond Cattell and Hans Eysenck are two other major names. See Digman, "Curious History," pp. 2-7, 10-11.

patient, dependable, and won't have her cell phone locked to her ear instead of listening to your kids!"

Words follow human need. Therefore the Five-Factor Model assumes that everyday language contains the necessary and sufficient vocabulary to define and distinguish crucial nuances of personality. Building out the model further follows a straightforward method. Language dictionaries are culled for the adjectives that capture enduring human characteristics. Vocabulary lists of personality descriptors are formed. These are then put to use building actual profiles within a diverse population. The results are sifted mathematically to sort terms into core elements by examining how the descriptors cluster together. Lexical personality models have a primarily linguistic base, not a psychological one. The procedures of investigation with human subjects, factor analysis and construct validation are plainly associated with the academic psychological enterprise. Ironically, the Five-Factor Model represents a sophisticated social engagement coaching system grounded in ordinary language.

The lexical premise should spark interest for those with a ministry mindset. The Christian community often hears about the tools of linguistic analysis in conjunction with arriving at the best meaning of a biblical text. This model considers individual differences using ordinary language, for the purpose of more deeply understanding creatures made in the *imago Dei*. Language not only belongs to human beings as one element of the *imago Dei*, but it also serves as a vehicle for general revelation.

How many broad attributes can generate reasonable depth and nuance in a personality description? Answers vary. On the low end, there are the scant Big Two superfactors identified as Neuroticism/Negative Emotionality (N/NE) and Extraversion/Positive Emotionality.[6] On the upper end, the generous Sixteen Personality Factors of Raymond Cattell illustrate the claim that without a generous supply of building blocks, personality is irresponsibly distorted and flattened. Cattell's Sixteen Personality Factor inventory (16PF) has been regularly updated and has a wide selection of available applications.[7] Given this range of two to sixteen core characteristics, the popular Big Five will be our working number. These factors, in distinguishing combinations, reflect enduring individual differences demonstrated in coherent and constant ways of thinking, feeling and

---

[6]David Watson, Roman Kotov and Wakiza Gamez, "Basic Dimensions of Temperament in Relation to Personality and Psychopathology," in *Personality and Psychopathology*, ed. Robert F. Kruger and Jennifer L. Tackett (New York: Guilford Press, 2006), pp. 7-38.

[7]Michael Karson, Samual Karson and Jerry O'Dell, *16PF Interpretation in Clinical Practice: A Guide to the Fifth Edition* (Champaign, Ill.: IPAT, 1997).

behaving.[8] Their significant empirical base actually extends worldwide and this model is not exclusive to the work of Costa and McCrae.[9] In fact, one major benefit of a lexical approach is that investigation in other languages need not rely on translation for study and use in another culture (etic method). Instead, researchers use the descriptive terms found within the indigenous language and culture itself to construct a comparable measure (emic method).[10] Cultural variations thus receive ongoing consideration as these factors are investigated, replicated and validated globally.

The acrostic OCEAN is the oft-cited mnemonic for recalling the FFM: (O) openness to experience, (C) conscientiousness, (E) extraversion, (A) agreeableness and (N) neuroticism.[11] The acrostic provides a compellingly convenient form. Unfortunately, it obscures a rather important feature that is built into the model. These factors are not equivalent regarding the weight of contribution that each makes to the overall personality. Therefore allow me to list and describe these in descending order, from the factor that makes the largest personality contribution to the one that makes the least.

Extraversion. People-oriented, energetic, talkative, optimistic and affectionate are the hallmarks of this quality. People described as extraverted not only thrive on being with others, but they also tend to be optimistic, laugh and enjoy having fun. One should not assume that introverts have opposite or negative emotions; they are simply low on extraversion. They are reserved but not necessarily unfriendly, quiet but not unhappy, and experience emotion but are not prone to outward display.

Agreeableness. Those on the high side of this quality are known to be trusting, helpful, altruistic, empathetic, eager to please and good-natured. Antagonism describes a characteristic found on the low side of this polarity. People described as antagonistic may be abrasive, suspicious, uncooperative and cynical. There can be a tendency on the low side to be manipulative, unforgiving and spiteful.

---

[8]Paul T. Costa and Thomas A. Widiger, "Introduction: Personality Disorders and the Five-Factor Model of Personality," in *Personality Disorders and the Five-Factor Model of Personality*, ed. Paul T. Costa and Thomas A. Widiger (Washington, D.C.: American Psychological Association, 1994), pp. 1-10; Costa and McCrae, *NEO Personality Inventory*.

[9]Robert R. McCrae and Paul T. Costa, "The NEO Personality Inventory: Using the Five-Factor Model in Counseling," *Journal of Counseling and Development* 69, no. 4 (1991): 367-72.

[10]Gerard Saucier and Lewis R. Goldberg, "The Language of Personality: Lexical Perspectives on the Five-Factor Model," in *The Five-Factor Model of Personality: Theoretical Perspectives*, ed. Jerry S. Wiggins (New York: Guilford Press, 1996), pp. 21-45.

[11]James R. Beck, *Jesus and Personality Theory: Exploring the Five-Factor Model* (Downers Grove, Ill.: InterVarsity Press, 1999).

Conscientiousness. Conscientious individuals are known to be hard-working, self-directed, punctual, ambitious, persistent and scrupulous. This attribute involves organization and drive toward achieving goals. Those low on conscientiousness are laid-back, easygoing to the extent of being negligent, and are drawn toward more pleasurable activities.

Neuroticism. The high side on this factor indicates that emotional unrest and instability is dominant. An alternate label is negative affectivity. These individuals are prone to feel emotions instantly and intensely. They have weak, inefficient coping skills for soothing or self-regulating, and this results in impulsive behavior. Low frustration tolerance may accompany unrealistic expectations and beliefs. People who are low on this factor have strong competencies and inner resources to manage desires and affect. Also on the low end, people show a readiness to accept flaws in themselves and others.

Openness to experience. This describes individuals who actively seek firsthand knowledge in encounter, for they find discovery of novel sensations intrinsically rewarding. Those high on openness are curious, imaginative and willing to entertain unusual ideas and values. A person low on openness tends to be conservative, conventional, dogmatic and rigid. The characteristic implies that those who tend toward being closed may be dependable while struggling with change and creativity.

It should be immediately obvious that the top two factors, extraversion and agreeableness are essentially interpersonal traits. The most telling markers of individual personality are exclusively relational. Group approaches, therefore, are ideal to bring out these formidable factors because of their embedded relational emphasis. Finally, while the FFM has considerable crosscultural verification, the dimension with the least amount of contribution to overall personality, openness to experience, has the most deviation in definition across cultures.[12] See the Five-Factor Model Summary for a graphical listing of these attributes and facets.

Each attribute is represented by a title indicative of the high end of its bipolar dimension. Neuroticism is consistent with this grid because it labels that dimension's high end. When referencing this factor, I prefer to describe the characteristic in a positive and appealing manner. This requires using the tag from the low end: *emotional stability*. The phrase *emotional reactivity* then functions best as an approximate substitute for the high side. These terms are acceptable

---

[12]Stephanie N. Mullins-Sweatt and Thomas A. Widiger, "The Five-Factor Model of Personality Disorder: A Translation Across Science and Practice," in *Personality and Psychopathology*, ed. Robert F. Krueger and Jennifer L. Tackett (New York: Guilford Press, 2006), pp. 39-70.

Table 10.1. Five-Factor Model Summary.

Factor Facets	High Dimension	Low Dimension
Extraversion	*Extraversion*	*Introversion*
Warmth	Cordial, affectionate, attached	Cold, aloof, indifferent
Gregariousness	Sociable, outgoing	Withdrawn, isolated
Assertiveness	Dominant, forceful	Unassuming, quiet, resigned
Activity	Vigorous, energetic, active	Passive, lethargic
Excitement-seeking	Reckless, daring	Cautious, monotonous, dull
Positive emotions	High-spirited	Placid, anhedonic
Agreeableness	*Agreeableness*	*Antagonism*
Trust	Gullible, naive, trusting	Skeptical, cynical, paranoid
Straightforwardness	Confiding, honest	Cunning, manipulative, deceitful
Altruism	Sacrificial, giving	Stingy, greedy, exploitative
Compliance	Docile, cooperative	Combative, aggressive
Modesty	Meek, self-effacing, humble	Confident, boastful, arrogant
Tender-Mindedness	Soft, empathic	Tough, callous, ruthless
Conscientiousness	*Conscientiousness*	*Undependability*
Competence	Perfectionist, efficient	Lax, negligent
Order	Ordered, methodical, organized	Haphazard, disorganized, sloppy
Dutifulness	Rigid, reliable, dependable	Casual, undependable, unethical
Achievement	Workaholic, ambitious	Aimless, desultory
Self-discipline	Dogged, devoted	Hedonistic, negligent
Deliberation	Ruminative, reflective	Hasty, careless, rash
Neuroticism	*Neuroticism*	*Emotional Stability*
Anxiousness	Fearful, apprehensive	Relaxed, unconcerned, cool
Angry hostility	Angry, bitter	Even-tempered
Depressiveness	Pessimistic, glum	Optimistic
Self-consciousness	Timid, embarrassed	Self-assured, glib, shameless
Impulsivity	Tempted, urgent	Controlled, restrained
Vulnerability	Helpless, fragile	Stalwart, fearless, unflappable
Openness	*Openness*	*Closedness to Experience*
Fantasy	Dreamer, unrealistic, imaginative	Practical, concrete
Aesthetics	Aberrant interests, aesthetic	Uninvolved, no aesthetic interest
Feelings	Sensitive, responsive	Constricted, unable to express emotion
Actions	Unconventional, adventurous	Predictable, stubborn, habitual
Ideas	Strange, odd, peculiar, creative	Pragmatic, rigid
Values	Permissive, broad-minded	Traditional, inflexible, dogmatic

(Based on Stephanie N. Mullins-Sweatt and Thomas A. Widiger, "The Five-Factor Model of Personality Disorder: A Translation Across Science and Practice," in *Personality and Psychopathology*, ed. Robert F. Krueger and Jennifer L. Tackett [New York: Guilford, 2006], p. 45.)

although neither readily conveys the stark, negative outlook of seeing the glass as half-empty, nor the steady pull toward anger, hostility and fear. Neuroticism carries all of these subtleties, thus explaining the term's staying power. Nonetheless, whether in a ministry or clinical group, I highly recommend the practice of pivoting this dimension on emotional stability, with the more problematic edge referencing a low threshold for reactivity.

Individuals vary considerably on each of these bipolar dimensions. Each person is an exceptional blend. But will these broad personality factors show up in a group with a prescribed life span? In other words, does a short-term experience allow enough freedom of expression for folks to be known as they ordinarily appear? I contend, with the following support from group literature, that from early on these facets of personality tend to make an appearance in the group. A team of researchers sought to improve the outcomes of group-based interventions. As there was no concern with global personality factors, they designed a specialized rating form to track member behavior within groups.[13] They wished to determine therapeutically enhancing performance, notice changes over the course of treatment and record these interactions. They developed a tool they called the Individual Group Member Interpersonal Process Scale (IGIPS), an instrument customized precisely for group therapy. The measure needed to be sensitive enough to detect progression and specific enough to pick up on any actions contributing to the eventual outcome. The IGIPS was put to use in seven groups that ran for fifteen sessions of ninety minutes each. Five experienced therapists directed the groups, which included fifty-two young adult patients who presented mild mental health issues and who were serviced by a major health maintenance organization. Examples of the behaviors recorded were: discusses own issues; receives input from other members; requests help from the group; provides other members with approval; and expresses anger, disappointment, disagreement, and frustration with the therapist, to name a few. In other words critical behaviors within a group were part of the reason people were participating in the research groups. Upon further examination, the IGIPS ratings indicated that five variables accounted for the variety of behavior: activity; interpersonal sensitivity; comfort with self; self-focused; and psychologically minded. The authors reported that they had absolutely no intention at the outset to build a bridge with a personality model such as the FFM. After all, the IGIPS was designed

---

[13]Stephen Soldz, Michael Davis, Simon Budman and Annette Demby, "Beyond the Interpersonal Circumplex in Group Psychotherapy: The Structure and Relationship to Outcome of the Individual Group Member Interpersonal Process Scale," *Journal of Clinical Psychology* 49 (1993): 551-63.

primarily to detect critical details of behavior in one setting, not identify factors as broad or far-reaching as personality. Nonetheless, the authors remarked with surprise that (1) the activity variable had similarities to extraversion; (2) interpersonal sensitivity had firm ties to agreeableness; (3) comfort with self ran alongside emotional stability; and (4) psychological mindedness corresponded to openness to experience. The remaining variable of being self-focused appeared to have an inverse relationship to conscientiousness. The researchers observed that conscientious members protected the group task and reached out to all, or were less focused on self.

This fascinating set of parallels between observed group behaviors and general personality traits lends credibility to the notion that the FFM presents an appropriate grid for consideration in group work. Clearly, a single study does not make the case certain. But it lends credibility to an approach that uses in-group behaviors to generalize personality patterns that affect relationships over the long term. Thus, leaders who become familiar with the FFM give themselves a flexible observation model that is both solid and simple. Leaders will undoubtedly develop an ad hoc method to take notice of and classify member behavior and interactions. Over time and use, their approach will become more systematic. The FFM is one practical, ready-made approach that fits with everyday language. These categories may build the bridge necessary to consider broader patterns.

The FFM can be a superb tool for leaders of ministry-based helping groups. Five explanations support the rationale for this recommendation.

1. Ease of use. The terminology of the FFM requires no specialized training. With the exception of neuroticism, it contains minimal jargon. The terms mean what they do in ordinary language. As a leader becomes acquainted with those on the journey, the categories exist as a reasonable method to rate how a member fits on a particular factor continuum. For example, those who are extraverted will typically stand out from those who are less so. Achieving a reasonable concept of individual tendencies does not require formal measurement. Once leaders establish a baseline impression, they refine it as more observations become available. Leaders avoid pigeonholing by holding their impressions cautiously and remaining open to developing formulations. Members can have customized progress markers. Take an individual who would best be portrayed as closed to experience, rigid and practical. If this person exhibits a reasonable effort to participate in an experiential or unstructured task, leaders must extend that individual considerable credit. He took a tough step that fell outside his comfort zone. A person typically open to experience, on the other hand, would have greeted the assignment with ease and enthusiasm.

If leaders wish to generate standardized scores or provide profile feedback on the FFM, such measures exist and can be used. For example, group therapists could administer the NEO Personality Inventory Revised (NEO PI-R) with reasonable reliability and validity.[14] The ethical parameters for using this type of psychological instrument dictate acceptable education to secure supplies, administer the tool and interpret the results. Common-theme groups do not require a full assessment profile. When members are granted a creative platform for self-introduction and the freedom to share stories, everyone reveals some outstanding characteristics. If a leader models an introduction or gives examples that describe these characteristics, others may follow suit in how they report. Using the FFM, leaders have a classification grid in which to mentally file these rough observations so that they can personalize growth expectations.[15]

2. *Focus on patterns, not destiny.* By definition, FFM characteristics remain consistent and stable across adulthood. Nothing requires individuals to consider these as variables that control destiny, however. A person may tend toward introversion, emotional reactivity or a relaxed, laid-back style; although these trends enable prediction, they are not automatically prophetic of future behavior. In evaluating personality models, observers may be inclined to think of individual reference points as deterministic. Characteristic modes of thinking, feeling and behavior formed in the past and operating in the present are the working parameters for the future. At the popular level, people cite traits and tendencies as rationalizations for problematic relating or behavior. "That's just how I am!" Or, "We had irreconcilable personality differences." This confuses propensity with necessity. The FFM does not necessarily imply rigid determinism. Default modes of thinking, feeling and behaving do tend to be maintained. These represent well-rehearsed scripts, imbedded preferences and natural inclinations. Routine components of personality tend to run along comfortable pathways, for this requires less effort and mental consideration. Nonetheless, a motivated will can indeed manage demonstrated behavior. And if the Holy Spirit is involved, an additional resource can empower personal action that moves one toward *shalom* in relationships.

3. *Address observations without attributing cause.* These factors have been so robust under investigation that numerous genetic studies regarding heredity also

---

[14]Costa and McCrae, "NEO Personality Inventory."
[15]In providing counselor education to future group leaders, I incorporate a measure that assesses the Big Five into the curriculum at a relevant juncture to increase self-awareness of these characteristics. This is a teaching technique to acquaint group leaders with this vocabulary.

reference the FFM. Personality traits, like the physical attributes of eye color or height, can be shown to correlate with one's genetic kin. Regardless of this established association or the volume of accumulated evidence, however, applying the FFM does not essentially assume causal properties.[16] In a chapter discussing lexical personality perspectives, Gerald Saucier and Lewis Goldberg press the point that what is observed and recorded by such a language-based approach is phenotype (surface characteristics) not genotype (causal or genetic). Using the FFM within groups equips leaders to recognize member uniqueness, and no compelling reason within the model itself requires a commitment to biological, environmental, interactive or spiritual causation.[17] While not a definitive stance on "nature verses nurture," the FFM simply describes traits. "The language of personality provides a framework for description, but not necessarily for explanation."[18] Research concedes that such patterns are sturdy and stubborn regardless of their source or cause. By grace, the Holy Spirit and human agency, individuals can direct their exhibited behavior according to their intentions, for the benefit of valued relationships.

4. Turn "problem members" into "unproductive patterns." The attributes within this framework can be presented with neutral, or at least not overly offensive, expressions. This is extremely important. Those entering helping groups may already have a substantial history of hearing, "You are the difficulty." A member who has demonstrated erratic and emotionally volatile behavior (low emotional stability) may accept having a penchant to experience emotions passionately, quickly and intensely. In addition, this person could eventually acknowledge hope and commit to inhibit instantaneous action that is destructive to self and lasting relationships. Or a withdrawn person who is perceived by others as cold, heartless and dull might embrace as a rewarding venture the notion of being reserved alongside the challenge to discover methods of communicating closeness to a select few.

Those who run groups have a tradition of representing members who parade

---

[16]These comments do not represent a dismissal of the concept of heritability. Rather, I separate an automatic association between the Five-Factor Model, trait theory and genetics in an attempt to head leaders off from rejecting the model merely because certain advocates argue for a biological basis for temperament. Nature and nurture debates can be set aside in the application of this framework.

[17]Based on Genesis 3, the lack of harmony within and between persons in the expression of these attributes would be the result of the Fall. I would resist any argument that attempts to press a specific factor trend as personal sin. On the other hand, Scripture admonishes the pursuit of wisdom and walking with the Creator as a way to resist ongoing sin.

[18]Saucier and Goldberg, "Language of Personality," p. 24.

disruptive interpersonal habits as *problem clients*. Yalom and Leszcz in their major text recognize that in actuality the problem is ultimately a combination of the client's unique psychological presentation, group dynamics, co-member and therapist interactions. Over 50 percent of those who lead groups rate "working with difficult patients" as a critical concern.[19] The *monopolist* is a prime example. Such persons are known to chatter away telling stories with unceasing energy. As a solution, Yalom and Leszcz recommend a combination strategy. First, leaders direct the group as a whole to consider its passive willingness to allow one member to carry the meeting. This places responsibility for management on the group itself. Second, leaders alert the member to the necessity of altering this established routine. The FFM may assist a leader to avoid any reference to monopolizing. The dilemma could be explained as extraverted enthusiasm to share about self. This energy needs modification to be relationally effective. The member could accomplish this by increasing the vitality of interaction while decreasing duration. Thus, the troublesome *monopolist* label never makes an entrance. In its place sits a member who requires challenge to tame extraverted—gregarious to the point of aggressive—behavior. This can be particularly effective if the member has demonstrated a productive disclosure on some occasion and a leader or other group member noted that exception. Should the trait relate to a concern outside of group, addressing it within the group might be an outstanding growth opportunity.

The term *help-rejecting complainer* describes another problematic participant style. This participant routinely brings forward crises worthy of group attention. When others grant the difficulty status, take it seriously and wrestle it to the ground, their best supportive endeavors and a wide assortment of helpful ideas are brushed aside or diminished in value. Using the FFM, such a participant may match on extraversion and low agreeableness or antagonism. The participant needs to hear that the desire to engage with others is important and commendable. Unfortunately, doubt, cynicism and the pain of past disappointments hurt others and hold back this member from taking productive action. Conceptualizing the pattern thus will not constitute a fast fix. The world of group therapy supplied the designation for this recurring and annoying interpersonal deadlock because facilitators have had regular visitors who request assistance then incessantly push others away using "yes, but." An understanding built on the FFM prevents leaders and participants both from entering the member's shadow view of the world and also from becoming susceptible to contracting compassion fatigue.

---

[19]Yalom and Leszcz, *Theory and Practice*, p. 391.

5. *Facilitate formation by uniquely applying the teachings of Jesus Christ.* These factors provide a means to discover pointed areas of need for spiritual matura-tion. On the downside of any group intervention, lackluster conformity could be mistaken for Christian maturity. Instead, a better governing norm would be to appreciate colorful individual development as a community with the love of Jesus Christ. The FFM intentionally curtails uniform advice or prescriptive formulas, a format routinely and regretfully played out in evangelical circles. A leader or an idealized member becomes the prototype associated with what it means to be Christlike. Such pressure toward uniformity rejects the notion that each person is a unique variation of the *imago Dei*, each undergoing re-creation for commu-nion within the church of Jesus Christ. The church body abounds with diversity and special gifting. Simplistic conformity pales in comparison to obeying the unique leading of the Holy Spirit.

A decade ago, psychologist and Christian scholar James R. Beck wrote *Jesus & Personality Theory: Exploring the Five-Factor Model.* The instruction from the Word that Beck articulates contains no indication that Jesus himself taught or endorsed this contemporary model of personality. Instead, he concentrates on a series of biblical themes Jesus regularly espoused that have direct bearing on how to turn each of these personality factors in a direction honoring to the Savior. These insights can stimulate individually oriented spiritual formation possibili-ties within a trek toward intimacy. Beck intends to encourage imitation of Jesus Christ by adherence to his teaching while endorsing human uniqueness.

CHANGE COURSE TO MATURE IN CHRIST

In chapter three, we examined the verse Wesley cited to anchor his bands; it supplied the foundation for his intensive small groups. "Therefore confess your sins to each other and pray for each other so that you may be healed" (Jas 5:16). Recall that confession extends beyond the open expression of a secret, internal state of sin to God or to a spiritual authority. The type of confessional conversa-tion encouraged here includes transparent revelation of solemn pledges of com-mitment, loyalty and faith. Sharing private sin and declaring intentional acts of devotion are intricately woven within this interpersonal exercise. This activity harmonizes with the heart of collective helping as collaborators strive to be au-thentic together. The professional counseling terminology would emphasize a member working on personal issues, agendas and goals. From the perspective of this admonition from James, believers confess or pledge their word before God and others. Our words precede our steps. The Holy Spirit moves us toward sanctification. A group provides an ideal venue to ascertain how activities, attitudes and expressions of love match our promises. When participants become a cohesive unit, a secure panel can guide the fulfillment of these pledges. Fellow sojourners grant a reliable source of progress appraisal based on immediate experience of relating, communicating and living.

Groups members find it crucial to strategically refine their statements of intention and pledge. These frame the criteria for motivation and accountability. The imperative to change is not, as is nearly universally believed, a correction of circumstances or redirection from an influential other. Contemporary culture fortifies the human proclivity to sniff out formulas, action plans or external interventions to resolve problems. People wish to coerce the offending other to cease or commence activities according to our expectations. But a more productive way exists for investing precious energy in these groups: are there cognitive rubrics, affective cycles or conduct pitfalls under self-jurisdiction to ponder and address? Serious reflection under these headings holds the potential for sustained change. Doing so does not implicate the person seeking assistance as responsible or culpable for any and all adversity that has befallen him. No one wishes to reenact the verbal sparring between Job and his comforters. Rather, sober reflection recognizes one's limited sphere of influence and control. People can and should still pray for the Lord to do his will, for God can and does intervene in external conditions, and he can orchestrate a change of heart within influential parties. Still, God's answer could indeed parallel the core message to Job. "The fear of the Lord—that is wisdom, and to shun evil is understanding" (Job 28:28). People and circumstances are not ours to manipulate. This includes indirect efforts to influence the Creator to heed our design. He has his own methods. He is the Creator and we are his creatures. What would respectful submission, trust and leaning on the Lord entail? Selecting biblical themes that speak to distinct personality attributes, as Beck does, presents a reasonable place to start.[20]

The two themes that Beck selects to give direction to those with distinctive highs or lows on extraversion are to *show love* and *be trustworthy*. The call to display love out of devotion to the Lord dominates the New Testament. Matthew 5:43-48 and Luke 6:27-28 stand out in the application of this specific personality feature. The passages charge readers and hearers to extend love worthy of Jesus Christ to our enemies, even those who persecute and cause harm.

The entire process of loving one's enemies, however, requires first admitting that we do have enemies, that people do hate or dislike us and that we are capable

---

[20]Beck, *Jesus and Personality Theory*, pp. 129-74.

of exceedingly sinful attitudes of malice, retribution and revenge. If we attempt to maintain that we love everyone, that everyone loves us and that we have no ill will toward anyone, we are not prepared to begin obeying Christ's command to love our enemies. Jesus had enemies; so do we.[21]

The inhabitants in our lives most likely to cross our minds or lips during a group exchange are those temporarily or permanently within the enemy camp. Consider how the extravert might cope with an estranged relationship. High drive, energy and extensive people skills could facilitate a bold move to pursue reconciliation. One who is introverted finds this a more strenuous maneuver. On the other hand, does the extravert ignore enemies as replacement relationships are gathered with ease? Are others enlisted to enter into the disdain or marginalization of the enemy? An extraverted individual has the means to recruit the goodwill of others without ever coming to terms with an enemy. For an introvert, the pattern of being detached, unconcerned or passive could hide inner damage as well as inhibit engagement that deals realistically with blows perceived or received. A withdrawn and less socially energetic person might have to labor intentionally to exhibit love even to those who are cherished and not enemies at all. Without deliberate deeds, the subtlety or absence of overt demonstration might leave love covered by a mask of unspoken affect.

The commandments Moses brought down from Mount Sinai clearly stated God's desire regarding the integrity and trustworthiness of his people (Ex 20:1-17). Jesus and James speak to the importance of words mirroring intention (Mt 5:33-37; Jas 5:12). The challenge of trustworthiness for the extra vert emanates from the constant press to impress, please and win popularity. This could contribute to distorting details, persuasive speech with limited depth and reduced reliability in the eyes of those counting on them to fulfill prior commitments. The production of white lies could be a concern. The introvert's silence could be mistaken for assent or the absence of commitment. Either direction compromises credibility and trust.

The agreeableness factor can be contemplated through the biblical lenses of *enjoying shalom* and *resting in acceptance* related to God's love.[22] Those who are high on agreeableness radiate empathy and compassion. These characteristics so tightly entwine with the current concept of what love actually looks like that an individual on the high side will undoubtedly be described as loving. In working out this attitude, an individual may multiply the experience of peace in self and

---

[21]Ibid., p. 150.
[22]Ibid., pp. 179-218.

others. If one is combative, full of strife and rough around the edges, the message to cooperate and be conciliatory will flow. Under the surface of each end of this dimension, individuals may misunderstand the message of the cross. The death of our Lord was an atoning sacrifice for sin that made reconciliation with God possible (see Rom 6:6; 1 Cor 1:18-25). Does the display of agreeableness or antagonism suggest a rejection of this message in continued attempts to crucify self to appease God or please others? Is *shalom*, the deep persuasive and holistic sense of peace, a reality? Or does a person seek superficial harmony at the hefty price of self-flagellation, loathing and begrudgingly bowing to others?

The creation stewardship command of Genesis 1:28-30 surely justifies conscientiousness, with its steady production and orderly appearance. Association of this dimension with the Protestant work ethic displays how fully this factor is interspersed with the Christian faith tradition and how dedication to overcoming a trend on the low end would be routine. The biblical themes with implications surrounding this factor are to *display mercy* and *pursue justice*.[23] The dangers of perfectionism, judgmental posture and righteous pride are not difficult to imagine. Christians need to monitor how this dimension affects their outgoing messages and attitudes toward others. Do they extend messages of consideration and acceptance? Or do impossible standards weigh them down with discouragement? One who is highly conscientious could conceivably struggle with how messy, risky and complex it is to change systems and conditions. This resistance may inadvertently contribute to tolerance of injustice. A laxness on this factor could contribute to taking others for granted, pursuing self-interest or ignoring the pleas of those in need.

Emotional instability does not by description convey practical appeal. But this facet of self-consciousness and the resulting engagement in self-scrutiny can bring substantial benefit if the process does not become crippling. Group leaders will recognize and anticipate that those high on this feature regularly travel aboard helping treks. In an article on the FFM of personality and the study of religion, Robert McCrae commented that those high on this neuroticism factor may turn to religion for relief and meaning.[24] The intensity of the struggle with inner emotional upheaval can find comfort and be granted purpose within a religious frame. McCrae was not referencing Christianity specifically. Still, the invitation of Jesus, "Come to me, all you who are weary and burdened, and I will

---

[23]Ibid., pp. 83-126.
[24]Robert McCrae, "Mainstream Personality Psychology and the Study of Religion," *Journal of Personality* 67, no. 6 (1999): 2109-18.

give you rest" (Mt 11:28), appeals particularly to persons high on this dimension. The individual high on this factor experiences unfortunate and painful disruptions on a regular basis, and therefore a religious orientation offers stability from the outside for the unrest within. The biblical themes that Beck suggests are relevant for this characteristic are to *offer and accept confession* as well as *seek and grant forgiveness*. These activities both soothe self and secure reconciliation. A group could conceivably provide step-by-step coaching and support on these imperative Christian practices. Further, members low on emotional stability will probably find an immediate opportunity to put these spiritually motivated interpersonal priorities into action.

The personality attribute of openness to experience represents an outlook on life. The two biblical themes that foster a Christian meta-attitude regarding the experience of life are *spread joy* and *experience hope*.[25] From his birth announcement that proclaimed good news of great joy to the shocking discovery that the grave could not hold him, the gospel of Jesus Christ casts a perspective of joy (see Mt 2:10; 28:8; Lk 1:14-15, 44, 46; 2:10; 19:37; 24:41, 52). From the prophecy of a Savior infused into the Genesis 3 curse of sin to the promise of no more tears under Jesus' rule in Revelation 21, the Christian message exudes an eschatological hope. The Creator holds this future. Through the plan of redemption, those who rest in the Savior share this hope. People on either end of this distinguishing characteristic can ponder how the Spirit may minister through the development of attitudes related to joy and hope. One who is generally closed may sense frightening risks all around, so much so that only adherence to customary or habitual rituals can prevail. For one high on this factor, the adrenaline rush of adventure and the thrill of beauty can become such a priority that novelty overrides faithfulness to cherished people and moral absolutes. Consider the addict who grieves the loss of joy as she turns away from the ecstasy of risk. A personality-altering substance can transform one who is generally closed into an experience seeker, removing his inhibitions. Upholding a marriage vow can be experienced as strangling cords of constraint for one who expectantly anticipates the experience of the forbidden or the unknown. A parent who leans toward being closed can react vigorously as the youth under his roof speaks of sprouting wings. Coping with an acquired physical restriction may be a particularly unbearable condemnation to one whose openness and hope rested in a now-lost capacity. How will such people embrace hope in the Lord?

The above illustrations give examples of how a leader's imagination may be ig-

---

[25]Beck, *Jesus and Personality Theory*, pp. 45-80.

nited by the recognition of an individual's features of distinction and one assortment of biblical themes.[26] Association of these attributes and themes does not
transfer into regimented treatment plans or ready-to-dispense recommendations.
This is not even remotely the case in Beck's presentation, nor in my brief sug-
gestive applications. Leaders do not assess tendencies toward either side of these
dimensions in order to instantly or forcefully confront them. Personality traits
can resist modification within the limits of a brief group experience. They are
normal characteristics with considerable traction and staying power. A common-
theme group experience raises awareness of autopilot patterns that conflict with
relational intentions or spiritual commitments. As the member fine-tunes her
own understanding, she may pledge to address the specific factor as it promul-
gates old behavior and to try on new ways of relating more effectively. Further,
personality is not one-dimensional. In groups, people more frequently see the
mixture of distinguishing tendencies, not single attributes. I propose, nonetheless, that these five factors will help guides notice members, and to do so with the
acuity to perceive behavioral depth. Finally, the method of cultivating awareness
of individual differences separates member activity into recognizable rings and
discernable acts, even though the leader is not a ringmaster responsible for the
execution of a flawless show. Individual members must discover what it will take
to realize fulfilling relationships and then to rest wholly in the Lord. The thrill
comes as the group assists its members to redirect their will in submission to the
Lord's direction. With this polarity adjusted, leaders can institute a corrective
course of relating to others in a way that honors Jesus Christ. This process often
demands members to bring their struggles to the surface and to grasp their inner
emotions and relational expectations. Thus the FFM frames one tool for leading
toward affect and attachment.

BAD BREAK; BETTER YOU

Rachael and Maria eagerly brainstormed themes, exercises and resources for their
budding group adventure aimed at women who knew all too well that "break-

---

[26]McCrae points out that this is the one factor that contributes significantly to placement of religious commitment as it reflects a desire for variety, aesthetic sensitivity and rejection of authoritarian values. He cites a study of liberal and fundamental Protestants that found this factor to
separate the two groups. Fundamentalists were less prepared to appreciate poetry, exhibit intellectual curiosity and try new foods. In my estimation this divide may be under revision and that
is why I have placed this comment in this footnote. My experience with Christian groups would
certainly support that those who are less open to experience, rigid and authoritarian are not as
pleased with a group method that relies on encounter, experience and relational communication.
See Robert McCrae, "Mainstream Personality Psychology," p. 1214.

ing up is hard to do." There was no shortage of material. Their own romantic histories had primed these women to lead such a recovery journey. Both worked as professional counselors in an agency specializing in women's issues. The staff readily agreed that spirituality quests are of prime import for self-discovery and optimal mental health when clients initiate them. The organization respected the overtly Christian counselors among these colleagues and endorsed them to expose faith values without imposing religious preferences. Referrals originated from other health professionals, clergy, the general community, a Christian college and even a nearby women's shelter. Not a week went by without a client choking up over a story of a romantic disaster or painful relational distancing. The steady stream of sufferers and relentless flow of tears made this guided mutual support experience appealing.

Bad Break; Better You

The end of a serious romantic relationship can release waves of intense emotional turmoil. This seminar and optional eight-session follow-up support group is designed to help women cope through a break-up without breaking down. Bad Break; Better You will emphasize self-care during relationship recovery. By exploring boundaries and behavior, dreams and desires, you may even find hope for growth.

Within this agency, groups were commissioned following a two-hour introductory didactic seminar. Attendance at a seminar presentation required no participation or commitment. For Bad Break; Better You, counselors would outline themes, explain self-destructive snares, share stories and list potentially helpful strategies. They would firmly endorse the support group as the ideal next step. The seminar had value and could itself be a sufficient boost to a renewed outlook. Individual counseling, with or without the group, was certainly an option. Joining the eight-session experience required attending the seminar plus an assessment and orientation session with one of the leaders. If the interested client was already in individual counseling, the agency permitted her counselor to admit her directly into the group, although it still recommended an orientation.

Bad Break; Better You was anticipated to be a journey that required an extra box of tissues. No one was likely to join without unfortunate and harsh reasons. Like similar time-limited groups, the leaders intended to direct concentrated care during a difficult period. Brief groups were no magical, curative elixir. Rachael and Maria understood that their undertaking invited women together in an effort to prevent anger from turning inward into depression. Instead, women might find a starting place for hope. The leaders carefully steered clear of communicating, "You're better off alone," instead trying to build on the strengths of each participant. These soon-to-be-coleaders were united on mission and major themes. But without much insight, they were miles apart on setting the essential structure and knowing how to exhibit unity when eliciting emotional material.

Rachael cautiously identified herself as a Christian and was judicious when bringing her faith into clinical work. Maria had the *Ichthus* fish symbol prominently on her business card and actively recruited clients favoring a Christian perspective into her caseload. During the initial planning session, Rachael came prepared with two articles, sample descriptions gleaned from an Internet search, and a list of possible exercises compiled from select sources. Maria moved to and fro, drawing on a handful of diverse first- or second-hand tales. Rachael was early. Maria's prior session ran over; she was delayed. Their distinctive styles were also strikingly evident during the seminar. Rachael taught with carefully selected words, supplied a handout complete with bibliography, and finished her assigned topics precisely at the designated minute. Maria shared several outrageous endings and eventual recovery stories in a spontaneous, winsome way. She ran long but finished well with a sensitive, moving illustration from her personal life. Bad Break; Better You drew several women who expressed a tentative willingness to begin. But the question remained, would Rachael's and Maria's personality strengths complement each another or were they bound for a painful blow-up?

The inevitable crash came in week four. When the crisis surfaced, Rachael and Maria were predominantly surprised. Two of the eight women announced a decision not to continue even though each had originally committed to attend the full series. One said that her life was too hectic. The other claimed that while the group had been useful early on, current discussion was holding her back and resurfacing old wounds. A third member suggested a compromise; these women should stay, but the whole group should conclude soon as many had successfully made important gains. Rachael and Maria used a pattern of taking turns at leadership. For this session, Maria was moderating. She attempted to sift through their specific grievances. Nothing came out into the open. She shared a story that illustrated the importance of remaining to the conclusion of the group sequence. The woman in favor of negotiating an abbreviated series of meetings then proceeded to take sides with those who were planning to depart. The membership divided between those who thought holding fast to the plan was best and those who accepted the legitimacy of the voiced reasons for departure along with the right to leave. Rachael was quiet. She softly asked Maria for permission to speak as the hour drew to a close. Her summary stated that if possible, all should return to the next session. Her rationale contained three questions. These were important to consider together: (1) Was there anything happening in the group that needed discussion or revision? (2) What feelings, if any, have these unexpected announcements of leaving surfaced? (3) As each one learns to achieve healthier goodbyes and to understand the limits of commitment, are there any lessons to be learned from this moment? Maria immediately jumped in to add her voice endorsing the view that those were terrific questions. "The issue for the group," she said, "is really about dealing with a premature, unexpected break-up!" She hastily ended with a promise to review everything with their supervisor who specialized in leading groups. The room felt tense. The session ended with most heads nodding, if only half-heartedly, in agreement to attend for at least one more week.

Supervision had already been planned for the group's halfway mark. The agency director kept updated on specific groups at set intervals. There was an informal drop-in oversight meeting for all group leaders each week for mutual support and ongoing problem solving. Rachael and Maria had not raised any major concerns in those chats thus far. There had been no obvious need. Midway through any group, a review supervision session was scheduled with Lil, the clinical director, to discuss the status of the group and make plans for the subsequent cycle. The supervisor listened to the reports on the trust level in the group, key events and the current viability crisis. The sessions so far had allowed the participating women to tell their grim stories, report on coping and address repetitive waves of emotion. There had been considerable anger in the room during Bad Break; Better You. Given the theme, the leaders had expected there would be good reasons for fury in members' reactions. Both Rachael and Maria provided input regarding this review. The supervisor leaned away from the events and dynamics within the group itself. To their shock, she started to detail the different styles of the leaders and the possible contributing influence on the rising tension. The supervisor then articulated three basic reminders about coleading groups.

1. Running a group helping experience can be draining. Productive coleaders can be a useful protection against counselor burnout.

2. Coleaders give participants the benefit of four eyes and ears. Less material falls through the cracks when coleaders offer joint coverage and attention.

3. If complicated group or member reactions occur toward one leader, the other is there to sort the tension out.[27]

Following this review of the basics, the supervisor gave her assessment. These principles of coleading were inhibited in their group. "During our conversation today, you, Maria, and you, Rachael, have both communicated extremely well. In my experience of listening to you, I have felt inwardly torn, like I needed to make a decisive choice to side with one or the other. There is no outward disagreement. Still, the raw heat of uncontrolled competition is in the air. This causes me to wonder if your women are sensing a rivalry between the two of you. If this is occurring, then they may be seeking to break free of any pull similar to what I have been exposed to and feel right now. Maria, you are energetic, always ready to emote and thrive on creativity. Rachael, I see you as cautious, calculating and concrete. It should be no astonishing news that your styles clash." Despite this statement, Rachael and Maria were profoundly stunned. And yet, they could not deny the sensations within. On the surface, they would not have admitted to holding any hostility toward each other. Inside, the trust between was low, in actuality, extremely low. The follow-up plan was to meet together before the next group to consider better ways to demonstrate and communicate a united front. The supervisor closed by placing a prohibition on any more turn-taking in leadership week by week. "You both need to lead each week, even if one ends up being more active than the other. Work out the meaning of the word *partnership*. Flip-flopping leadership each meeting can be confusing for members. Seek to combine your styles in a complementary manner each time the group assembles."

As Rachael and Maria were leaving, the supervisor let down her customary, professional guard. She tossed out an off-hand comment as she chuckled, "It is so fascinating. I always knew that you two were wired differently. But I have always been struck by how you both take your spiritual faith so seriously. How interesting is it that I just expected that miraculously you two would somehow be a strong team. Sorry, my assuming that miracle was a big mistake. No matter. Differences naturally show up in groups and that's why we run them."

For lunch the next day, Maria and Rachael made a plan to eat, talk and take a walk together. Before they started, there was a long pause.

Rachael began, "I had a restless sleep last night."

---

[27]Marianne Corey and Gerald Corey, *Groups: Process & Practice*, 7th ed. (Belmont, Calif.: Brooks/ Cole, 2006), pp. 48-49.

Maria looked right into Rachael's eyes and replied, "I think I know what you are going to say. What Lil said at the end of our meeting got to you. Am I right?"

"Amazing, I'm astounded that you knew that. Her miracle comment left a bitter aftertaste. My insides have been churning and sour ever since. I don't think she meant anything harsh by it; except that we are both actually normal. It made me upset because . . ." Rachael broke mid-sentence. Even though she had planned out precisely what she expected to say phrase by phrase, she began to choke up. Maria could not recall ever having seen Rachael cry.

"The group is going to be fine," Maria said softly, "but that's not what's going to be hard. I am starting to realize that I actually need what you bring into the room. That was not obvious to me until you gave that awesome summary at the end of the last session."

Hearing those words of recognition by her coleader permitted an inner release. Slowly Rachael found the phrases she had practiced. "I feel like I don't know what to expect from you. That makes me anxious even though I can appreciate that your instincts are good. It will take Lil's big miracle for us to become a team. If that happens, it's not going to happen for this agency or for any group. I believe that the Lord would like us to bring honor to him."

With these words, Rachael and Maria were ready to pray, eat and take a stroll. Bad Break; Better You would run out its planned rotation with a set of leaders ready to relate behind one purpose: being helpful. Affect and attitude had surfaced. Attachments were reshaped. All this occurred within a bold intention to bring glory to the God of the universe. The Holy Spirit stepped in to assist.

Section Five

LEADING TOWARD MEANING

11

MEANING IN THE BREAKTHROUGH

LANDMARKS AHEAD

Guided trekking is temporary and limited. When defining questions burst on life's scene and into these short-term groups, opportunities abound for spiritual breakthroughs with lasting impact. Such breakthroughs mark the epitome in group trekking. This chapter gleans conceptual gems from gifted giants who hold a deep and profound existential orientation for therapeutic groups. The essence of meaning attribution within the group encounter, however, brings the bend in the road signaling our need to depart the company of these generous pioneers. We pursue uniquely Christian applications. Within this leader function, our distinctively Christian worldview becomes boldly transparent. Following the precedent of previous chapters, this excursion begins and ends with a group recollection that illustrates the leader function of guiding toward meaning within interpersonal encounter.

FROM CRISIS TO COMMUNITY

The room was empty, the session completed. I peacefully gathered up my things. This motion symbolically mirrored the collection of my thoughts. When I paused to look around, I could hear echoes of the voices that had only recently filled the room. Much of the meeting had been occupied with an orderly advancement through the requests for consultation made during our standard check-in. This particular group was composed of bright, high-functioning counselors-in-training who met for the purpose of collaboration, instruction and oversight. My role in this setting was supervisor, professor and trekking guide. We had traveled together enough to establish expectations and a reasonable routine. That last word regrettably described nearly all of this session—*routine*. The exchanges were so predictable that my mind yearned to wander. The final member to bring forward a concern posed yet another straightforward case question. There were a couple of interesting angles but responses aroused only minimal investment. This explains my logic for reserving it until later in the meeting. The final topic was a legitimate concern but not a burning priority. When I heard the clinical question and considered Shelly, the person who had posed it, the reaction that instantly popped into my mind was, "This is so elementary; she knows ways to research a solution." From another perspective, however, there had been a recent lull in the material Shelly brought into this supervision group. This question could be a return to engagement. Besides, her request for input would allow several other members with reasonable expertise to step up and shine during the exchange. The remaining portion of the allotted time would amply account for brainstorming options, sorting critically through them, providing feedback and summarizing. The session would land smoothly. We would disembark and be happily on our way. The inquiry would afford a fine finish for a clean working session. All would be routine, reasonable and respectable.

Why then had I been laboring to squelch an internal rumble that urged me to pursue one of the doubts ringing the alarm on my inner alert meter? Shelly packaged her question too neatly. Perhaps she knew the answer and was looking for an opening to display her own prowess. Matt, a normally muted but potential presence, requested clarifying information from Shelly. This afforded a reprieve for me to deliberate on the implications of my instincts. Then I began to hear how Matt's press for Shelly to further expose and add detail was validating my own instincts that she could have an unspoken agenda. Was there an intervening variable? Matt's polite inquiries stayed in safe territory as he elegantly hinted at his uncertainty in taking a swing at this easy pitch. This confirmed the necessity to check out a hunch. I jumped in. "Shelly, would you mind talking about your recent conversations with your supervisor or agency director? Tell us how this clinical issue has been previously addressed in your setting."[1] This intervention was nothing striking. Surprisingly, fresh material rapidly surfaced. It moved the topic from counselor choices regarding technique to functional and relational dynamics. The intensity increased and turbulence ensued. The "fasten seat belt" sign came on. The session moved from its appropriate content focus on defining a treatment procedure to a process moment exploring relational communication.

---

[1]My intervention query might suggest outside knowledge of the supervisor's performance assessment. This was not the case. Coordination between the academic and on-site supervisor is the ideal and fortunately the norm. In the event that triggered this composite scenario, the request for consultation from this supervision group reflects a procedure that is a standard protocol within the setting. My initial hypothesis was that Shelly was attempting to challenge an existing agency procedure. While that specific hypothesis proved to be unfounded, the domain of the relational tension between supervisor and supervisee was correct. The intervention stemmed from her immediate way of relating to the group, not on any content specifics I knew ahead of time.

The session's landing would now be precarious and certainly beyond the ordinary.

An underlying storyline unfolded. This counselor-in-training explained that the base concern had remained unexamined because she had lacked sufficient opportunity to raise it with her field supervisor. She needed no further query or challenge. Shelly proceeded to unveil her burden over an urgent, serious and recent evaluation. She had been sternly rebuked and was silently hurting. With reluctant honesty, this struggling apprentice admitted a prevailing sense of disorientation and discouragement. Her dismay had resulted in frequent lateness, missed meetings, regularly fumbling through appointments and the hopelessness that accompanies the tiring treadmill of playing endless catch-up. A dreaded phrase from her director had catapulted Shelly back to reality: "Your current performance level has fallen below reasonable standards for a professional helper." Shelly choked up and confessed, "My supervisor is actually right." The atmosphere came alive with an emotional charge as the other members pumped support, concern, empathy and additional self-disclosure into the exchange. Serving a peer in crisis was more energizing than reiterating a memorized series of procedural steps to address a clinical concern. This counselor was capable, in fact abundantly so. The voices in the room unanimously expressed that conviction with no resort to contrived endorsements.

Due to the late arrival of this potent revelation, the group identified much material as good stuff to revisit, perhaps even on a regular basis. Reassurance was plentiful. One central compelling issue remained to be addressed: the stalled disclosure of this crisis to peers and myself. Considering Shelly's acute hunger for support, not asking for peers to pass the potatoes was a sure tactic for starvation. The need had been growing for weeks. Given the apparent severity of the director's message, avoiding me as her academic supervisor marked a breach in the expectations of that relationship.[2] This hurting helper recognized that the preferred approach would have been to raise this sensitive area of vulnerability during check-in. Unfortunately, she had given in to a frightfully familiar and admittedly destructive pattern of procrastination and avoidance. Her dominant philosophy was to put on a good front, push aside the uncomfortable and proceed as if all was or would be well. This pattern was bolstered by a tendency toward perfectionism that made exposing weakness prohibitively difficult. Her entire

---

[2]There are allusions in these lines to the relational provision of bread as basic nurturance and support (Jn 6:35, 48) and shepherding due to the need for an advocate, protector and provider (Jn 10:11).

self-preservation system showed signs of crumbling. The session may have ended abruptly but the emotional tenor reverberated with hope, compassion and assurance. The reason we had all gathered was evident. The session successfully reached its destination. Shelly stepped out of the shadows. Others were sympathetic, not shocked, disappointed or condemning. The group could trust with intensity and enjoy community.

I initiated few moves in the encounter. But while I was only minimally active, this leader's presence did instill an essential contribution. Having a safe person around to deflect hurtful or useless conflicts encourages risk taking. In this collection of novice helpers, members possessed the requisite skills but did not have the firmest grasp of when or how to apply them. A defensive barrier had kept the underlying concern at bay. This might be viewed as a purely individual issue; Shelly was holding back to her own detriment. But such a personal attribution would hide the effect of the overall group interaction. The tone of the meeting had not heartily invited the type of disclosure that Shelly needed to make. Projecting top-notch performance had held precedence over exposing vulnerabilities. My role was to enable the development of a culture where admirable effort was associated with the pursuit of growth in professional skills, including the appropriate use of self. With the words I selected for my summary, I sought to instill a vocabulary and a visual illustration of what the group needed to be. This meant affirming a transparency about the participants' development as clinicians, particularly on issues that could be readily defined by what transpired as we met. "We assemble because becoming people helpers requires a dedicated commitment to grow personally while we establish a wide range of skills to perform professionally. If each of us had it completely together, there would be no benefit to supervision or this meeting. My thanks to those who risked by divulging a ragged edge today—that includes you, Shelly. All around there were solid efforts to stay direct, persist and speak toward enhanced confidence. Nice invitation to expand our work, Matt." A short, touching prayer by Matt served as the finale. On a spiritual level, another dimension was undeniably in operation but not explicitly so. Wisdom was working its way into this gathered community. Bread and Living Water were in good supply.

The central dilemma of this session might appear to be limited to this population of aspiring counselors, or tied to an idiosyncratic individual tendency to maintain a flawless facade. However, on the contrary, it describes a pervasive and typical struggle for helping groups. The yearning to make a good impression and the craving to be perceived as competent by others inhibits the openness required to immerse fully into the pool of fellow strugglers. This chapter now turns to the fourth leader function that helps participants take this plunge. Leaders assist in the discovery of meaning as they weave the here and now with the group's overarching purpose. Themes that emerge from the immediate implication of working together can and do relate to the motivating force that brought participants into the group. As leaders expand the depth of meaning to encompass current challenges, participants form a mental picture of the impact of their behavior inside and outside of the group. Guides strive to aid the group and its members to translate "feelings and experiences into ideas."[3] This chapter discusses three aspects of the leader function *discovering meaning:* supplying the ingredients for cognitive structure, solidifying a cognitive framework and stimulating spiritual formation though expanding one's faith journey narrative.

Helping group leaders do well to understand refinement of meaning in a group setting as a wisdom-oriented activity. This equation may initially strike readers as too psychologically or self-insight focused for ministry-targeted groups. But allow a marvelous theological classic to inform the link. John Calvin's oft-quoted opening to his *Institutes of the Christian Religion* summarizes his mission to articulate numerous theological doctrines to inform those seeking to live to the glory of God. As his exposition begins, he acknowledges the juxtaposition of two plausible starting points. The pursuit of either ends up at the identical objective. Calvin's premise has a critical application in the attribution of meaning to experiences shared within groups.

> Our wisdom, in so far as it ought to be deemed true and solid Wisdom, consists almost entirely of two parts: the knowledge of God and of ourselves. But as these are connected together by many ties, it is not easy to determine which of the two precedes and gives birth to the other. For, in the first place, no man can survey himself without forthwith turning his thoughts toward the God in whom he lives and moves; because it is perfectly obvious, that the endowments which we possess cannot possibly be from ourselves; nay, that our very being is nothing else than subsistence in God alone. In the second place, those blessings which unceasingly distil to us from heaven, are like streams conducting us to the fountain. Here again the infinitude of good which resides in God becomes more apparent from our poverty.[4]

---

[3]Irvin D. Yalom and Molyn Leszcz, *The Theory and Practice of Group Psychotherapy*, 5th ed. (New York: Basic Books, 2005), p. 536.
[4]John Calvin, *Institutes of the Christian Religion*, trans. Henry Beveridge (Oak Harbor, Wash.: Logos Research Systems, 1997), S. 1.1.1. CD-ROM.

Calvin recognizes that contemplation to produce self-understanding will eventually progress to two premises: (1) human complexity and experience denotes a Divine Creator and (2) human brokenness reveals the gracious blessings bestowed by that Creator. Self-knowledge is never sought as an end in itself; rather it is endorsed for the fundamental spiritual questions that are likely to surface. Consider this implication: Group encounters uncover meaning within relational patterns that proceed from internal processes. Such exchanges open up internal explanatory and relational regulation systems for review. In the scenario presented, the group experience helped Shelly resolve an imminent crisis as she grew in her awareness of how her high expectations and desire for approval actually prevented her from the engagement and closeness she craved. She exposed her own frailty and hurt. A trek toward wholeness by design enables participants to expand their self-understanding. As Calvin perceives, self is a crucial but single source of knowledge. Ultimately, any enhancement in self-understanding resulting from a group trek should evoke a deeper dependence on God and on what he has revealed. These journeys open our eyes to our inner brokenness, fears, dreams and wishes. Wholeness comes not from the group experiences of commonality in these fractured hopes and flawed intentions but from placing them within our lifelong spiritual journey. We complete this application only by looking to the other knowledge source, God's self-revelation through Scripture. These comments set the parameters for exploring the existential foundation of the leader function known as *meaning attribution*.

TRIBUTE AND ALLEGIANCE

For me, the daylong workshop about to unfold was a much-anticipated privilege. On our campus, speaking to my colleagues, students and local community clinicians was Molyn Leszcz, M.D., psychiatrist-in-chief at Mount Sinai Hospital, associate professor and head of group psychotherapy at the University of Toronto Department of Psychiatry. Dr. Leszcz is the coauthor with Irvin Yalom of celebrated text *The Theory and Practice of Group Psychotherapy* (5th ed.).[5] Besides leading a traditional ongoing outpatient process group for many years, Dr. Leszcz has ongoing responsibility for training psychiatric residents in the techniques of group therapy. He regularly participates in groups with women diagnosed with metastatic breast cancer; that is, those with the most devastating and deadly diagnosis. He has also conducted groups with senior adults confronting the trials

---

[5]Much appreciation to colleague Keith Bjorge for arranging this one-day conference on the Trinity International University Campus, in Deerfield, Illinois, April 13, 2007.

of aging and crippling depression. These are admirable qualifications. In my estimation, most helping professionals cling to an outdated, false belief that group interventions are the inferior stepchild, a diluted version of dyadic conversations. This view persists despite ample empirical evidence to the contrary. The message this authoritative expert would bring via lecture and demonstration would take that false notion down by more than a few notches. From the instant that this training had been planned, the occasion served as a resource on the horizon for my own investigation into the kingdom potential of group applications. Expectation fueled encouragement. Six and one-half hours would not be adequate to turn prevailing professional winds. But fortunately, it would sufficiently fan the fire ignited within me and focus the heat in a productive direction.

The announced title for the day was "An Evolving Approach to Group Therapy: The Integration of Interpersonal and Existential Approaches."[6] As promised, the speaker accented assumptions of interpersonally oriented groups. Leszcz articulated with precision the principle that people consistently have blind spots that are in sync with their personality presentation. As these patterns are the natural outflow of our constitution, we are too often unable to distinguish the impact of those blind spots, particularly in the midst of adversity. Groups permit blind spots to be seen, evaluated according to intention, assessed critically by outcome and then modified with firsthand support. This helping approach makes strategic use of meta-communication or talk about the shared experience of being in the interpersonal pattern. In the workshop, live group demonstrations amplified the message. As I self-monitored my experience throughout the presentation, the absorption of the review felt comforting and soothing. Familiar concepts were rehearsed and explained. Each nuance and accent felt confirming as well as stimulating. Leszcz exhibited a genuine enactment of the academic axiom that those with extensive expertise and subject mastery are those most capable of representing it simply and succinctly.

When Leszcz brought the existential perspective into the forum, the activation of my mind and emotions was heightened. "Lord, will you be speaking to me during this time? I pray for the ability to pay intensely close attention to the presenter and still hear the prompting of your Holy Spirit." The notes I recorded on my laptop that day bear a closer resemblance to free association than verbatim transcription. Having delved heavily into Yalom's published material, I traversed

---

[6]Molyn Leszcz, "An Evolving Approach to Group Therapy: The Integration of Interpersonal and Existential Approaches" (paper presented at Trinity International University Counseling Conference, Deerfield, Ill., April 13, 2007).

familiar ground in listening to his reputable coauthor explain ways of applying existential philosophy to constructive, up-close, person-to-person helping.

Yalom defines existential psychotherapy as dynamically oriented, meaning it presumes that motivational forces beneath the surface can erupt into the throes of life to draw attention to ultimate, core concerns.[7] The deep questions of life produce profound anxiety over being and existence, limits and transcendence. Yalom writes:

> The existential psychotherapy approach posits that the inner conflict be-deviling us issues not only from our struggle with suppressed instinctual strivings or internalized significant adults or shards of forgotten traumatic memories, but also *from our confrontation with the "givens" of existence.*
>
> And what are these "givens" of existence? If we permit ourselves to screen out or "bracket" the everyday concerns of life and reflect deeply upon our *situation in the world,* we inevitably arrive at the deep structures of existence (the "ultimate concerns," to use theologian Paul Tillich's sa-lubrious term). Four ultimate concerns, to my view, are highly germane to psychotherapy: death, isolation, meaning in life, and freedom.[8]

The advantages and tension in the application of these ideas to group ap-proaches are poignantly depicted on the pages of Yalom's novel *The Schopenhauer Cure.*[9] This fictional work is packed with considerable group theory, technique and drama. It portrays the tale of a prominent psychiatrist, Julius Hertzfeld, who confronts his own cancer diagnosis in the midst of directing an intensive psycho-therapy group. One antagonistic group member is a devout adherent to the pes-simistic existential philosopher, Arthur Schopenhauer (1788-1860). Beneath the transcripts of stimulating group therapy, a dispute rages between extreme and moderate, bleak and celebratory existential philosophy. This contest between the group psychiatrist and the Schopenhauer protégée is the stage that presents the duel between these competing forms of existentialism.

I admit purchasing my copy of *The Schopenhauer Cure* when it was fresh on the bookstore shelf. For one who finds group counseling exciting, this was sizzling summer reading. I turned its pages on the identical lake where the fishhook-in-

---

[7]Irvin D. Yalom, "Religion and Psychiatry," acceptance speech to the American Psychiatric As-sociation 2000 Oscar Pfister Award for important contributions to religion and psychiatry, May 2000 <http://www.yalom.com/lectures>. See also Irvin D. Yalom, *Existential Psychotherapy* (New York: Basic Books, 1980).

[8]Yalom, "Religion and Psychiatry," p. 6. Emphasis added.

[9]Irvin D. Yalom, *The Schopenhauer Cure* (New York: HarperCollins, 2005).

finger episode had taken place. You may recall that getting my hands joined by a set of treble hooks forced a return to the hospital where I had early on applied myself to leading a helping group. Much of *The Schopenhauer Cure* penetrated deep into my heart and mind while I was supposedly fishing on my bass boat. Not much takes my attention off fishing, but the novel consumed my thoughts so thoroughly that nearby fish remained unharmed. As I poured over Yalom's unfolding story with a group therapist as the unlikely hero, no unsuspecting fish were forced to contemplate issues of mortality. I concentrated fully on in-depth intensive group experience, ignoring beeps from the depths indicated by the fish finder and ultimately returning from my trip with no fish for the grill. What did return with me was an appreciation for ways that earnest pursuit of self-understanding, stirred by mundane dissatisfaction, crisis or relational disaster, can awaken concerns of existence in everyday reality. Existential philosophy percolates throughout guided group conversations.

That remarkable reading experience informed my digestion of the workshop presentation. I easily discerned how Leszcz followed the path of his mentor and textbook collaborator. He too appealed for an existential foundation for group interventions. Leszcz brought these to life as he wove together his own story through personal anecdotes and memorable quotations. Eventually, he arrived at a conclusion similar to Yalom's regarding existential philosophy's usefulness in supplying a broader context for an interpersonal approach within groups. Although I recall his stories vividly and might even be able to recount them relatively accurately, I prefer to leave those formative events as Leszcz's alone to retell. With personal recollections of family members who survived the horrors of the Holocaust and patients who faced the most dreaded diseases of our day, it is not difficult to imagine the intensity of his content. Leszcz's tone was steadfastly quiet and his approach was unswervingly sincere. He never veered toward the sensational. He modeled a vulnerable transparency exceptionally well. There were echoes of prevalent existential phrases: use death as a cotherapist to foster the pursuit of life; the act of death ends life, the idea of death vitalizes life; engage life, not immortality; live time or kill time; act with strategic agency rather than allow prevailing circumstances to make decisions. Leszcz exhorted the audience to help people become the authors of their own life story and pursue relational vitality to inspire the narrative. This message dominated the intersection between the interpersonal and the existential: "Personal ownership of the active and willful dedication to one's relational matrix is a crucial prerequisite to authentic engagement and a broadening of one's interpersonal repertoire."[10] Based on the stirring of my own motivation and reviews by others in attendance, Molyn Leszcz conveyed his message successfully.

Although caught up in the experience with enthusiasm, I was not so much enthralled with these existential themes as I was pounding against the limits of the philosophy. I again recollected the day I had closed the cover of *The Schopenhauer Cure* while out on my favorite lake. There was enjoyable satisfaction in reaching the end of a good read with the accompanying disappointment that the pages had run out too soon. I gazed up at the steep hills that met the shore and felt the warmth of the breeze that was easing the boat softly across the surface of the water. "I lift up my eyes to the hills—where does my help come from? My help comes from the LORD, the Maker of heaven and earth" (Ps 121:1-2). Listening in on the inner narrative of an extraordinary group therapist as he copes with mortality was indeed a gift.[11] The use of the word *gift* invokes a term Yalom frequently employs to represent the nurturance that surges from one to another within an intimate interpersonal exchange. Following his chronicle of a collection of group participants, even these fictitious ones, felt more like participation than eavesdropping. The characters engaged in a therapeutic group to bring meaning to the experience of being tossed into the universe to live out their lives. I am grateful for the gift; still I sense a limitation. "Lord, thank you that the storyline of my own life rests on a different meta-narrative, one that you have supplied," I prayed. The protagonist in *The Schopenhauer Cure* summarizes an underlying and recurring premise that occurs as the mantra of existential psychotherapy. "How shall we live? How to face our mortality? How to live with the knowledge that we are simply life-forms, thrown into an indifferent universe, with no preordained purpose?"[12] The participants investigate their lives to discover meaning and live intentionally within these parameters. A different phrase drives the search and sets the structure that binds my own thoughts into a semblance of cohesion. "In the beginning, God created the heavens and the earth" (Gen 1:1).[13]

---

[10]Leszcz, "Evolving Approach to Group Therapy," April 13, 2007.
[11]Here my reference is to Julius, the psychiatrist in Yalom's novel, a character of fiction.
[12]Yalom, *Schopenhauer Cure*, p. 331.
[13]In a work by Kevin J. Vanhoozer, the phrase "thrown into existence" is attributed to Martin Heidegger, *Being and Time*, trans. John Macquarrie and Edward Robinson (Oxford: Basil Blackwell, 1980), p. 321. Vanhoozer builds off this existential phrase to assert that theological doctrine is how the church makes sense of where it has been thrown and what role it is to play. This introduces the divine drama of redemption, which plays out in a series of acts from creation to the consummation or eschaton. See Kevin J. Vanhoozer, *The Drama of Doctrine: A Canonical Linguistic Approach to Christian Theology* (Louisville, Ky.: Westminster John Knox, 2005).

Remaining solely within the existential frame would be like restricting Scripture reading exclusively to the book of Ecclesiastes! The Teacher firmly debunks a life centered on wealth, pleasure, toil, learning, power and achievement, but an alternate basis for wisdom is barely articulated. The method of the Teacher parallels man's philosophical search for meaning across time. The ending of Ecclesiastes does conclude, with measured passion, that remembering the Creator in youth is best. Wise people will make this commitment before the body wears down (Eccles 12:1-12). Fearing God and keeping his commandments represents the whole duty of man (Eccles 12:13). The answer is correct but the embrace feels forced. A faith response based on the whole of Scripture, however, captures an inviting, comprehensive and future-oriented hope. Adopting the entire gospel story gives coherence to life, work, relationships and the struggle to grapple with foundational questions. Recalling God's call to Adam as he walked in the garden compels me to find meaning in the biblical narrative from Genesis to Revelation: "Where are you?"(Gen 3:9).

This religious orientation within me could arise from my seminary education with its emphasis on the centuries of thought that assembled and assessed knowledge with theistic footings. This propensity could also be credited to my childhood, since I grew up in a family that honored faith in God as a good way and valued tradition. Yalom cites Schopenhauer who wrote: "The capacity for faith is at its strongest in childhood; which is why religions apply themselves before all else to getting those tender years into their possession."[14] Additionally, Schopenhauer asserts that:

> Religion has everything on its side: revelation, prophecies, government protection, the highest dignity and eminence . . . and more than this, the invaluable prerogative of being allowed to imprint its doctrines on the mind at a tender age of childhood, whereby they become almost innate ideas.[15]

These words—perhaps even accusations—may also apply. Yet I find no reason to resist or resent the implications. Revelation is a good thing to have on one's side. Ultimately, I attribute my faith to the divine ministry of the Holy Spirit who brought together people, experiences and the peculiarities of my inner narrative to culminate in my conversion, declaring dependence on Jesus Christ and committing allegiance to the gospel. This loyalty has resulted in expanding the

---

[14]Arnold Schopenhauer, as cited in Yalom, "Religion and Psychiatry," May 2000 <www.yalom .com/lectures>.
[15]Yalom, *Schopenhauer Cure*, p. 55.

relational polarities that govern my schemas from a stark two: self and others, to a sufficient three: self, others and God. The profound questions raised within the exploration of the first two, connecting with self and others, do not overwhelm the third polarity, relating to God. Instead, the third sphere offers relationally based, fulfilling answers to complement and correct the limitation of the other two.

The interpersonal model flourishes within a group and rests neatly on an existential foundation. In settings where I must restrict my procedure to mining the big questions and assisting each member to find personal meaning, interpersonal tools are well suited for excavating the deeper issues of an existentially oriented search. Once the larger questions are on the surface, though, my heart prays that the Holy Spirit will intervene and supply wisdom. The therapeutic agreement that I voluntarily accept at the outset of a healing journey governs how I pray. This influences whether I pray silently or aloud, privately or in community, immediately or afterwards. A verbal contract, written policy or assumed agreement between helper and client determines if religious values are to have an explicit place or only a remote bearing on the personal investigation conducted together. I place a high priority on maintaining integrity regarding this agreement, as do others in my profession. Doing so has important ethical implications when operating in such a capacity and with this authority. Helping efforts may remain within the two relational polarities or by arrangement and setting, encompass all three. Stated differently, a medical, community or secular agency setting ideally matches interpersonal groups that blend in an existential quest. It will address core concerns and is quite feasible, desirable and therapeutically effective. Group participants locate meaning in what they face in order to motivate and sustain growth. Seeking out and showing up for a group demonstrates their agreement to improve functioning, health, family ties or their quality of life, and in some cases to relieve distress. The learning voyage applies meaning into one's ongoing relational story as shaped by the internal working model. This crucial aspect generates renewable fuel for maintaining revised expectations, emotions and behavior. A ministry setting where people desire a Christian orientation can and will use the gospel message to address the third relational polarity.

That one-day workshop conducted by Leszcz crystallized for me the call to articulate this alternate foundation on which to rest the use of the interpersonal group method. Why only seize a moment to live authentically when one can also squeeze the hand of the Savior, sense the ministry of the Holy Spirit and return to the *shalom* intended by our heavenly Father? Unfortunately, the brokenness of human beings abundantly gives evidence that adherence to certain religious ideals, even presumably Christian ones, can perpetuate a deadening status quo. The sad evidence shows up when people live by ritual, in blind imitation and without authentic love. This undesirable occurrence, although widespread, does not provide a sufficient reason to rule out genuine Christian faith. The good news of the gospel makes possible a renewed relationship with the Creator through the death and resurrection of Jesus Christ as made effective by the Holy Spirit. This restores created human beings made in the *imago Dei* to intimacy with the very Creator reflected in them. Further, the call to love genuinely and selflessly gives meaning to a full range of interpersonal relationships. A Christian framework does not settle with extrapolating meaning to fill out our finite days as the clock ticks away. Instead, Christian faith makes abundant life available for a communal experience in anticipation of an eternity in the presence of Jesus Christ.

In 2000, the American Psychiatric Association (APA) awarded Irvin Yalom the Oscar Pfister prize for important contributions to religion and psychiatry. As a recipient of his literary contributions, I eagerly affirm the APA's conclusion. His approaches and perceptions move a scientifically anchored procedure to an intersection where life and religious matters converge. It is at this crossroads where a helper with Christian convictions will experience constraint in the boundaries of an existential approach. In his acceptance speech, Yalom reported that those who made the award decision predicated it on the belief that he had dedicated himself to religious questions.[16] Yet he fully recognizes the tension in the linkage between existential psychotherapy and religious consolation.

I believe these two approaches have a complex, strained relationship. In a sense, they are cousins with the same ancestors and concerns; they share the common mission of ministering to the intrinsic despair of the human condition. Sometimes they share common methods: the one-to-one relationship, the modes of confession, inner scrutiny, forgiveness of others and self. In fact, more and more as I've grown older, I consider psychotherapy a calling, not a profession. And yet still, the core beliefs and basic practical approaches of psychotherapy and religious consolation are often truly at odds with one another.[17]

The principal conflict area that surfaces immediately and consistently for one with a Christian faith is acknowledging a loving Creator who has revealed himself

---

[16]Yalom, "Religion and Psychiatry."
[17]Ibid.

in history and through his Son's entrance into the world. This explains my earlier reference to Calvin's introductory assertion of the two sources of knowledge. An honest quest for self-understanding through the exploration of experience eventually arrives at core questions regarding existence, limits, loneliness, death and transcendence. Full answers only come with intense examination of the knowledge revealed by the Creator himself. *Trekking Toward Wholeness* follows the faith tradition of the multitude of seekers across history and culture who have tapped into both veins of knowledge to secure wisdom. Taking this path when an empirically supported method raises religious questions allows the Creator to respond by grace. His answers call for an authentic, loving walk with him, the abandonment of wandering in sin that destroys self along with all that one attempts to love, and the pursuit of wisdom to relate with others in love. The eyes of faith recognize this as a realistic and, more important, a radically relational choice.[18]

I have great gratitude to those who have profoundly shaped my perspectives by thorough, reliable and engaging communication. The faith alliance expressed and the turn at this crossroads does not diminish appreciation for the contribution that these men have made nor the debt we owe them. Countless helpers are equipped to assist others based on the meticulous application of science, carefully crafted constructs, empirical consolidation and engrossing stories. This is my tribute to Irvin Yalom and his recent coauthor, Molyn Leszcz, as I set a course to guide treks down a different road.

WHEN MOTIVATIONAL TRAILS MERGE

There are intersections in life where a variety of forces merge to convince or convict a person that this is the optimal juncture to listen, hear, risk and act (see Mt 7:24-27; Lk 6:46-49).

There is a time for everything,
and a season for every activity under heaven:
a time to be born and a time to die,
a time to plant and a time to uproot,
a time to kill and a time to heal,
a time to tear down and a time to build,

---

[18]The following statement appears in Yalom's 2000 acceptance speech: "*I believe that these extraordinary claims require extraordinary evidence*—and I mean by that *evidence beyond pure experience* which as we therapists know is fragile, fallible, rapidly shifting, and vastly influenceable." It is Yalom's dedication to evidence as a basis for clinical decisions that make his material such a valuable empirically based resource. In relation to faith, a rational basis may require a different lens. Emphasis added.

a time to weep and a time to laugh,

a time to mourn and a time to dance,

a time to scatter stones and a time to gather them,

a time to embrace and a time to refrain,

a time to search and a time to give up,

a time to keep and a time to throw away,

a time to tear and a time to mend,

a time to be silent and a time to speak,

a time to love and a time to hate,

a time for war and a time for peace. (Eccles 3:1-8)

Tension and transition accompany any change in season. These shifts are as sure as the rotation of the earth. The ancient poetic language of the Old Testament exposes human activity indicative of the dilemmas everyday folks bring into today's helping groups. Each season reveals a basic struggle within the underlying relational polarities. Thus each stimulates contemplation of how patterns within one facet or factor of personality can inhibit the attainment of intimacy. Many common-theme helping groups address concerns imbedded within the turn of a season.

The term *perturbation* expresses the restlessness incited by a situational crisis, relational strain, internal disruption or role adjustment. The static state of the status quo is disrupted. The schemas that secure our grip on reality tremble as the surrounding world quakes. Naturally, this results in cognitive and emotional turmoil. Our prevailing equilibrium is disturbed and a successful return to normal appears impossible, or what is even more unsettling, undesirable. Discontentment instigates a trek with others facing analogous disorientation.

Certain cycles of perturbation require only select innovative information. Encouraging voices help quell the turbulence. Applying these welcome ideas brings a satisfying awareness. A pleasant sensation follows. This is like noticing that the furniture in a room has been stylishly rearranged, the house has been given a fresh coat of paint or the person in the mirror has received a decent haircut. Attainable action steps usher in the return of a reassuring equilibrium as a person assimilates inventive approaches into customary habits and perspectives. Knowledge and relational support yield relief.[19] People internalize meaning through

---

[19]Applying the integrative psychotherapy approach of McMinn and Campbell, this level of change could be classified as symptom-focused or functional. See Mark McMinn and Clark D. Campbell, *Integrative Psychotherapy: Toward a Comprehensive Christian Approach* (Downers Grove, Ill.: IVP Academic, 2007), pp. 113-43.

the acquisition of words, terms and descriptions. They may adopt a language of recovery, identify their intensive swings in mood with stages of grief and loss, or intentionally apply and label a range of communication techniques and affective experiences. The stories others tell form an internal database of motifs, plots and phrases to enliven one's own. Their new experiences and vocabulary supply ingredients to revise and update cognitive structure. Cognitive materials such as these indicate that people have indeed been led toward meaning, since they are now linking raw feelings with experiences and ideas.

What if the annoying perturbation and jolt to the status quo feels less like a restless ripple and more like a relentless riptide? Realizing a remedy may require substantial restructuring. The necessary renovation deeply penetrates one's inner conversations, emotional trenches, degrees of connectedness and readiness to love. This type of reconstruction results in new inner accommodation, usually involving multiple alterations in cognition, emotion and relational expectation. Forget rearranging the furniture or splashing on new paint; this is about walls tumbling down, dust flying, and grueling, creative work. When the construction crew departs, not only will the house look and feel different, the entire world may boast a brighter hue. The person in the mirror stares back with a renewed countenance.[20] People find meaning as paradigms and models, previously unknown, become readily accessible. Insight to explain events and establish long-term goals directs daily decisions. People own the solutions and are responsibly aware of when they need to implement them. When someone adjusts a wide assortment of behavior patterns and relational wishes, he demonstrates having attained meaningful and pragmatic cognitive structure.

The application of the term *perturbation* again illustrates the importance of moving toward affect as a compelling leader function. Establishing equilibrium will entail exploration within emotional territory. Generally, a chasm exists between the desire to behave comfortably while maintaining autonomy and the need for change coupled with the longing to enjoy connection. Even just considering this conflict will detonate emotion. The wonder of a group approach is that while modest repair or major reformation occurs within the individual, the undertaking unfolds within an interpersonal context. Entering into this miniature social network to engage in reciprocal assistance assumes that help is contingent upon getting personal with strangers. This methodology perturbs relational patterns even when participants feel no initial compulsion to develop increased

---

[20]Ibid. This level of change would represent the structural or schema-level domain since core beliefs and the methods to manage life that emerge from them are affected.

relational awareness or skill. Recall that interpersonal bonds contain centrally engrained associations and apprehensions within the internal working model. Any examination and push to realign the expectations of the IWM releases emotional heat.[21] A Christian resolution insists that reaching equilibrium is not merely balancing forces within the soul but strengthening love between the polarities of self, others and God. Corrective emotional relationships experienced within the cohesion of the group soothe stirred-up emotions, reduce anxiety and give meaning to the encounter.

A Christian perspective on group trekking locates meaning in the association between what has brought an individual into a group and the ongoing spiritual journey of each member. In constructing this linkage, I consider the concept of perturbation alongside a set of stages classically associated with spiritual formation. These terms hold an enduring and dignified history within Christian soul care: purgation, illumination and union.[22] Throughout church history and across doctrinal and denominational traditions, this progressive sequence has been applied to a pilgrimage of faith.[23] In the fast pace and anticipated ease of contemporary life, people perceive perturbation—the production of uncomfortable symptoms brought about by the pressure of difficult circumstances—to be an oppressive intrusion. Such a season requires strength beyond a person's current means. Behind the immediate need, perturbation may contain an ulterior, elevated purpose. It can be a time for movement toward deeper connections, dependency and perhaps even spiritual renewal. Perturbation may signal an opportunity for purgation. James 1:2 exhorts believers to count the entire experience stemming from perturbation as joy. This perspective can be applied with eyes of faith and careful determination. Perturbation provokes instinctual responses that

---

[21]The third level of change is interpersonally focused since it addresses relational wounds, character change and spiritual longings. McMinn and Campbell associate this third level of engagement as soul care or depth psychotherapy. While the integrative psychotherapy model has much appeal, its application to group interventions is not straightforward. In groups, the relational level is fused into the treatment method itself. It is not relegated to a mode of therapy, timeline or stylistic choice. Groups are an inherently relational enterprise. The purpose of the group will establish how overt or covert the processing of relational experience will be within the helping experience. I contend that group work can engage these three levels simultaneously. Perhaps this helps explain the circus metaphor in chapter ten to tap the imagery of "three rings." Note that while group work may touch all three areas, the time-limited format suggested serves as a catalyst, not as a journey to completion.

[22]Gary W. Moon and David G. Benner, eds., *Spiritual Direction and the Care of Souls: A Guide to Christian Approaches and Practice* (Downers Grove, Ill.: InterVarsity Press, 2004), p. 19.

[23]An extensive recent appraisal and exploration of these traditional formation stages is available and recommended. See F. Leron Shults and Steven J. Sandage, *Transforming Spirituality: Integrating Theology and Psychology* (Grand Rapids: Baker, 2006).

can intensely push trekkers in any direction that promises to reduce the distress. Choosing to try out a presumed shortcut may eventually corrupt or waylay faith development. The Holy Spirit can instead transform this unrest into a period of receptivity where he can minister. A group experience furnishes a supportive forum where people are encouraged to resist superficial respite in favor of adopting a Spirit-infused agenda for change. By grace, this trail merger can have eternal repercussions.

A Christian view of suffering associates terrible struggle as the means for God to accomplish a greater good (Rom 8:28). The pain may be transformed to assist others, reflecting the way in which Jesus' death benefits all humanity. It may also strengthen the person coming through the adversity.[24] "We also rejoice in our sufferings, because we know that suffering produces perseverance; perseverance, character; and character, hope. And hope does not disappoint us, because God has poured out his love into our hearts by the Holy Spirit, whom he has given us" (Rom 5:3-5). The disturbance represents a test, challenge or trial. The Word assures God's children that the Lord can use this period to shape convictions, character and kingdom worthiness (Jas 1:1-18). I adamantly assert, nonetheless, that while this frame may be useful in securing and applying meaning, there are most definitely occasions where the purpose of suffering is left an open and unsolved mystery. None can discern a reason; no good results. Left with only unanswered and painful questions, people find comfort in one another and in the assurance that God does hear the cries of those who seek Him (see Ps 66:16-20; 102:1-2, 17; Mk 11:24; 2 Cor 1:8-11; Phil 1:19-20).

Purgation, or this active period of purification, combines an awareness of need with repentance, renewal and reaching out. The desired cleansing dictates that we steer away from any sinful practices that have encroached on critical aspects of our being. They may have become routines or regular practices without our conscious recognition or consent. The soul searching of purgation extends to all the relational polarities of self, others and God. Our awakened awareness that the status quo is no longer a desirable state marks the onset of renewed spiritual vitality. The realization that a portion of self must die brings sources of security, values and beliefs under serious scrutiny and rigorous reflection. For example, consider unrealistic attachment expectations or attachment aversions. When groups explore relational communication, members may notice problems in the immediate experience of relating. The barriers to connection with others

---

[24]Paul J. Achtemeier, *Society of Biblical Literature: Harper's Bible Dictionary*, 1st ed. (San Francisco: HarperCollins, 1985), p. 999.

may shed light on how one is resting in the Lord for security. Resistance to accept God's supreme gift love may become evident. Irregularities within the IWM that prevent a transparent walk with the Lord likewise become subject to confession. People may disclose their regret, but declaring an invigorated reliance on the Holy Spirit is more essential. Doing so primarily involves holding forth hope in what God will do in the days ahead. It is not about shifting through the reasons for the irregularities that stem from relationships in the past. The polarity of relating to God under false illusions or dependent prayer undergoes renewal as Truth makes an authoritative visit (Jn 14:6).

By grace, cleansing and confession invigorate a longing to experience God as the psalmist beautifully expressed. "As the deer pants for streams of water, / so my soul pants for you, O God. / My soul thirsts for God, for the living God. / When can I go and meet with God?" (Ps 42:1-2). One's perception is transformed to see self, others and God from God's view. This laser correction of spiritual vision has been referred to as *illumination*. Worship pours from our increasing clarity about personal brokenness and the mercy available from a holy, loving God. A holistic response extends beyond passive gains in the integration of one's inner life. A spiritual quest within a Christian framework does not offer a crude form of self-enrichment; it is a season during which God enlightens all three relational polarities. Illumination brings spiritual sight where once there was blindness, and a yielded determination of will where stubbornness formerly reigned. There is surrender to the presence and desires of God.

The third formation stage is referred to as *union* and is associated with deeper certainty and enjoyment of communion with the triune God. This side of heaven, unity with God is never complete. Steady approximation of the restored *imago Dei* marks the progression. An invigorated and intensified unity with the Father, Son and Holy Spirit is the destination of all kingdom-oriented treks. The immediate working through of misunderstanding and misconstruction on a human plane may be the method, but the hope is for renewal in this divine-human pole of relationality. Corrective emotional relationships are experiences that approximate in a partial but prophetic way God's perfect love. Those finite experiences open us more fully to the infinite love of God.

These formation stages repeat in cycles spiraling further into holiness. A refreshed walk with the Lord brings *shalom* and the release of perturbation. As a result, people humbly rest in solitude, a free-flowing hospitality and a self available for genuine communion with the Lord in prayer.[25]

---

[25]Shults and Sandage recast the formation stage of purgation as *intensification*, illumination as *in-*

Customarily, believers associate these traditional formation stages with independent practices such as meditation, contemplation, worship, fasting and devoted submission to the Word of God. These time-honored spiritual disciplines evoke reflective introspection. The watchful eye of a spiritual director can grant private, personalized guidance. Formation conjures images of separation, retreating and God meeting the wanderer who is lost in the desert. However, the benefits of solo devotional training with the Lord must not be pitted against interpersonal intimacy transformed into communion. In his active ministry, Jesus invested three years with his disciples, taught in public, and went out early in the morning to commune in private prayer with his heavenly Father (Mk 1:15-35). The deeds and activities of Jesus' earthly life exhibited a range of social activities. Further, the great commandment inextricably binds the relational polarities of self, others and God (Mt 22:37-40; Mk 12:29-31; Lk 10:27). Thus including practices both of solitude and of solidarity may enhance exercises associated with spiritual formation.

A season of purgation enriched by contributions from guided interpersonal work can bring one's underlying pattern for expressing and receiving love into immediate awareness. The surrounding social framework is conducive to reflection and encounter. If interference or distortions bound within the IWM block the intention to love, discovering this via exploration of relational process is possible. Faulty relational assumptions, predictions, beliefs and interpersonal styles contribute to misreading and misinterpreting communication. Restricting the capacity to authentically relate with ourselves, others and God results in ongoing sinful activity of omission or commission. Defensive patterns perpetuate distancing from God and others. Our familiar but inhibiting responses and default reflexes cause preemptive assaults or a refusal to reach out. Illumination may arise as others speak truth in love and offer corrective emotional relationships. People can embrace union as they encounter unity afresh in communion.

SPIRITUAL JOURNEYS FOR A SEASON

Previously, in considering the relational polarities, I blended the Lewis reference to gift love and need love with the benefits exchanged in close and com-

---

tentionality, and union as *intimacy*. Not only is their update useful for bridging the theological and psychological, but it also supports the benefits of reciprocal relational process associated with the groups as having a formation purpose. My intention is to inspire more groups in churches and ministry settings. Therefore I have elected to maintain the traditional formation terms for the sake of familiarity and to display a tight continuity with longstanding faith development traditions. Shults and Sandage, *Transforming Spirituality*, p. 24.

munity relationships. I described group treks as a method to quicken members' alertness to unwanted barriers that inhibit the reception and granting of gift or need love. I also employed the generic term *relational adaptability*. This references our readiness to enjoy and spread love at a variety of relational intersections. These intersections include everything from a supportive acquaintance to a marriage partner to fellow members of the body of Christ. Rather than view love as a composite set of discrete attitudes or distinct forces that can be broken down into separate components, perhaps we should view relationships holistically within one's ongoing self-narrative.[26] Instead of repeatedly attempting to isolate emotions and attitudes, a helper takes in an entire relational story with its collection of characters, plots, themes and expectations. Stepping back from rational, logical, analytical and abstract approaches to consider intuitions, illogical expectations, repetitive scripts and self-validating assumptions provides significant advantages.[27] When it comes to pondering spiritual journeys, let us listen to a still-unfolding story for critical themes, recurring lessons and dramatic highlights. A small group can be the ideal setting to share spiritual journeys in such a way that similar or overlapping plots expand understanding and increase faith. Learn to discern where loneliness robs peace from solitude, where hostility erodes hospitality and where illusion overpowers an attitude of prayer. Such themes point toward creative relational work.

An intriguing pilot research investigation looked at how expectations central to one's human relational stories, either romantic or familial, indicate a believer's relationship with God.[28] The intent was to examine the striking similarities between human love experience and love of God. The construct of an internal working model as a central relational template is consistent with the premise of this research. Researchers modified three measurement tools utilized in separate theoretical research traditions (attachment, object-relations and triangular love perspective) to switch the focus from an interpersonal to divine relationship. When data was collected and compiled, two factors emerged as potential explanations of the correlations across the distinct measures. The initial factor was labeled *communion* and encompassed features such as intimacy, regular feelings of presence, warmth, closeness, dependency and trust. The other factor was

---

[26]Robert J. Sternberg, *Love Is a Story: A New Theory of Relationships* (New York: Oxford University Press, 1998).
[27]Ibid., p. 24.
[28]Richard Beck, "Communion and Complaint: Attachment, Object-Relations, and Triangular Love Perspectives on Relationship with God," *Journal of Psychology and Theology* 34, no. 1 (2006): 43-52.

granted the title *complaint* for it captured aspects of disappointment, frustration, lack of attention or promise keeping, and insecurity regarding loving care.

The appearance of two separate factors, communion and complaint, would suggest that both are contributing features to a relationship with God, not opposite extremes on a single dimension. A step deeper into communion may not reduce attitudes of complaint or vice versa. Recognizing these as distinct themes provides comfort and gives perspective to the resulting emotional turbulence. This assists in meaning attribution. This study only laid down a direction for additional research and was not intended to stand solo as conclusive for validating or merging theories. For our purposes, the introduced terms instruct, even in their preliminary form, those who listen in on spiritual journeys. Our walk with the Lord contains dynamic experiences of intimacy, security and trust along with emotional sensations of sadness, tension and mystery. A mature relationship with God does not suppress or silence issues of complaint pertaining to perturbing experience and struggle. One learns with the help of the Holy Spirit to express these open questions to God in humble prayer. The joy of communion inspires trust and the courage to explore territory where misunderstanding and dissatisfaction prevail. The candid and tender communication that brings stability to human relationships can add similar depth to one's relationship with God. Richer communion does not entail squelching complaint; it invites transparency and awe. "Your will be done" (Mt 6:10).

Linking immediate demonstrations to long-term relational narrative themes can enrich the attribution of meaning to behaviors and experience. There may well be extensive interplay between the interpersonal learning that occurs within the group to relationships outside and even to one's spiritual walk with the Lord. Wrestling with deeper questions within a kingdom perspective suggests the age-old quest for wisdom (Prov 1:1-6; 2).

In order to bring this chapter to a close, I would like to return and consider the opening recollection involving Shelly, Matt and the others in a former counselor supervision group. Shelly submitted a content question to the group dialogue that hid a looming struggle within her. She was anxious over the extreme performance concerns she had as a novice helper. Her desire to maintain a perfectionist posture held her back from tapping into the support that was readily present in this group of peers. In addition, the superficial conversation within the group on that day did not invite Shelly to expose her pain and apparent failures. My recounting of the story ended without any consideration of the long-term benefits. What meaning did Shelly uncover in that instance of personal exposure? Was her relational narrative adjusted; were her polarities affected? A fitting closure to that scenario would relate extensive detail about Shelly's maturation in her walk with the Lord within the group and under my watchful shepherding. After all, hiding from helpful resources to maintain a false facade and being crushed under the weight of perfectionism surely has significant spiritual overtones. In what ways did she eventually approach or avoid God? The reason that I have relatively little to share along these lines will expose areas where my own faith as a group guide has undergone extensive struggle and shaping by the Holy Spirit. The insights of Dietrich Bonhoeffer in his classic work *Life Together* have bearing.[29]

Bonhoeffer cites the identical verse that Wesley did to promote public confession (Jas 5:16). Three ways of "breaking through" are possible when those in Jesus Christ disclose sin and failure to one another. First, there is a breakthrough to community. Bonhoeffer contends that when the act of confession breaks through isolation and abandons self-justification, the fellowship exists to distribute the weight of sin. The forgiveness experienced in the fellowship makes tangible the grace that God has granted. As all present are sinners, a bond of community is affirmed. Second, confession breaks through to the cross. It signals the renunciation of pride in favor of depending on the salvation provided through the cross. Third, confession breaks through to the certainty of forgiveness. This does not shift the source of forgiveness from God to the fellow believers. Instead, open confession and community accountability complete the cycle of forgiveness. Shelly's eventual disclosure of hidden shame to the group marked a breakthrough to community. Why not press further into her life to ascertain if Shelly broke through to the cross and into the beautiful certainty where grace is experienced?[30]

The explanation for not searching out these implications has much to do with the parameters of this particular group. It has everything to do with maintaining integrity as a group leader. This supervision group was, and still is, hosted in a seminary setting, so references to spiritual concerns, principles and biblical truth are both relevant and expected. However, the primary intent of the group is clinical supervision. Thus the criteria for content inclusion essentially limit the basic scope to matters of professional development. When important spiritual

---

[29]Dietrich Bonhoeffer, *Life Together*, trans. John W. Doberstein (New York: Harper & Row, 1954), pp. 110-18.
[30]Ibid., pp. 26-39. Bonhoeffer was extremely concerned regarding any mixture of psychological technique into Christian community. Although I cannot maintain the rigid distinctions he advocated during his day, his perspective regarding a leader's engagement in work not motivated by the Holy Spirit is a sobering and useful reminder.

formation questions are raised, most of the actual follow-through is referred for direct attention elsewhere. The breaking through may begin in the group but it is encouraged to continue in another relational context. This begs an imperative question. Does not the disclosed spiritual need of a particular member supersede all established priorities and agreements? This is a serious matter that every leader of a specialized small group will have to earnestly pray through. An unqualified *yes* could destroy the parameters that define roles and ensure the psychological safety essential for group cohesion. If a leader cannot set and then accept those boundaries and limits, the conditions that foster group development are seriously compromised. Cohesion itself may become impossible. In common-theme, time-limited groups, there will be an agreed-upon scope for the content addressed. This implies that not all of the possibilities exposed can be fully explored. Some matters that members bring to the surface will not be feasible or advisable to confront within a group where the trek framework includes deliberate agreed-upon restrictions. Leaders mark the breakthrough, recognize its importance and point out other relational contexts where it can be investigated and enjoyed further. Once again, this indicates how common-theme, leader-directed groups do not replace or diminish other supportive or study-oriented ministry offerings. They instead refer or return members to those other forums. Lord willing, members are better prepared to benefit from what such fellowship gatherings truly offer.

Once Shelly developed a plan with the clinical supervision group to address her situation, there were only two items left for occasional and quick follow-up: (1) Shelly, is your time and task management plan progressing? Are you and your supervisor communicating regarding your development in that area? (2) Is your accountability team working for you? Her own personal intervention plan did include a spiritual mentor who functioned in the role of pastoral authority. Shelly also remained engaged in friendships within the peer group. This is the extent of what I know about where the meaning found in that group encounter progressed. As leader, my role was not to move from supervisor to spiritual director. Instead, I highlighted the moment of spiritual formation that emerged on that group trek as a breakthrough. The Holy Spirit then took that interpersonal encounter and used it to further his redemptive purposes. This is how the meaning found in the immediate can influence the spiritual journey of a lifetime. If the perturbation set off a transformation of purgation, illumination and union, this group and this leader were not designed to go down that road. My duty and function were instead to make the immediate interpersonal experience accessible and meaningful.

As a small group leader, I monitor the following key matters, seeking after wisdom regarding them and attempting to keep them and myself transparent before the Lord.

1. The Holy Spirit is a reliable source for wisdom to discern when to raise a concern, expose vulnerabilities or acknowledge growth. The needs and goals of members must remain the priority in order to curb any and all irresponsible, sinful displays of power or pride as a leader. This is service within agreed-upon boundaries and time constraints.

2. A brief group leader is present to serve in a specific way, setting and mission. Other pastoral, professional, therapeutic and personal relationships will hold precedence in the life of a member. John the Baptist is an ideal role model for a brief group leader; he was quick to step back and give Jesus Christ preeminence.

3. Since the role of trekking guide is temporary and narrowly focused, assess holistically but intervene strategically. Ask the Holy Spirit to reveal next steps and resist the temptation to overwhelm participants with unrealistic expectations. Explorations for future formation activity can be identified in a fashion that projects and maintains hope.

4. A temporary group assists members to identify supports and resources available over the long term. A leader does not draw members into a destructive reliance on the group as an end in itself but only as a temporary means to learn how to relate more effectively.

5. A group operates at its best when members serve other members. The entire experience is for participants, never to showcase the leader. Good guides rely on and trust group process.

6. Spiritual formation is the exclusive work of the Holy Spirit who will draw the seeker closer to the Great Shepherd. A group leader as pastoral shepherd has the honor of participation and observation, but must never force or presume upon the Spirit's freedom. Psychological principles may be appropriated as useful tools, but progress and results are under the domain of the Spirit.

"Being confident of this, that he who began a good work in you will carry it on to completion until the day of Christ Jesus" (Phil 1:6).

12

TREKKING IN THE GAPS

LANDMARKS AHEAD

The best treks finish strong so that memories crystallize with energy and enthusiasm. This final chapter recalls a personal trek that produced deep conviction regarding three critical guiding premises. These are: the essential vitality of Christian fellowship, the elusiveness of genuine therapeutic community and service as the signature of a maturing wholeness in Christ. These concepts not only ground ministry-minded trekking, they also bridge the experience gap between focused treks and our lifelong journey to expressly honor our Lord. Detailing each premise grants an opening for a short review of the related resources already described along our path. This final trekking segment demonstrates further the importance of the fourth leader function, weaving purpose and meaning into the ongoing story of each member's walk with Jesus Christ.

GUIDING PREMISES

Getting to covenant group by six o'clock in the morning was frequently a trying ordeal. The alarm sounded well before night properly ended and had to be silenced immediately. The twins were in their terrible twos and our apartment was tiny. If awakened in the wee hours of the morning and released from their crib, the consequences could be unpleasant. My wife, who worked late into the evening, would have too little sleep, extra hours of energetic childcare and less than a sparkling welcome on my return. The petite Honda 125cc Scrambler had to be rolled down the dark ally before being kick-started to avoid disturbing tenants behind paper-thin apartment walls. The ride down city streets contained hazards in the pre-dawn haze. One morning, a roving dog brought the motorcycle down, while I lifted up into flight. The dog was unharmed. Then there were those snowy mornings. Nonetheless, with audible groaning and a semblance of dedication, I would faithfully make the challenging commute to the small group meeting on the seminary campus. This was a rare privilege, not a formal requirement.

The faculty office where we assembled was cramped. Numerous stacks of books multiplied like rabbits, leaving scant room for seating. We poured our coffee, found a clear patch of floor for our folding chairs and commenced our discussion of weighty matters. Donuts were a draw during my first semester. Then our trusted professor Vernon Grounds stimulated a controversial dialogue surrounding the simple life as a Christian virtue. Somehow, in a symbolic gesture to commit and embrace this message, healthy homemade bread became the dreary substitute for those sweet delights. The atmosphere was always permeated with affirmation, perhaps emanating from the persona of the host. This was contagious and generated a climate where vision could take root. A pervasive gentleness kept the peace among participants even during vigorous disagreements. I prized those dedicated minutes and they disappeared all too rapidly. The membership routinely evolved, but the cohesion those gatherings attained stamped a deep impression on my inner template for that elusive and cherished experience of Christian communion. I could credit the charisma of the host, whose warmth and memory for people are legendary. Dr. Grounds was president of Denver Seminary from 1956-1979 and remains chancellor to this day. Even after crossing into his nineties, Dr. Grounds spends hours on campus and still has that contagious, winsome presence. The library has long since established a more suitable location for his prolific collection of books. Despite the remarkable qualities of this distinguished pioneer in Christian counseling, his esteem of participants and ascription of worth to our contributions made the obstacles to attendance less formidable. For those contemplating convening a trek, there will be significant obstacles for you and your imagined members to overcome before stepping off. Will the experience of community cause those obstacles to fade into the background as entirely inconsequential? If the immediate trek builds a bridge to ongoing communion, the obstacles will be remembered as a shadow of the vision obtained.

That seminary-setting breakfast club was not a prototype for the full spectrum of leader-guided ministry treks referenced here. This one would ideally fit under the class of groups aimed at advancement. Dr. Grounds sought to disciple seminarians to prosper in their unique giftedness and enter ministry with a coherent sense of calling. Certainly redemptive- and adjustment-level chatter occurred over the course of our being together, but the character of the meetings did not have those destinations in view. Honestly, if you inquired of any member what those morning excursions were designed to accomplish, I suspect that responses could be summed up in boring and blunt terms. Covenant group was about enjoying a cup of coffee and breaking bread with a valued mentor. The element of leader attractiveness cannot be separated from this particular group. Still, the experience of participation in *koinonia*, Christian fellowship, and the expectation it established within is noteworthy. The substance of these encounters speaks to the crucial value of leader-guided treks with mediated feedback. These experiences lift immediate burdens by easing current needs through informational and instrumental support. If corrective emotional experiences arise, people gain a permanent sense of anticipation over what those redemptive connections can contribute to ongoing sanctification and maturation in Christ. Conversely, toxic exchanges take a severe toll and hinder one's willingness to later press into the intensity and transformation that true fellowship can afford. Therefore guides do well to visualize meaning as emanating elsewhere than from immediate redemptive intimacy. Meaning reaches fruition by establishing the desire, will and education to enter future spiritually enhancing communities. This sustains strength and holy fervor for the life journey ahead.

Three gems associated with those seminal daybreak dialogues form the structure for this final chapter. Each initiates a summary of a range of group applications and indicates the significance of them. These core ministry premises, passed along via the modeling from my beloved professor, have breathed intention into this undertaking from its inception. I conclude with these concepts in hopes of inspiring future trekking guides to use every trekking opportunity to the fullest extent. Group leaders aim to pursue genuine Christian fellowship, arouse therapeutic community and motivate service to others. In realizing these purposes, leaders ideally fulfill the function of moving members toward meaning.

Fellowship is the vital energizing force of the local church. To qualify as fellowship and not mere socializing, these interpersonal associations must be Word-centered. Our seminary covenant group invested heartily in Scripture reading and once took on the contemplation of a classic text, *Life Together.* We mulled over the delights of fellowship, past and present, according to Dietrich Bonhoeffer's observations on the essence of Christian kinship as expressed in divinely directed unity. That modern-day martyr, condemned to prison for acting boldly on his faith, spoke with piercing passion about fellowship as if it were an absolute necessity for life itself. We consumed selections of that treasure as we chewed on chunks of natural, whole wheat bread. Further, *therapeutic community* actively draws seekers into the living body of Jesus Christ, the church. The extraordinary love within Christian community is a healing balm central to the attraction of the gospel. Experiencing the love of Christ in a socially cooperative unit furthers the re-creation of broken but redeemed people. Our small group worked to understand authentic ministry's need to entwine sustenance from the Word with the relational encounter of existence in the body of Christ. The influence of Spener's pietism and even of Wesley, by way of Bonhoeffer, made its presence felt among us as contemporary evangelicals. Last, we internalized Christian *service* to the surrounding culture as the purest method to validate a vibrant faith. When Christ-honoring fellowship flourishes, it touches the vulnerable, hurting, poor and marginalized. That enlightening covenant group banter consistently commingled the spread of the gospel with the practice of social justice. We understood that separating service from fellowship represented both a personal and a spiritual liability. Bonhoeffer had internalized the call to Christian service so seriously that it cost him his pastorate, freedom and eventually his life.[1]

BRIDGES OVER TROUBLING GAPS

"Christianity means community through Jesus Christ and in Jesus Christ."[2] These words display the essential tie between faith and *fellowship*, or sharing the same faith as others. Bonhoeffer defines this communal bond and in doing so, describes the foundation for such *koinonia*.

> What does this mean? It means, first, that a Christian needs others because of Jesus Christ. It means, second, that a Christian comes to others only through Jesus Christ. It means, third, that in Jesus Christ we have been chosen from eternity, accepted in time, and united for eternity.[3]

Bonhoeffer articulates a premise that is basic and essential to reformation thought. Salvation, justification and righteousness have no roots within an isolated human being. There are no internal seeds; Jesus Christ only bestows them from the outside. And yet others participate. God places his Word in the mouths of acquaintances, friends and family to speak to the one redeemed and blessed. The Christian community serves as the vehicle for this communication, or bestowing of the Word. The match between good news bearer and receiver signals

---

[1]It is heartily recommended to those serious about *Trekking Toward Wholeness* to review the Bonhoeffer classic firsthand.

[2]Dietrich Bonhoeffer, *Life Together,* trans. John W. Doberstein (New York: Harper & Row, 1954), p. 21.

[3]Ibid., p. 21.

the Holy Spirit's ingenuity. Human hands, vocal cords and various configurations of human agency are employed. Divine-human reconciliation has an interpersonal touch. The exchange binds believers in Jesus Christ. The one who became flesh to remedy the penalty for sin restores divine-human relationship. The union fused by being in Christ and Christ being in believers elevates fellowship to its position of vital importance. Togetherness in Christ is a mystical union central to the restoration of the *imago Dei* and fellowship for eternity (2 Cor 13:5; Eph 3:17; Col 1:27).

John records this message at the pinnacle of Jesus' high priestly prayer (Jn 17:20-26). Jesus prays that his oneness with the Father will be the experience and the model of intimacy enjoyed by believers for eternity. What Jesus prays will be so. The experience of fellowship graciously ushers us into the unity of relations within the triune God. Two extremes point out the fine distinctions: unity is not an individual accomplishment, nor does it negate individual responsibility. Unity implies harmony, synchrony and partnership, not absorption, dissolution or fusion. Nonetheless, the individual relies on gift love to become eligible for participation in ongoing Christian communion. In that community, individuals become whole.

Theologian Stanley Grenz makes the case for a parallel between the New Testament conception of being *in Christ* and what contemporary psychology regards as central to the establishment of self.[4] Self is not formed solo or constructed in isolation. The individual does not gradually release identity by unfolding material packaged neatly inside. Development is best pictured as assembly within community as opposed to autonomous self-discovery. The exploration that exhibits self-agency occurs in utter dependence on the immediate social network for the means and material to become a functioning personal identity. Human development is a reciprocal endeavor even though the exchange contains a mix of gift and need love. Likewise spiritual formation means abandoning self to dependence on Christ. The Holy Spirit sustains all agency, and participation within the new humanity provides the means of identity construction. The *imago Dei* is renewed within the fellowship of the church, those who are "called out" to commence a future of being with Christ. This mutuality blends our internal sense of narrative identity with that of being a new creature in Christ.

Being "in Christ" entails participating in the narrative of Jesus, with its focus on the cross and the resurrection (see Rom 6:1-14). It involves retelling one's own narrative, and hence making sense out of one's life, through the lens of the Jesus

---

[4]Stanley J. Grenz, *The Social God and the Relational Self: A Trinitarian Theology of the Imago Dei* (Louisville, Ky.: Westminster John Knox, 2001), p. 325.

narrative. Consequently, those who find their identity in Christ come to understand themselves by viewing their lives through the lens of the language of the
old life and the new life that lies at the heart of the New Testament interpretation
of Jesus' coming and its significance.[5]

The ongoing story of Jesus Christ collecting a people unto himself across
generations runs alongside the gospel narrative as recorded in Scripture. The
perpetual gift and activity of the Comforter permeates the human-divine drama.
The continuous narrative of the Christian community, not just the current activity of the Holy Spirit, enfolds the believer. The universal church throughout history—even with its fumbles, flaws and blemishes—provides secure grounding.
Believers are merged into an extensive blended family with ancestral ties dating
back to Pentecost. Church history converges with one man's personal historical
narrative in the gospel. Future blessing depends on the perfection of Jesus Christ
and his resurrection, not on achievement or autonomous development. This is
identification with those in Christ. "The Christian identity is to be a shared
identity."[6] Individuality is forever bound with the destiny of the redeemed. The
new humanity fulfills the Creator's intention; within this communion in Christ,
those made in the *imago Dei* reflect the loving relationality and character of the
triune God.[7]

What then happens in Christian fellowship within the family of God? Jesus Christ is experienced in the here and now as Word, Bread, Truth, Vine,
Light, Shepherd, etc. These nurturing ingredients can be explained on a human
plane in the demonstration of social bonds providing attachment, reliable alliance, belonging, worth, altruism and guidance. When humans experience the
exchange of love, they experience ideal relational process in action, the means
to self-construction and the route to *imago Dei* renewal. Whether results last for
a season, a lifetime or eternity depends on the source. On a purely human level,
human nature makes God's immanence apparent. Social creatures imitate the
Creator in caring for one another. If the Holy Spirit reveals the presence of Jesus
Christ in the interpersonal, the encounter becomes transpersonal. Thus on the
spiritual dimension, God nurtures a human bond with himself and reveals his
transcendence.

Fellowship and the relational activity within ministry helping groups are not
necessarily synonymous. In function and outcome, they may be linked. Fellow-

---

[5]Ibid., p. 329.
[6]Ibid., p. 331.
[7]Ibid. Grenz makes extensive use of the term *ecclesial self* to reference the individual in redeemed
community undergoing steady transformation to spend eternity with Christ.

ship is a vital component of the Christian life. Yet many seekers have a distorted view of relationships due to a tainted or isolating past. Consider also those believers with a fair inner relational schema of what fellowship could be, but whose inner model has been disconnected from the present due to a recent rough life transition. A troublesome gap may exist between the notion of fellowship and actual familiarity with this spiritual reality. Some may require a strategic crossover to allow folks in turmoil a fresh experience of intimacy, gift love and support. Ultimately this should stimulate an urgency to become active participants within the family of God. Helping groups can encourage an increased readiness to partake and engage with others in fellowship. This is where we can observe and be amazed at the advantages of leader-guided, focused groups. Such group treks can be remedial, complementary, preparatory or formative for fellowship. Tended social interactions increase participants' skills and readiness to be alive in community as participants

1. achieve insight into the crisis or transition currently provoking turmoil
2. investigate personal openness and limits to trust
3. take ownership of behavior, blind spots and responsible investment in growth
4. notice, tolerate and utilize relational tension for interpersonal learning
5. work through transparent exploration of relational fears, expectations, patterns and default assumptions
6. enjoy collaboration in community as corrective emotional relationships
7. explore the polarities of self (solitude and loneliness), others (hospitality and hostility) and God (prayer and illusion)
8. revise and expand inner, identity-sustaining narratives

Such supportive interpersonal experiences, by grace, can result in an appetite for communion. Corrective emotional relationships are an invitation to be in Christ and join in fellowship where Jesus Christ openly glorifies himself. In summary, these brief leader-guided treks are planned outings that not only communicate relief and introduce resources but coach along the way to improve intimacy with others. The fellowship that follows lays out the route to *shalom*.

Acknowledging the use of repetition for emphasis, please catch this critical nuance. The leader-facilitated common-theme treks illustrated across the last eleven chapters are no fast track to wholeness or alternate method for spiritual formation. Their potential promise lies in contributing to the multifaceted group offerings already available by enriching the relational depth of Christian fellowship. Further, when ministries deliberately design specialized groups to minister to important needs, they preserve and protect the integrity of other care groups. These focused treks are intentionally weighted toward the full experience of community whereas other small groups foster a wholesome and necessary balance between nurture (through the study of the Word), worship (including prayer and praise), mission and community care. Unique treks must not dead-end or terminate in a cul-de-sac. Members are refreshed and directed to a loop that connects to the broad array of fellowship experiences in the body of Christ.

The concept of local fellowship as *therapeutic community* prompted vibrant discussion in my former seminary covenant group. While this remains a refreshing ideal, it is profoundly old news. The concept requires an updated frame to account for current conditions. Leaders find the implementation of restorative *koinonia* surprisingly evasive, and even when such fellowship is realized, it too often falls well below its actual potential. A decade ago, Larry Crabb promoted an identical thesis under a different heading when he asserted that the Lord has granted each believer an incredible means to heal and be healed via blessed connections.[8] Crabb stressed that struggles in life are rooted in disconnection caused by "flesh-driven responses" to life's disappointments. These are issues of the soul even though modern, psychologically oriented language contains phrases like mood disorders, emotional instability, relational brokenness and marital breakdown. Healing happens both between individuals in congruent alignment and also within small communities linked to a visible body of Christ. Interpersonal bonds formed in love nurture holistic soul refurbishing and maturity. Crabb purported that believers find "connectedness" in the activity of God's healing work by the touch of the Holy Spirit. Would it be possible or even desirable to differentiate Crabb's construct of connectedness with the phrase adopted in these pages as corrective emotional relationships CER? These concepts indeed overlap. My use of CER attempts to pull the broadly accepted, group-curative therapeutic factor of corrective emotional experience in a direction that ties faithfully with theological convictions. Connectedness is a more global expression while CER places a definite accent on redemptive relational process. The principle beneath connectedness and CER unites the two. Both occur on a human level but when

---

[8]Larry Crabb, *Connecting: Healing for Ourselves and Our Relationships, A Radical New Vision* (Nashville: Word, 1997).

the Holy Spirit anoints the activity, God accomplishes his transcendent healing purpose.

The message of therapeutic potential in closely-knit, spiritually oriented groups is well known and widely circulated. Small groups have been a dominant influential force on the American religious scene. Robert Wuthnow observed that these grassroots efforts make faith accessible to masses with parched souls. "Small groups are thus a means of extending the ministries of established congregations into the crevices of society."[9] Despite the popularity, resourcefulness and advantages of religiously oriented ventures, Wuthnow articulated four all-too-familiar soft spots following his empirical investigation into diverse, spiritually driven groups. These shortcomings do not negate the numerous gains that intimate gatherings have contributed to religious life and personal spirituality. However, these observations poignantly identify critical detours that trekking guides should prepare to avoid. Even in small groups with good intentions and well-meaning members, Wuthnow concludes that the following spiritually inhibiting attitudes can become entrenched:

1. "Me-first" religion can thrive. Maintaining interest and involvement can sway prayer toward personal need and biblical study to individual contributions. This style of spiritual quest reduces God to a method for making life better.

2. "Anything-goes spirituality" may be tolerated. When personal experience and individual differences become the ultimate criteria for moral and absolute truth, groups that hold subjective contributions in high regard can unfortunately mutate into the blind leading the blind.

3. "Cheap-grace" spirituality is equated with unconditional acceptance, including that of self. When reaching for righteousness is not prized, authority is diffuse, and being non-judgmental is a virtue, moral standards fade into ethereal aspirations.

4. "Rosier-than-thou" perspectives can dominate spirituality. Emphasis on positive feelings and a persistent pressure to be happy restricts permission for suffering. Claiming God's promises and victorious Christian living prevail over directly and courageously facing together intense fear, doubt and pain.[10]

---

[9]Robert Wuthnow, "The Small-Group Movement in the Context of American Religion," in *I Come Away Stronger: How Small Groups are Shaping American Religion*, ed. Robert Wuthnow (Grand Rapids: Eerdmans, 1994), p. 351.
[10]Ibid., pp. 344-66.

These trends run counter to growth in Christian maturity by falsely inflating the relational polarity of the self without adjustments in the other two polarities. Working exclusively to bring comfort to the self dimension alone may have intuitive appeal as it seems to soothe distressed self-esteem. It is ultimately destructive, however, because it does not build a bridge to move members toward others or God. Thus groups with a Christ-centered kingdom vision will seek to curtail these outcomes. Realistically, groups arise in realms of the informal and diffuse, in neighborhood space and cyberspace. Thus problematic distortions that arise from self-oriented small groups are likely to be replicated unless someone sets a counter movement in motion.

Those four self-enhancing, imitation spirituality trends undermine dependence on the authority of God and his Word. Are such biases necessary in small group experiences? A glance back at the two historical movements already referenced may offer perspective. Similar critiques were applied to pietistic movements. Subjectivism, or the use of immediate personal experience to determine right from wrong and truth from error, could overpower the tenants of sound doctrine derived by diligent scriptural exegesis. Likewise within the encounter group movement that Oden referred to as the New Pietism, parallel practices gave permission to any and all desires in the interest of self-expression. This paved the way for a multitude of personal spiritualities. Groups exhibit an undeniable bias to ratify risk taking without satisfactory value-based reflection. The vulnerabilities within small groups run close to their strengths.[11]

A further variable warrants consideration as well. Relational disruptions run rampant in the current atomistic cultural landscape. Limited, fragile, long distance and transitional community experience is a substantial if not the prevailing norm. These are days of fragmented and permeable families, extensive geographic mobility, multiple career changes, employment migrations, unknown neighbors and shifting demographics. Ministries expand and contract in rapid progression, reacting to alterations in leadership, worship style, vision or building programs. People treat stable relationships and community ties as disposable accessories. The unfortunate byproduct of weakening extended family and social fabric are increased pitfalls for isolation. The prevalence of perturbation from fractured social ties bodes well for semi-organized intimacy opportunities incorporating spirituality searches. Despite an ample and ready supply of communication, people are starved for connection. Sojourners across the American

---

[11]Thomas C. Oden, *The Intensive Group Experience: The New Pietism* (Philadelphia: Westminster Press, 1972).

landscape often discover the despair derived from traveling single-handedly. The same current that draws individuals into groups, however, can also bolster extremes in individual freedom and autonomy. These increase at the expense of readiness for mutual trekking. Lasting, meaningful, longitudinal relationships appear rare. I do not wish to extrapolate the elements of exploding alienation during an era when technology has made instantaneous global connection viable. Instead, I suggest that we must not confuse accessibility, potential and quantity of group offerings with realized community and quality relating. Sin-tainted loving, trusting and connecting create the distortion and distancing that result in intimacy barriers. People enter groups isolated and broken. Some enter with limited, skewed or traumatic experience in addressing relational concerns. People may have unrealistic expectations or low exposure to healthy relational models. The prevailing folklore suggests that people grow out of relationships rather than through them. Interpersonal conflict can be seen as the signal to exit, not an opportunity to pursue reconciliation or the internal recreation that revises one's relational patterns.

The body of Christ can indeed remedy problems like alienation, brokenness and stunted spiritual maturation; as a healing balm, the church furnishes the necessary and sufficient conditions for growth. A perplexing dilemma persists, however, as to the actual method of creating conditions favorable to this potential. How can a church or ministry foster a quality Christ-honoring group in the disjointed lives of seekers? Yet leaders can and must develop portioned, accountable communities where the priesthood of believers comes to life. In a sense, doing so reasserts the premises of Pietism where people directly experience compassion and caring in clusters derived from a larger congregation or loosely tied community. Through intentional efforts to be transparent, honest and submitted to the influence of the Holy Spirit, believers share spiritual encouragement to supplement corporate worship and the proclamation of the Word. When fledgling believers minister through soul care, the effort requires concentrated discipleship and apprenticeship. The concept of reciprocal care within the interpersonal is predicated on the inclusion of the third relational polarity, namely, remaining dependent on the Lord through conversation and prayer. When the Holy Spirit takes up residence in a believer, few understand or claim the concept of a ministering peer-to-peer priesthood as a Christian birthright. This honor accompanies maturation under the ministry of the Holy Spirit.

Herein lies the current concern over seeing the church of Jesus Christ as a potential therapeutic community: the promise of small group fellowship inherently risks fostering a self-oriented spirituality. We name and address this distracting delusion by returning to the three biblical motifs described early on as trekking fundamentals: walking, wandering and wisdom. These were lifted from Genesis 3 where God comes to walk in the garden and seeks out Adam and Eve, who are hiding in the bushes: "Where are you?" (Gen 3:8-9). Group trekking trains members to walk with self, neighbor, enemy and God through remediation of the relational ruptures that persist as the residue of sin. A group potentially allows leaders to observe and address actual ruptures as these deter connection. Members find meaning in responding to the invitations to walk with others and the Lord. Accessing both content- and relational-level communication can generate insight into patterns of hiding and wandering. What triggers the discrepancy between genuine fellowship and self-serving spirituality searches? In a desperate attempt to reduce shame, Adam and Eve partnered to sew coverings out of fig leaves. When cohorts in supportive groups silently conspire to subdue shame and its relational repercussions, they reenact this frantic response to nakedness in the biblical storyline. Shabby coverings attempt to disguise shame. Humans subtly relieve their shame by wandering further from the Lord and into more sophisticated hiding places. Rationalization and blame serve as shields that inhibit meaning and echo the ancient excuses that Adam and Eve attempted to pose to God. Recall Cain, who wandered further and further from the Lord, eventually building his own city and raising a family where doing evil was the main mode of life. Human beings industriously cover up and choose their own courses. A group can become a community that wanders or a nurturing system for a wanderer. On the surface, this can appear therapeutic; the one burdened by shame instantaneously enjoys relief through interpersonal support. But if members disregard the relational polarity of submission to the Lord, the short-term gains will produce a long-term loss. The peace, *shalom*, that God wishes to supply through fellowship requires a person to confess her relational rupture with God and initiate a walk with him. Jesus Christ bestows wisdom by the Spirit as he blesses the bond of love and communication that honors him. In addition, with no attempt to restore and enhance relationships along the other polarity, isolation is bound to recur.

The metaphor of church as therapeutic community or source of personal healing remains valid. Unfortunately, when invitations to this kind of community are merged with pop culture terminology, the phrases that attract will mimic advertisements for a day spa or upscale getaway vacation. Walking with the Lord in wisdom does not allow for self-indulgence or designer spirituality. To trek toward wholeness is to love God and others while growing authentically every day into eternity. Nothing guarantees that the path will be easy or traveled by clamoring crowds. The way can be treacherous due to the darkness of the human heart. The King decides where and how the voyage proceeds. Due to the unpredictability of travel conditions, emphasis on the delight of the journey and the open destination, I adopted *trekking* as a contemporary and appropriate metaphor. Christian fellowship becomes therapeutic community as we journey, make pilgrimages and walk together in Christ. Trekking with those who come alongside has therapeutic and healing value. The trip is about the community experience, not self-sufficiency, independence and happiness. Intimate treks provide an opportunity to travel with acquaintances, friends and companions in Christ as the *imago Dei* undergoes restoration. The destination is not an end, only a means to invigorate natural relationships within the broad range of intimacy levels expressed by the four loves (affection, friendships, romantic bonds and Christian fellowship).[12] Lord willing, a brief, focused group temporarily aides members by instilling a passion for and preparing them to pursue lifelong fellowship. Once again, introducing or increasing leader-directed short-term groups can add a distinctive layer to pastoral care, self-help, step, study and service group offerings. Implementing this layer of ministry will, I hope, yield thoughtful perspective to and clarify the vision of the group projects now available within contemporary ministries. The type of groups proposed here could navigate still-open community care gaps. This bridge recognizes and utilizes relational communication as a means for healing. And ultimately, it connects trekkers to other care group opportunities.

The last concept my seminary covenant group exposed deals with the promise ministry helping groups hold for blessing people in Jesus' name, or *service to others*. In applying this premise, I survey two tracks: (1) direct service-using groups and (2) indirect service where trekking guides prepare servants for outreach. Consider first the struggle or risk that expanded group offerings can alleviate. The extensive hurts represented within congregations and ministry communities display a panorama of opportunities. Guides who launch a worthy undertaking must conduct an assessment of need areas, consider existing resources and learn as much as possible about the population they seek to engage. Ready-made solutions have not formed the foundation of this particular book, yet curriculum and protocols for groups are irrefutably worthwhile. I contend that those who firmly grasp what the leader brings to the forum will skillfully wield such tools.

---

[12]C. S. Lewis, *The Four Loves* (New York: Harcourt, Brace & World, 1960).

Conditions within each unique convened company change with every ensuing interaction. Leaders with an advanced understanding of their role and function are prepared to customize techniques that realize optimal relational communication. Standardized protocols, workbooks and manuals for distinctive groups exist to structure content while steering conversations toward interpersonal support. When customized and applied with thought, such resources can maximize time, identify useful techniques, inform the themes of discourse and assist in crafting conditions where the fruits of intimacy are ripe for harvest.

Leaders can also investigate documented pioneering group efforts from other helping contexts. Effectiveness in these fields informs wise implementation in ministry. Medical literature abounds with references to group interventions for training, health promotion and disease treatment. Social service agencies and educational systems make extensive use of psycho-educational groups that report favorable outcomes. There are considerable gaps in the research into the efficacy of groups within a Christian context. How does participation in the fullness of the Christian life—including meditation on the Word, worship and prayer—enhance the experience of divine support and thus contribute to the benefits of social support?

My heart yearns for Christians to promote excellence in providing holistic soul care as solace for sojourners. My conviction, readers should now understand, rests on biblical teaching, appreciation for the integrity of Christ-honoring fellowship and weighty empirical evidence in the counseling literature. Group interventions with advancement, adjustment and remedial agendas have considerable merit. Wide opportunities exist for even greater variety and improved quality in group offerings that make use of skilled leadership. While examples can be located, this methodology remains underutilized in kingdom-oriented Christian counseling and pastoral care settings. This prayer pours out: "Lord, would it be your will to raise up informed, dedicated and consecrated trekking guides to serve others in your name?" Such leaders would allow the Holy Spirit to build an awareness regarding gaps in the levels, types and styles of service available. These guides will merge compassion with social perceptiveness and skill in response to a call from the Lord to intervene. If this sounds like a familiar whisper from the Holy Spirit to your heart, these pages have been written to encourage you to echo Isaiah's submission: "Here am I. Send me!" (Is 6:8).

Take responsibility to implement necessary procedures and communication to ensure the optimal opportunity for success. A reader who intends to fill the leadership role would do well to proceed by entering into prayerful dialogue with the Lord regarding vision, calling and preparation. Trekking guides in ministry function as shepherds. The term not only implies a pastoral caregiver, but it also carries with it the beautiful imagery of our Lord as the Great Shepherd (see Jn 10:1-18; Heb 13:20; 1 Pet 2:25; 5:4). A shepherd tends to the vulnerabilities and promotes the well-being of sheep. Metaphorically this title has been honorably applied to those who assume political, religious and moral governing authority.[13] In the timeless Psalm of comfort, Psalm 23, the Lord is our Shepherd who instills rest in green pastures, refreshment beside quiet waters, restoration of the weary soul, renewed wisdom through anointing, and a readiness to walk with his sheep in the extreme, even through the valley of death. This provides us with a worthy model and inspiration. Answering a privileged call and assuming responsibility for a helping group mandates a commitment to remain consistently under the authority of the Great Shepherd, a continual walk of faith with him at your side and good standing in a fellowship community. How awe-inspiring it would be for the Lord to reveal gaps in ministry service to those with these priorities.

Conceptualizing possibilities for intimate helping treks wonderfully blurs the line between congregational care and community outreach. Such ventures frequently pool participants from across traditional organizational lines. The good news of a quality group for those with chronic illnesses, for displaced workers retooling after a forced career change or for foster parents will travel fast. When these expeditions gel, expect word to spread both inside and beyond the congregation. Those deep in marital distress or discouraged by an adolescent's acting out may welcome the invitation for a shared group experience. Since common-theme groups are usually time-limited, the commitment investment is acceptable and realistic. Negative reports of an effort that contained only good intentions will also spread. Once word is out, a marred reputation takes monumental effort to restore. Therefore prepare well, love those who respond and become known as a credible community where newcomers are respected, understood, valued and assisted.

It is essential that orientation materials, meetings and interviews clearly reveal agendas, limitations, risks, leader qualifications and member responsibilities. Members' trust erodes when manipulative tactics or unsubstantiated claims entice participation. Ethical codes for professional disciplines adopt the important value of obtaining fully informed consent.[14] Potential participants must be

---

[13]In the New Testament, the role of shepherd is not a self-assumed position. Rather, this anointing is of the Lord and recognized and ratified by a community of believers or ecclesial authority (see Jn 21:16; Acts 20:28; 1 Pet 5:2).

[14]Marianne Corey and Gerald Corey, *Groups: Process & Practice*, 7th ed. (Pacific Grove, Calif.:

educated to make a personal and deliberate choice regarding entry into a treatment or growth experience. Doing so constitutes sound practice for recruiting for a ministry focused group, even if it is not required by a professional license or organizational membership. This principle is a foremost cultural expectation and thus will likely affect a participant's outlook. Further, an orientation in which trekkers evaluate the investment they are about to make builds community and ensures success well before they even know others in the cohort.

Ministries may also position themselves to creatively bridge abundant gaps in community outreach. A group may form the basis for a new beginning, yet a single offering does not necessarily need to cover all issues or themes. Options that layer assistance from seminars to self-help to leader-led to advanced support groups might be both advisable and feasible. Such ventures influence communities and touch lives. Most important, these demonstrate how believers act justly, love mercy and walk humbly with the Lord in service to others (Mic 6:8). Sponsoring a leader or team to run a quality group several times a year may represent outstanding ministry stewardship when the alternative is rationed referral of a select few to individual counseling.

Will a retreat, preaching series or area-wide event address a critical or sensitive behavioral or relational area? Ministries should consider offering follow-up services like groups or a series of groups introduced over time. Self-help ministries routinely begin with facilitated leadership until they activate a critical pool of support and prepare a network of veterans to carry on that service to others. In fact, the beautiful progression from supported one to mutual supporter demonstrates how service offerings can reap multiple harvests.

Ministries that have a basic care or cell-group format, or those that gather clusters around families' developmental phases, will encounter crises that exceed the resources of the average prayer and study meeting. Rather than stress the structure of these congregational building blocks, burn out a dedicated facilitator or grant inadequate attention to hurting members, a periodic trek can specifically target the identified concern. Groups that deal with loss, grief, marriage, vision, addictions or family struggles can accept referrals from home Bible studies or fellowship meetings. Gender-specific men's and women's ministries consistently uncover incipient concerns such as explosive anger, unaddressed trauma or sexual purity battles. Pastoral caregivers may find that they routinely refer individuals to professional counselors for a particular perplexing problem. Might this represent a niche well suited for a leader-orchestrated group? Finally, leaders may

Brooks/Cole, 2006), pp. 63-102.

launch a specialized group to rouse the imaginations of Christ followers who wish to dedicate concentrated effort to dig deeply into a core aspect of their spiritual lives. The application of guided groups for formation efforts and spiritual direction deserves concentrated attention. These pathways enable group treks to fulfill a direct service mission. But these various examples fail to capture another aspect of service that groups can provide.

Indirect service looks beyond the internal group needs. Perhaps the following illustration—my recollection of a wilderness trip that expanded the crosscultural horizons of youth from a rural town—suffices to introduce this concept.

The Adirondack shoreline displayed majestic hemlocks hovering over the water's edge. They gave the sandy beach at the portage opening an elegant and inviting frame. What an unlikely spot for a mutiny! Our canoe expedition had been meticulously planned from route to provisions, swimming holes to pit toilets. Not only was this big blast intended to kick off the summer youth program, it marked the beginning of a year of preparation for an ambitious overseas short-term mission trip. The over two dozen teens and chaperons who were out paddling aspired to board an international flight to a distant land and to represent the Lord and our little country church. Outdoor wilderness excursions were considered imperative conditioning for service projects. As leader, I was surprised to arrive at this substantial one-half-mile canoe carry. This was not a planned break, and was certainly not the campsite selected for day's end. Several canoe partners were unloading and they quickly announced their reason. They had determined the distance traveled thus far to be overwhelming. Majority rules; enough was enough. The group stops here. There were tears, girls hugging and considerable adolescent drama. Not all the boys were present as their canoes, belongings and bodies were securely resting at the launch site over by the next pond. With considerable effort, I assembled everyone for an on-the-spot defusing. I intended to reiterate the itinerary, rest, give a pep talk and move out. Contrary to my goals, these youth were ready to inaugurate a roast and not of marshmallows. "Why do we have to paddle so far?" "Look at these blisters!" "We want to camp here." "Why does our canoe have to hold all the food for tomorrow night's dinner?" Defense of the objective or any explanation about camping permits would have been futile. My credibility as a leader was shot and my sanity was under review. Other chaperons were quiet. Evidently they were praying silently—to what end, I remain uncertain.

If the canoe trip had been a purely recreational outing, this was my cue to pack up, return to the drop-in point and enjoy a leisurely afternoon swim before heading home. I couldn't deny the legitimacy of the challenge; this ambitious travel segment had been planned without accounting for the slight breeze or the inexperience of the crew. Would this paddling strike prove to be a disaster? No one had planned or provoked the incident, but still I anticipated some sparks. In adventure therapy terms, what was about to unfold was *eustress*, the healthy use of stress to ascertain how people solve problems, form trust and process communication.[15] I would prefer not to have flames toasting my tender skin. On the other hand, I knew that I should seize this teachable moment, not squirm out of or squander it. My trekking savvy was put to the test, far from assuring positive results. Eventually, I spit out some questions like these: How were the stronger assisting the weaker? Did being first actually matter? Was it smart to keep friends together or was there a more strategic way to design paddling teams? How much did the packing list actually stipulate that personal belongings should weigh? Were six packs of soda the ideal refreshment and worth the weight? How could the team implement attitude checks? Is it all right to question procedures, plans or authority? How so?

Stress challenge experiences produce metaphors for life and immediate responses indicate personal styles or issues. Better to sort out our stuff here, beside these overweight canoes, than in a third world country. A year from this mountain jaunt, needy and expectant recipients would depend on a team to complete a project and fulfill a promise spoken in the name of the Lord. In the end, this leader roast produced only an uneasy sensation in me, on par with the sting of sunburn. The cannibals left hungry. At least they left and carried on. We redistributed our packs, paired up differently and planned trade-offs. I reduced the route for the next day by selecting a less ambitious destination. The team learned a prayer lesson. Even to this day, if the miraculous or mysterious allowed me to rewind years or relive history, I would travel anywhere and in any way with the cohesive team that emerged a year later to serve our Lord. What we learned together on those pristine ponds became the bonds that held us close when faced by adversity on the mission field. We never were perfectly polished. We did come to know our stuff, our strengths and our Lord. We had few complaints, shared many smiles and lifted up Jesus Christ.

Evangelical ministries emphasize outreach endeavors. Wilderness adventure

---

[15]H. L. "Lee" Gillis and Michael A. Gass, "Adventure Therapy with Groups," in *Handbook of Group Counseling and Psychotherapy,* ed. Janice L. Delucia-Waack et al. (Thousand Oaks, Calif.: Sage, 2004), pp. 593-605.

exhibitions and short-term mission projects are popular. In these activities, a wise trekking guide can often fill a reflective learning gap. Camps and youth facilities publicize outdoor education, obstacle or ropes courses, or like venues requiring cooperation coupled with individual stamina in order to complete a complex series of physically and mentally demanding tasks. These activities have entertainment appeal. In addition, they afford exercise, acceptably messy fun and productive adventure. Leaders often overlook these as a viable means to incite lively group dynamics. Under these conditions, the intensity of interaction can produce unprecedented development within individuals while building rich camaraderie between. The risk taking and unusual tasks require reliance on previously untested associations. Group members visibly and palpably grant or withhold their trust, or else convey being stuck in ambivalence. These outings are a choice method to facilitate self, peer and community awareness, not only in youth but also in adults. When leaders are competent not only in the mandatory physical safety requirements and outdoor demands but excel in accessing group dynamics to propel intra and interpersonal growth, the group can achieve maximum gain from the experience. Astute leaders build on these activities and create hearty conversations. Wise use of here-and-now sensations related to trust, insecurity and vulnerabilities establishes the basis for the service team of the future. Quality psycho-educational and interpersonal debriefing can strike learning gold in these unconventional classrooms.

In a similar fashion, leaders can assist teams tackling a mission trip or service project by embracing sudden degree shifts related to group dynamics. Typical signs could be disputes over decisions, grumbling over harsh conditions, tension between sub-groupings and jealousy over assignments or recognition. Without relief or remediation, nasty and unexpected people problems sabotage worthwhile and well-organized charitable efforts. Heightened arousal occurs from the dramatic change in roles, surroundings, novel partnerships and loss of accustomed comforts. The combination can heat into a combustible concoction of interpersonal friction. The service project itself may represent a courageous battle to curtail the devastating effects of sin in our fallen world. The explosions between participants unmask the pervasive clutch-hold that sin has even on those determined to announce redemption and proclaim the gospel. Leaders can incorporate the motivation for service into the immediate experience of awkward relating and thereby further interpersonal and spiritual maturation to accomplish kingdom service. Identify the bridge between present learning and future ministry. Harness the emotional stimulation to further growth and formation. Here-and-now encounters yield metaphors overflowing with meaning for service, life and beyond.[16]

Group guides benefit from appreciating encounters where relational experiences are born. Consider the group pace categories of cooperation, competition, collaboration and consolidation that this book discussed earlier. The quality and impact of the relational connections have ongoing use. Three caveats should be taken to heart: First, there are no shortcuts to deriving benefit from intimate interpersonal experience. A leader may propose a good route but cannot impose or transpose relational conditions for the within and between. The messy stuff in the relational matrix is real, robust and risky. The unique mission inspires each collection of participants; it is theirs alone to untangle then clinch. Second, leader empathy, genuineness and creativity give support that may be imitated. When original members become empathetic, genuine and creative, a leader has succeeded. Last, a group may build a collection of powerful memories but it cannot maintain momentum on victories from its past. The only way to make use of the here and now is to be in the here and now.

OVERCOMING OBSTACLES, REALIZING VISION

In order to make my seminary covenant group a priority, I had to abruptly abandon a warm comfortable bed only to endure a thrill ride on a zippy little motorcycle, winding between delivery trucks and predawn urban traffic. Reflecting on its life impact, the hurdles and sacrifice are only laughable, but the lasting gifts stir profound emotion. My steadfast shepherd and fellow early risers provided support each week when I needed it more than I could possibly know. We passed around more than that dense whole wheat bread in those meetings. The names and faces have faded, but the impression on my soul has not dimmed but brightened. Subsequent group experiences have enriched those memories and added their own contribution. As this trek comes to a close, consider the guides and mentors, formal and informal, who have left impressions on the relational templates within your own internal schemas for intimacy and fellowship. Where do your convictions converge with your experiences of mutual care, corrective

---

[16]There is a legitimate concern and controversy in mission leadership circles over short-term trips that may yield a greater benefit to those traveling than those who are receiving service. Funds raised for such travel are collected in the name of evangelism or discipleship. Thus it behooves leaders to articulate objectives and purposes. From an interpersonal learning perspective, much can be gained from planned team service close to home or within an adventure setting. A beyond-the-border experience can then be planned and assessed with stewardship of the Lord's resources. My contention is that leaders maximize the benefits to those being served and those doing the service by coaching well when these treks are underway.

emotional relationships and true *koinonia?* When did you exchange gift love and need love? How have you blessed, extended and enriched that chain?

Guides face legitimate obstacles to realizing a vision for groups that encourage mediated feedback. Funding poses a perpetual problem. The American cultural preference for personalized attention does not stir enthusiastic crowds vying to enter groups. Marketing, recruiting, screening and building a referral network are labor-intensive, thankless tasks. And yet the resources offered here make possible the engineering required to build bridges over these challenges. Leaders inspired by this vision can feel confident in embracing the group enterprises I suggest here, making use of the four leader functions to forge ground-breaking and useful ministry enterprises.

I have sought to traverse objections to incorporating group therapy practices in Christian ministry. While other service systems have made extensive use of the leader-function framework, evangelical ministries and Christian counselors have not invested as heavily in this level of productive care. I believe that gaps in the range of pastoral care offered arise from questions about the legitimacy of a similar enterprise. But should common-theme groups that make forays into interpersonal learning be left to the exclusive domain of professional disciplines utilizing a medical, existential or social service model? The training, ethical standards and supervision of related disciplines offer distinct advantages. Professional guidelines can foster the heightened interpersonal awareness and objectivity necessary to manage relationality in close quarters. Such management lies at the core of groups that make use of immediate struggles surrounding intimacy attempts, connections and misses. Clergy and Christian leaders may or may not have received similar training through coursework, chaplaincy internships or fieldwork. Given the array of Christian universities, seminaries and doctoral programs that host degree programs with a dual emphasis on a biblically grounded, Christian eschatological vision and professional competency, I anticipate that a sizable pool of potential guides currently exists and will continue to expand.

One of my major purposes has been to explore the question of Christian applicability of psychologically based concepts. I have tried to address potential pitfalls honestly while introducing unmistakable Christian correlations. The living, relational process for growth and healing can be described as corrective emotional relationships or as the love of Christ brought into immediate reality via interpersonal encounter. Explaining these as interchangeable concepts for use in a ministry context explicitly bridges empirical approaches and the Christian worldview, the Christian community and a future heavenly fulfillment. The vision of small groups as contemporary continuations of our pietistic heritage—offerings that rightly occupy a place within other Word-centered ministries—gives treks toward wholeness a renewed foothold. Beyond the therapeutic, relational process lies the promise of gradually restoring the *imago Dei* with which each person is created. What begins as personality support or reconstruction can be transformed by the Holy Spirit into redemptive activity. Relational communication and intimate experience that moves individuals toward *shalom* applies to the personal and the spiritual domains. Progress over time may appear negligible or sluggish but the assurance of eternity with Jesus Christ maintains our hope to persevere. Guided treks can relieve distress, offer comfort and foster relational adaptability. Such relational facility implies the expression of love across the three relational polarities. Given this kingdom-oriented perspective on relational process, how reasonable and promising it is to host these groups within a ministry context!

Perhaps the obstacles most difficult to resolve reside within. Leading this style of group does require the courage to address insecurities and interpersonal fears. Quality groups have no corners where participants can hide. Likewise leaders have no protective screens. Trekking guides must step up to the four leader functions. They must fulfill the demanding work of developing vision and structure. Each steps out to bring caring hospitality where hostility has prevailed. A guide must then stand firm under conditions conducive to affective expression and attachment formation. And when these finally merge in those magnificent movements of a collaborating group, a sensitive leader steps back so that members can practice acquired intimacy in the exchange of gift and need love. This allows for steady revision of inner narratives and the arrival of a lucid message with both personal, corporate and kingdom meaning.

I consider my own experience in equipping and encouraging guides for such helping groups to be an honor. It produces considerable joy to recall one who guides men's groups in a correctional facility. Another cares for those with self-destructive tendencies and deeply damaged attachments. One leads a novel trek dealing with previously unrealized loss, a venture she imagined and nurtured into being. Her reports are nothing short of delightful. I experience such excitement over the international helper whose culture prefers the group modality to individual treatment. Each is ready to rely on Jesus Christ to minister through self and despite self. They share an unyielding confidence that their group forums offer a dynamic dimension not readily available in traditional dyadic models. Trekking guides like these inspire hope, not in what has been or exists, but in what the Lord will accomplish through journeys that persist until he returns. Therefore even greater joy flows from anticipating those whom the Lord will raise up to participate in the formation of intimacy bonds that reflect his grace and presence. Might this include you?

Let us hold unswervingly to the hope we profess, for he who promised is faithful. And let us consider how we may spur one another on toward love and good deeds. Let us not give up meeting together, as some are in the habit of doing, but let us encourage one another—and all the more as you see the Day approaching. (Heb 10:23-25)

RECOMMENDED READING

*Indicates a Christian ministry resource.

*Arnold, Jeffrey. *The Big Book on Small Groups*. Rev. ed. Downers Grove, Ill.: InterVarsity Press, 2004. Start with Arnold for a sturdy introduction to small groups for any ministry setting. The benefits, structure, vision and balance are all addressed and are absolutely fundamental. This is the "home page" for learning about the ingredients of worship and prayer, community, Bible study, and mission.

Brabender, Virginia. *Introduction to Group Therapy*. New York: John Wiley & Sons, 2002. This comprehensive academic text presents an organized and readable overview of the variety of group theories and approaches currently in use. The four leader functions that structure *Trekking Toward Wholeness* are described extremely well.

Brabender, Virginia, Andrew I. Smolar and April E. Fallon. *Essentials of Group Therapy*. Hoboken, N.J.: Wiley, 2004. This is the installment on group from a series of condensed works that boil down the essentials for mental health practice. Thus the approach is designed to provide a brief look at everything one would need to know in order to run a counseling-style undertaking. This paperback admirably covers considerable territory. It could serve well as a firm introduction or as an ample refresher on the basics of constructing and leading a helping group.

*Bonhoeffer, Dietrich. *Life Together*. Translated by John W. Doberstein. New York: Harper, 1954. Here is the manifesto for a vibrant underground seminary during the Nazi period that resisted the dominant culture due to faith convictions. It remains a crucial inspirational reading for all Christians. Bonhoeffer values all that the community can be and become in Jesus Christ. Still, he maintains a staunch position on the necessity of letting the Lord and Scripture have supreme authority.

*Cloud, Henry, and John Townsend. *Making Small Groups Work: What Every Small Group Leader Needs to Know*. Grand Rapids: Zondervan, 2003. These well-known authors discuss how Christians grow and thrive in small groups. The accent is on support-style groups that have a community care orientation. The emphasis is practical as it contains a down-to-earth approach while casting a ministry vision.

Corey, Marianne Schneider, and Gerald Corey. *Groups: Process and Practice.* 7th ed. Belmont, Calif.: Thomson/Brooks Cole, 2006. This primarily academic textbook is so readable that it would make a useful foundation for group work in a wide range of settings. The eclectic model offered maintains an explicit stage progression that tends to be a reasonable fit with time-limited, focused groups. The how-to material on customizing groups to address specific life developmental phases and helping themes clearly informed the discussion on common-theme, leader-directed groups promoted in these pages. The text would indeed partner well with *Trekking Toward Wholeness* for counseling courses in settings where a Christian worldview and ministry applications are valued.

Corey, Gerald. *Theory & Practice of Group Counseling.* 9th ed. Belmont, Calif.: Thomson/Brooks Cole, forthcoming. The feature of this text is its strong ethics chapter along with systematic chapters on theory-specific approaches. A full range of counseling theories are represented such as person-centered, gestalt, psychodynamic, etc. The group modality within each theory is outlined.

*Donahue, Bill. *Leading Life-Changing Small Groups.* Grand Rapids: Zondervan, 2002. This practical and enthusiastic guide for ministry-oriented discipleship groups has long sustained the momentum of these ventures within the Willow Creek Association. This is a terrific tool for those ever-important faith-nurturing groups where Scripture enriches the Christian life within an intimate and caring setting.

*Icenogle, Gareth W. *Biblical Foundations for Small Group Ministry: An Integrational Approach.* Downers Grove, Ill.: InterVarsity Press, 1994. For one book that aligns contemporary group ministry with the text of Scripture, consult Icenogle. This is a prime theological and biblical resource for pastors and trainers looking to inform those facilitating these shepherding efforts week-to-week. Consider this an imperative classic for leaders of any ministry group.

Ivey, Allen E., Paul B. Pedersen and Mary Bradford Ivey. *Intentional Group Counseling: A Microskills Approach.* Belmont, Calif.: Wadsworth/Thomson,

2001. Straightforward skill demonstration and abundant language samples are the strength of this text. Any aspiring group leader would benefit from the basic, accessible, first-person leader statements placed neatly alongside helpful diagrams, charts and explanations.

Kine, William B. *Interactive Group Counseling and Therapy*. Upper Saddle River, N.J.: Pearson Education, 2003. This particular academic counseling text places emphasis on the unique social dynamics of group work. It is recommended for its useful balance of material on the roots of contemporary therapeutic groups, interpersonal theory, facilitation techniques and intervention skills.

*McMinn, Mark R., and Clark D. Campbell. *Integrative Psychotherapy: Toward a Comprehensive Christian Approach*. Downers Grove, Ill.: InterVarsity Press, 2007. This one is *not* on groups. It makes this list for two compelling reasons. First, the intervention approaches outlined with good detail pull the best from the scientific psychological literature while remaining under the authority of Scripture. There is a commitment throughout to cooperate with the Holy Spirit in the redemption of the *imago Dei*. Second, though the examples are set in individual counseling, the stress on therapeutic interpersonal connection is consistent with the relational experiences that groups offer. Common-theme groups often begin with the functional domain as a unifying focus. The method itself then presses further into the schema and relational domains. These domains give the book its structure in conjunction with a theology of *imago Dei*.

Yalom, Irvin D., and Leszcz, Molyn. *The Theory and Practice of Group Psychotherapy*. 5th ed. New York: Basic Books, 2005. Beyond doubt, this is the classic and authoritative tome on group psychotherapy for helping professionals. There is extensive review of the mental health empirical literature along with discussion of theoretical constructs. This is an ideal *advanced* reference for those with considerable familiarity with psychologically informed, clinical group applications for the treatment of mental health issues embedded in personality concerns.

Name Index

Scripture Index